T0365649

Fostering CREATIVITY

THE FULL DAY KINDERGARTEN CLASSROOM IN ONTARIO: LEARNING THROUGH INQUIRY AND PLAY AND ITS IMPLICATIONS FOR CHILD DEVELOPMENT

Ella Karia, Ed.D.

FOSTERING CREATIVITY
THE FULL DAY KINDERGARTEN CLASSROOM IN
ONTARIO: LEARNING THROUGH INQUIRY AND PLAY
AND ITS IMPLICATIONS FOR CHILD DEVELOPMENT

iUniverse books may be ordered through booksellers or by contacting:

iUniverse
1663 Liberty Drive
Bloomington, IN 47403
www.iuniverse.com
1-800-Authors (1-800-288-4677)

Because of the dynamic nature of the Internet, any web addresses or links contained in this book may have changed since publication and may no longer be valid. The views expressed in this work are solely those of the author and do not necessarily reflect the views of the publisher, and the publisher hereby disclaims any responsibility for them.

Any people depicted in stock imagery provided by Thinkstock are models, and such images are being used for illustrative purposes only. Certain stock imagery © Thinkstock.

ISBN: 978-1-4917-7396-3 (sc)
ISBN: 978-1-4917-7397-0 (e)

Print information available on the last page.

iUniverse rev. date: 11/18/2015

Play is the purest, the most spiritual product of man at this stage and is at once the pre-figuration and imitation of the total human life, of the inner secret, natural life in man and in all things. It produces, therefore, joy, freedom, satisfaction, repose within and without, and peace with the world. The springs of all good rest within it and go out from it.

(Friedrich Froebel, 1889, p.25)

CONTENTS

I dedicate this work to my daughter, Esha, and son, Krishan. To all the love, laughter, and learning they both bring into my life. We continue to grow, learn and build precious memories filled with the joy of imagination, spark of creativity and energy of play. Continue to be inquisitive, imaginative and inventive as you embrace the love of learning.

Chapter 1

CANADIAN PERSPECTIVES: AN INTRODUCTION

Let us begin by imagining a day in Kindergarten. A child comes to school each day and is excited to play. Sifting sand, pouring water, pressing and molding clay. Later the child is experimenting with ramps, stacking blocks and exploring shapes. Painting with brushes and dabbing with sponges they mix colors and explore art. Drawing their thoughts in their journal book they express what is on their mind. Expanding and building on their ideas all the time. Sketching on clipboards and drawing on whiteboards. Cutting with scissors, sticking with glue, coloring with markers and crayons. Throughout the day they are constructing and creating with a variety of materials in many ways. Eventually, a masterpiece, something unique, unfolds in front of their eyes. With great pride and joy they talk about their creation. During indoor and outdoor play children socialize, interact and role-play in a truly natural and informal way. Climbing, running, jumping are all a part of their play. Outside they dig in the garden, collect rocks, hug a tree and closely look at living things. Gazing with a stillness, calmness and a deep sense of awe and wonder. They carefully engage and interact with nature.

Kindergarten learning opportunities are based on discovery learning and being fully present. Knowing there are no right or wrong answers in this place of wonder and creativity makes it safe and comforting. The child's curiosities lead the direction and focus of the learning. At times, it is their first encounter that sparks conversations, excitement during these 'wonder years'. Kindergarten children have many choices and materials with lots to see, hear, feel and do. Educators in the classroom are mindful of the natural flow of play, minimizing transitions and letting the process of inquiry learning unfold. Children are happy and engaged. Teachers nurture, guide and care, they help students build and extend their own ideas, freely engage and deeply explore. Children begin to find their own connections to the learning.

Greater opportunities for this type of authentic, quality and varied play are essential for children between the ages of 3 and 6 years of age. Children come with an inner openness to ideas and their own thinking and if given opportunities to express their thinking the individual uniqueness within each child shines. Children naturally invent, create and experiment in their own personal ways. The Kindergarten years lay a strong foundation for success in future schooling, and looking closely at teaching and learning practices in the classroom brings awareness to the best early years experiences and the importance of nurturing the use of the imagination at an early age. Fostering one's creativity also defines personal identity, individuality and self-esteem. Innovation emerges from combining disparate ideas. Research studies validate this premise.

Over the last decade, research in Canada on early childhood education and brain development has focused on the importance of laying a solid foundation in the early years of a child's life for improved learning in the later years (Mustard, 2006; Pascal, 2009a, 2009b; Shonkoff & Phillips, 2000). As a result, the government of Ontario has made policy changes that have affected Kindergarten programs in public schools in Ontario. The Full-Day Kindergarten (FDK) learning model was introduced after a new law amendment was passed. In September 2010, Bill 242—Full-Day Early Learning Statue—Law Amendment Act (Legislative Assembly of Ontario,

2010)—came into effect and started the process of changing Kindergarten learning in Ontario public schools from a half-day to a full-day program with a greater focus on inquiry and play.

The Ministry of Education (MOE) updated the Kindergarten curriculum document and named it *FDELKP—The Full-Day Early Learning-Kindergarten Program* (*Draft Version-2010*). The *FDELKP* outlined the vision, purpose, and goals of the new FDK curriculum. According to Leona Dombrowsky, then Minister of Education, Full-Day Kindergarten learning was part of an overall plan to help more children have a strong start in school. She asserted that "[b]y giving them more opportunities at a young age we're giving our children a brighter future" (Ontario Ministry of Education, 2010, p. 1). Establishing excellence in early years pedagogy gained focus and priority and as we await the release of the final version of the Kindergarten curriculum document we see the value and lessons from research about young children.

In Ontario, the *Early Learning for Every Child Today* (2006)—also called ELECT—was a framework for the Ontario early years childhood settings written by the Best Start Expert Panel on Early Learning. The researchers from this expert panel compiled brain development studies and compared early years programs from around the world. Professor Mustard (2006) conducted studies showing that early brain development sets the foundation for lifelong learning, behavior, and health. Research findings in Mustard's report were based on detailed evidence from the neuroscience, developmental psychology, and educational fields of study. Evidence showed that a child's brain development is connected to early years education and experience. Furthermore, Mustard found that:

> There are critical periods when a young child requires appropriate stimulation for the brain to establish the neural pathways in the brain for optimum development. Many of these critical periods are over or waning by the time a child is six years old. These early critical periods include: binocular vision, emotional

control, habitual ways of responding, language and
literacy, symbols and relative quantity. (2006, p. 5)

According to Mustard (2006), the brain's architecture is built
from the bottom up, and although the sequence of development
in a child's brain is similar from one child to the next, the rate of
development and the variety of pathways vary. Understanding how
children learn best will optimize the early years learning. Professor
Shonkoff (2010) showed that genes set the parameters for the basic
structures of the developing brain, but a child's interactions and
relationships with his or her parents and significant others establish
neural circuits and shape the brain. Many brain research studies
(Greenspan & Shanker, 2004; Mustard, 2006; Shonkoff & Philips,
2000) have also revealed that opportunities for children to learn
through play assist with the development of multiple pathways in the
brain. Over the last decade, child brain development research studies
(Rushton & Larkin, 2001; Rutledge, 2000; Washington, 2002) have
produced more knowledge about neuro-scientific data than in several
centuries. Clearly, the scientific evidence points to the importance of
quality early years education programs. It also shows that we need
to better understand what is actually happening in the classrooms.

In addition, the American Association of Pediatrics released
a report in 2007 about the importance of play in the early years
(American Association of Pediatrics, 2007). The report showed
that starting from birth, play serves to strengthen the synaptic
connections in the brain, especially the motor and sensory areas. It
stated that there are also areas of rapid growth in the frontal cortex
(cognitive thinking, problem-solving, and logic skills), and that it is
through play that children can demonstrate their abilities (Bergen,
2007; Bodrova & Leong, 2007). Thus, this report showed that a
wide variety of play experiences is necessary in order to develop
a complex and integrated brain (see Appendix A for Glossary of
Terms). Research studies (Bergen, 2007; Diamond, Barnett, Thomas
& Munro, 2007; Kostelnik & Grady, 2009) also affirmed that

play is important in the development of self-regulation, cognition, language, social, emotional, and creativity skills.

Fostering Creativity investigates and analyzes Ontario's FDK teaching practices. Through conversations with FDK teachers and visits to their Kindergarten classrooms, this book gathered information that would help one better understand how the Kindergarten practices are taking shape. The Ontario Ministry of Education's FDK curriculum document outlined specific expectations and embedded a play-based philosophy in Kindergarten programs. Teaching practices in the FDK classroom started to take a new direction. Learning through inquiry, learning in real-life contexts, and learning through exploration proved to be more and more important. Early childhood development takes place in the context of families, communities, and schooling and is shaped by the day-to-day experiences and environments of early life.

The most significant findings in *Fostering Creativity* are that quality teaching and learning practices are based on the following features: (a) learning through play-based, inquiry-based and experiential-based exploration; (b) making the educational experiences child-centered and authentic; (c) building on children's past experiences, nurturing self-expression and identity; (d) strengthening relationships and connections; and (e) creating stimulating environments, both indoor and outdoor, for children's learning and development. Teachers' perspectives and specific practices are described, analyzed, and discussed. Theory informed practice and practice informed theory, as models were developed and designed during this research journey. *Fostering Creativity* is a great resource for teachers, early years educators, policy-makers and parents.

The Ministry of Education (2010) states that children learn best through activities and develop their knowledge by building on past experiences. "Children are naturally curious. The new Kindergarten program, therefore, is supposed to feed this curiosity by providing opportunities for learning, self-expression, self-regulation, and self-discovery in a variety of ways" (Ontario Ministry of Education, 2010,

p. 6). This could be through talking, reading, predicting, inquiring, exploring, pretending, experimenting, building, role-playing, and socializing. Each child should grow and develop in a number of interrelated areas—social, emotional, communicative, cognitive, and physical. In fact, the United Nations has recognized play as a specific right for all children (UNICEF, 2010). Furthermore, according to the Canadian Council on Learning (CCL), "[p]lay nourishes every aspect of children's development—it forms the foundation of intellectual, social, physical, and emotional skills necessary for success in school and in life. Play paves the way for learning" (2006, p. 2).

While the idea of Kindergarten—a program of education for young children, usually four to six years of age—was first brought forward more than a century ago, the continued focus of the program has shifted among educators. The type of play materials in the classroom was examined more closely to see if that made a difference. The specific practices and analysis of how children were helped to attain higher potentials were considered. The question of the length and quality of day also became a topic of further interest and discussion. All of these topics remain important in examining Kindergarten practices today. At this point in time, it seems that both the quantity of time and the quality of the program make a difference. Furthermore, in recent decades, increased emphasis has been placed on the need for educational opportunities for children at the earliest possible age. Therefore, it is imperative to research how to maximize children's learning experiences at the Kindergarten level.

Learning happens when a child can explore and experiment in a friendly, safe, and exciting environment. Finding the best teaching approaches for young children requires looking at what all the different philosophies of education highlight. These will be discussed in this research study. Does the new Full-Day Kindergarten (FDK) model follow one specific philosophy, or is it a combination of best practices from several theorists? Which teaching approaches and practices are adopted in the FDK classrooms? The section below provides some general information on the Full-Day Kindergarten program, and more details can be found on the Ontario Ministry of Education website (www.edu.gov.on.ca). The main benefits of the FDK program include improved literacy skills (Vanderlee et al., 2013, NCES, 2004), greater independence (Plucker, 2004), school readiness skills (Pelletier 2012a, 2012b) and improved peer interaction (Walsten & West, 2004), especially for at-risk children. There is also greater school success in Grade 1 (Cryan et al., 1992) resulting in building an overall stronger foundation for children. Therefore, the more time children spend with classmates and exposed to the school environment, the better their self-regulation, academic, and social skills. A seamless and integrated day makes the day smoother and easier for parents and children. This flow and consistency can really help with the child's confidence and security.

The relationship children develop with their peers as well as with their teachers is an important part of learning to build trust with others. Aside from parents, other relationships can add value to a child's development. The Ontario Ministry of Education's *Full-Day Early Learning—Kindergarten Program* (2010) emphasises the need for interrelated systems that include family, the school, the broader community, and the world. The assumption is that partnerships with families and communities strengthen the ability of an early childhood setting to meet the needs of young children. Meeting their needs includes respect for diversity, equity, and inclusion. These are prerequisites for optimal development and learning. Teachers can proactively build positive affirming relationships, connect families with services in the community, and collaborate with outside agencies when needed. Good communication can foster good relationships. This increases awareness about ways to meet students' needs and will eventually improve student success.

In the policy vision, the Ontario Ministry of Education proposed that "early childhood settings can organize programming to use diversity of the participants as an asset that enriches the environment for everyone" (2010, p. 42). Making a concerted effort to integrate and represent learning in a meaningful context to the community of learners helps deepen connections for children and supports the integrity of their families. Is this policy vision a reality in the classroom? Are we truly integrating and considering cultural identity in the curriculum and the classroom? These are concerns that will be brought to light throughout this book.

Lastly, the FDK program is built upon the partnership between the teacher and the Early Childhood Educator (ECE). This is a significant shift from the half-day programs' classroom management model. The government established this partnership between the teacher and the ECE as part of the policy change and stipulates that each FDK classroom in Ontario be managed accordingly. The idea of two educators in one classroom was intended to improve the teacher-student ratio and the quality of the Kindergarten program. This was a significant change for teachers, who in the past solely managed their own Kindergarten program.

Five years ago the Ontario Ministry of Education embarked on a five year process that revolutionized Ontario's Kindergarten program. During this time we have increased the depth and breadth of understanding of inquiry-based and play-based learning. Now that the new Full-Day Kindergarten program has begun taking shape, we can learn from the implementation phase (see Tips for Teachers – Appendix D). Each teacher is unique in his / her own way. By hearing the stories of Kindergarten teachers and how they went about adapting to the educational policy changes, we can gain a better understanding of the pedagogical implications and specific teaching practices as well as the outcomes of the changes proposed in the FDK curriculum.

Background on Kindergarten in Ontario

The history of early years education in Ontario is important background information for this research study. The political debates on the topic of education for children under the age of six started back in the 1960s and 1970s, and the pendulum has swung back and forth with regards to support for funding for the Kindergarten years. However, in the twenty-first century, there have been significant shifts, and the public debates on early years education have intensified as the Ontario Liberal government invested over a billion dollars in this endeavor.

There were many significant events over the years that characterized the nature of child-care and Kindergarten programs in the province of Ontario. The Best Start Expert Panel on Early Learning, which consisted of professionals from the early childhood education in Ontario, introduced the document entitled *The Early Learning for Every Child Today*. Published in 2007, this document presented a framework to guide the development of Ontario early childhood settings. It considered many early childhood settings such as childcare centers, regulated home child care, nursery schools, Kindergarten, Ontario Early Years Centers, family resource programs, parenting centers, and child development programs in the community. Through the research conducted by academics, government agencies, unions and educators, it is possible to outline some key documents, government decisions, and the general path that led to where we are today with FDK initiatives in the province (See Appendix C). This present study aims to focus on the section relating to the Kindergarten years. In a document entitled *Kindergarten Matters: The Importance of Kindergarten in the Development of Young Children* published by the Elementary Teachers Federation of Ontario (ETFO), there is a brief summary of historical facts about Kindergarten in Ontario, presented as follows:

> Kindergarten first took root in Ontario in the early 1870s. Kindergarten programs developed in communities in different parts of the province during the early 1900s and expanded significantly during the Second World War and afterwards. The first junior Kindergarten programs were established in Ottawa in 1943–44 and then in Toronto four years later. By the late 1970s, close to 100 per cent

of five-year-olds were enrolled in Kindergarten programs. By 1995, about 95 per cent of four-year-olds were attending junior Kindergarten programs.

(ETFO, 2001, p. 3)

The social movements of the 1950s–1970s brought awareness to the public about early years education. However, it was only after the 1980s that the Liberal government introduced policy to expand Junior and Senior Kindergarten programs. The Liberal policies were continued and enhanced into the 1990s by the succeeding New Democratic Party (NDP), resulting in the government considering greater infrastructure and funding to support the development of early years educational programs across Ontario. In fact, there was a pendulum shift during those years as the political parties changed powers, which influenced the history and development of the Kindergarten program in Ontario. With the change of government again in 1995, when the Progressive Conservatives took office, this new government tried to undo most of the policy initiatives and cut funding for Junior Kindergarten in half.

By the late 1960s, Half-Day Kindergarten was well-established in Ontario cities, and it was increasingly available in rural communities as the result of school consolidation. In 1979, close to 100 per cent of five-year-old children in Ontario were enrolled in Kindergarten programs while 39 per cent of four-year olds attended Junior Kindergarten. The mid-1970's also marked the development of Montessori programs and schools in Canada. The Montessori environment was a unique classroom setup with specific materials. The classroom environment was prepared with small shelves for ease of access to learning materials that would encourage children to become independent and move freely. Children were taught how to use materials correctly, often in a particular order and as they were developmentally ready.

In 1989, the Liberal government announced that school boards would be required to offer Half-Day Junior and Senior Kindergarten programs. The concept of requiring school boards to offer Junior Kindergarten programs had recently been proposed in the *Report of the Early Primary Education Project* commissioned by the Progressive Conservative government of Bill Davis. The 1989 Throne Speech also committed the government to funding full-day Senior Kindergarten programs where classroom space permitted. The policies were to take effect over the next five years.

A general election was held in September 1990 when the New Democratic Party led by Bob Rae took office. The NDP government, however, implemented the Liberal policy and even supported the policy with additional funding. The Education Ministry provided 100 per cent funding for Junior Kindergarten students, regardless of school boards' level of provincial grants. In 1994, the government also established a $35 million capital fund to assist boards to build or renovate Junior Kindergarten classrooms. School boards were given until September 1997 to fully implement the Kindergarten policy.

It was not only until the late 1990s that the Liberals once again gained power and pushed forward the early years program development in the Province of Ontario and in 1998 introduced *The Kindergarten Program*, the first policy document for Ontario Kindergarten curriculum development (ETFO, 2001). *The Kindergarten Program (1998)* provided specific expectations for children's learning in Kindergarten and the knowledge and skills that children should develop by the end of Kindergarten. Within the provincial levels, there was a significant gain that got the ball rolling. Not only was this early years educational movement a political and provincial phenomenon, but it was also a national and global one. Other provinces and countries were also looking at early years educational policy changes. Additionally, in 2003, expert panels on early reading and early math released reports in Ontario (Ontario Ministry of Education, 2003a, 2003b) and other Ministry documents were released (Ontario Ministry of Education, 2006a, 2006b). For a summary of titles of main reports and for further information, see Appendix B.

However, according to the Elementary Teachers Federation of Ontario (2001), the PC government moved quickly to undo most of the policy initiatives of its predecessors, including the policy to expand Junior Kindergarten. In November 1995, the government announced that it would be cutting $400million from elementary and secondary education grants, including a $100 million cut to Junior Kindergarten, a reduction of about 50 per cent. The change of provincial government in 1995 meant more changes for early childhood education. Reversing the 1989 policy, the government announced that school boards no longer were required to provide Junior Kindergarten for 4-year-olds and changed the amount of grant funding per child. When 22 boards exited the program, communities lost more than 20,000 Junior Kindergarten spaces, with an accompanying loss of 1,400 teacher jobs. The early childhood pilot project initiative was cancelled, as was the capital funding for child care space in new schools. Start-up grants are no longer available, replaced by a health and safety fund to take care of only urgently needed repairs. The Education Act was amended once again to prohibit education spending on child care.

Moving into the 2000s, there was revised hope for the early years movement that would lead to changes that would stay and be supported by the Ontario government. Studies such as the *Early Years Study* and *Best Start Initiatives* were taking shape, and integrated and play-based learning programs were getting attention. Also, other provinces were moving forward with significant changes in early years programs. The government supported Early Years Centers and free access for families with children from birth to the age of six. Investing in the early years seems prudent as it offers children a better foundation for learning. Once children were in public school programs this also meant more parents could go back to work with seamless child-care arrangements. In 2003, The Ontario Early Years Framework began to guide the plan for early years program development and delivery for families and children. This included a comprehensive plan for early years initiatives across the province. With greater priority and initiatives from the government for high-quality family-centered programs and services, accompanied with greater support and resources, early years education made considerable progress.

In 2006, *The Kindergarten Program (1998)* was revised and replaced by a new curriculum document. The national and international early years development programs were researched and studied more closely by the Ontario government and finally, with greater collaboration and support, early years development started becoming a reality. The biggest gains were in the twenty-first century with the introduction of Full-Day Kindergarten for both Junior and Senior Kindergarten. *The Full-Day Early Learning Kindergarten Program—Draft Version* (2010–11) was released to begin the implementation of the FDK program across the province of Ontario. It is interesting to note that we moved from a twenty-page curriculum document to one that was almost two hundred pages in length. There is no doubt that the importance and value of early years education was being provincially recognized and the study of early years pedagogy was continuing to evolve.

The Half-Day Kindergarten (HDK) program integrated more formal teaching and teacher-directed classroom practices. The children were involved in center-based learning, which may have been more formally organized by having the teacher and children rotate through various centers throughout the week. There was more of a requirement that all children would complete certain activities each week. Therefore, there was a more formal structure with direct instruction, and the rules and routines were more rigidly enforced. The FDK program shifted the learning in Kindergarten to less formal and more organic with flexibility, choice, and variety for the child and less teacher-directed learning. Not only did the amount of time that children were involved in the school environment change, but the way they were being taught also changed as FDK was established in Ontario schools.

On September 7, 2010, Ontario made history when Premier Dalton McGuinty moved ahead with FDK and as Boards launched

Ella Karia, Ed.D.

Full-Day Early Learning Kindergarten in 600 schools across the province. Approximately 35,000 four- and five-year-old children benefitted from the first phase of full-day learning as part of the province's plan to build a stronger school system and a well-educated workforce. The province has made a commitment to fully implement the Full-Day Kindergarten Program in all schools by 2015–2016. The introduction of FDK in 2010 has resulted in increased enrollment each year in Kindergarten. In Table 1 below is a summary of Junior Kindergarten (JK) and Senior Kindergarten (SK) public school enrollment in Kindergarten in Ontario.

Table 1
Public Schools Enrolment in Kindergarten in Ontario

Year	Junior Kindergarten (JK)	Senior Kindergarten (SK)
2012-13	117 829	124 576
2011-12	87 120	90 127
2010-11	84 254	87 991
2009-10	81 598	86 903
2008-09	80 617	85 359
2007-08	79 025	83 769

Source: Ontario Ministry of Education. (2007–2013) *Ontario Schools: Quick Facts.* Toronto: Queen's Printer. (Data obtained from the Ontario School Information System).

Looking Across Canada: Provincial Comparisons

Seven provinces and one territory in Canada have implemented FDK programs. Some only have FDK for five-year-olds. The province of Ontario introduced FDK in 2010 along with British Columbia (BC) for both four- and five-year-olds. In the past, Quebec and New Brunswick have developed an FDK program for five-year-olds. In addition, Nova Scotia has had FDK since 1995 for five-year-olds. Prince Edward Island and Northwest Territories (NWT) are piloting

14

some FDK programs, but Manitoba has yet to get on the bandwagon for FDK. Class size is highest among Ontario schools. With the election of Liberal Prime Minister Justin Trudeau in November 2015 and majority Liberal party at the provincial level we hope for more support for educational endeavors and positive change in the future. Below in Table 2 is a summary of class size limits in different provinces.

Table 2
Summary of Statistics on FDK Plans across Canada

Province	FDK start	Maximum Class Size
Quebec	1999 for 5-year-olds	20
New Brunswick	1999 for 5-year-olds	22
Nova Scotia	1995 for 5-year-olds; some sites piloting JK programs	25
Ontario	2010 for 4- and 5-year-olds	26
British Columbia	2010 for 4- and 5-year-olds	22
Prince Edward Island	2010 offers some FDK for 4- and 5-year-olds, primarily in child care. (15 with one teacher and 24 maximum with two qualified teachers)	24
Manitoba	Only some (Francophone schools)	20
Northwest Territories	FDK for 5 year olds (16 for one teacher in Education Act) Note: Phasing in for 4-year-olds in Sept. 2014).	16

Justification and Significance of the Study

Since the mid-1980s, a great deal of public attention has been focused on educational systems, and the importance of early years educational programs for four- and five-year-old children across Canada. Questions about the length of the program and the content of the curriculum were raised (Best Start Expert Panel on Early Learning, 2007). Controversial issues that have also been raised over the years include inappropriate formal teaching techniques for young children and an overemphasis on the achievement of narrowly defined academic skills

(Canadian Council on Learning, 1996, 2006; McQuail, Mooney et al., 2003). This all influenced the shift in Kindergarten practices in Ontario schools at the turn of the century. Dr. Charles Pascal, the Premier's Special Advisor on Early Learning, released a report, *With our Best Future in Mind: Implementing Early Learning in Ontario* on June 15, 2009. The advice and consultation with Dr. Pascal was instrumental in moving Ontario forward with FDK. In the past, many research studies have compared the impact of HDK with FDK.

Table 3
Research Showing Impact of FDK vs. HDK

Research Study	FDK – Major Benefits and Effects
NCES, 2004	Integrating learning with activities – all eight participants adapted to a centre-based learning approach
Cleveland et al., 2006 Walsten & West, 2004	Room layout, setup, access to materials, variety of play, both indoor and outdoor spaces stimulating
Plucker, 2004; Janus M et. al. 2012	Inquiry-based learning, encourage problem-solving and critical thinking and finding ways to extend learning and use different senses
Cryan et. al. 1992	Whole-child focus – look closer at natural sciences, engaging in nature as a classroom for learning, building on different perspectives, focusing on children's own ideas and thinking
Da Costa & Bell, 2001	FDK has demonstrated positive academic effects for at-risk children
Pelletier 2012a,b, 2014	Improved self-regulation and readiness skills
Vanderlee et. al., 2013	Similar basic literacy – letter recognition, but improved advanced oral communication skills, phonetics, and reading
Da Costa, 2005	FDK appeared to eliminate the gap between high and low socio-economic status children in reading and writing, but not in numeracy. This effect was sustained until end of grade 3, although diminishing

After the introduction of the draft version of the Full-Day Kindergarten (FDK) policy change, there has been growing attention on understanding what is actually happening in the Kindergarten classrooms. Thus, it is valuable to talk to those who implement the change—the teachers. Teachers can share perspectives on the implementation phase, its impact in the classroom, and the overall outcome of the policy change. Furthermore, in light of current knowledge of child development and play-based Kindergarten learning programs, there is a growing body of emerging research affirming that children learn more effectively through concrete, play-oriented approaches to early childhood education. By looking more closely at how young children learn in Kindergarten programs, we can see that programs should be more tailored to meet children's needs (e.g., play-based learning) rather than expecting them to adjust to the demands of adult-tailored programs. The trend now seems to be moving toward actually observing children in classrooms and thereby gaining a better understanding of how they learn best. Viewing the child as curious, competent and capable of complex thinking has been the overarching vision and the predominant outlook shaping early years pedagogy. Educators continue to respond and shift teaching and learning practices providing more meaningful environments and experiences for children to explore and investigate.

The historical trends in teaching styles are displayed below. There is a shift in mindset among some Kindergarten teachers from the 'old' instructivist way of thinking to the 'new' constructivist way of teaching, which includes more play-based learning pedagogy. The 'new' growth mind-set adapts to change, builds in more imagination, critical thinking, creative thinking and individual differences. For some teachers, there is a lack of clarity about what the new model really looks like in the classroom. As such, they feel that they are not familiar with what is actually supposed to be done. Many FDK teachers are still experimenting with curriculum changes and are learning as they go. Consequently, as the policy change is recent and implementation is new, there is a need for more evidence, research, and discussion on Kindergarten teaching practices and the 'High Scope' path as we move forward.

The 'High Scope' curriculum is based on active learning through key experiences that can be adapted in countries around the world. 'High Scope' curriculum has been extensively researched and demonstrated positive results over the long term (Best Start Expert Panel on Early Learning, 2007). It is widely used in Ontario and adapted for use in Quebec. The overall vision is that children learn best at all ages with active experiences with people, materials, events and ideas rather than through direct instruction. It has a strong constructivist focus. It is used in many Kindergarten programs throughout Ontario. The present research study provides some insight into this educational policy change.

Each teacher interprets, focuses, and develops a Kindergarten program in his / her own way. Thus, the different teachers' voices will be based on their own personal experiences. In the future, we can redesign, rethink, and even remove practices as we get a clearer picture of FDK classroom expectations and experiences. Improving quality in education means understanding existing teaching practices thoroughly before reshaping and improving upon what already exists. We need to see exactly what exists in FDK classrooms. What does it look like in the classroom when teachers implement the FDK model? What specific activities or centers are present in the Kindergarten classroom? The research was intended to gain a better understanding of current pedagogical methods such as play-based learning in Kindergarten.

Our observations of the child inform us that educators need to respond, extend and enhance development through play and inquiry. Educators need to respect the multiple cultural ways of knowing, seeing and living and the uniqueness of each child. Educators need to understand and honor the curiosities and questions of each child. These are some significant ways they can support the needs of each child. As educators push their thinking and practice they are redefining their role and finding better ways to improve learning.

The internalization of theory and its application and practice synthesizes our beliefs and inspires our vision of what should be. The purpose of this research study was, in part, to gain a better understanding of Kindergarten teaching practices. It was driven by the desire to understand the early years development and the life of the child in his / her formative years. It is crucial to start with what children know and to understand more about how they learn at this age. Therefore, reviewing literature, studies, and educational philosophies informed my research. Talking to different Kindergarten teachers who are developing their classroom practices to integrate FDK would shed light on what teachers are thinking and how they can help policy-makers better understand the ways in which they want to improve the Kindergarten learning experience for children (see Appendix E). Further, by using the teachers' accounts and to understand what students want to know and what motivates them, teachers' can be more aware of how to make the environment more conducive to meeting the needs of children. This research is intended to be of value to all stakeholders in education: parents, students, teachers, principals, board employees, researchers, academics, and policy makers.

The problem examined in this study is directly linked to the quality of teaching and learning practices in the classroom and the need to clearly articulate the key elements of quality FDK. A quality program needs to be comprehensive and integrated. In the past, research has focused more on quantitative research and the impact of the FDK program on children. This qualitative research study fills a gap by providing rich descriptive data and insight on the learning process itself from the perspective of the teachers. The focus is on the approaches, practices, and key elements of building an FDK program. This research is highly significant, timely and relevant at this crucial time of honing the FDK model and before the release of the final version of *FDELK* document by the government.

The book is important and timely in informing others within the province, but also across Canada as some provinces are still moving in the direction of FDK.

Research Goals

Fostering Creativity explores the rich dialogue with Kindergarten teachers by looking closely at teachers' experiences in the classroom and their understanding and development of play-based instruction and learning. The research highlights how some teachers have planned their program in the Kindergarten classroom, focused on play-based centers and activities. Using the case study methodology, examples of FDK teaching practices are shared. The study reveals how teachers facilitate and scaffold learning in FDK. The focus of the research is the following: (a) the Kindergarten teachers' teaching experiences; (b) the understanding of teachers' interpretation of play-based instruction and learning; (c) the exploration of Kindergarten teachers' teaching practices in their own classroom; (d) finding out teachers' opinions, perspectives, and personal teaching style; (e) discussing early years educational philosophies.

The main emphasis of *Fostering Creativity* is to provide insight on the new shifts in Kindergarten teaching and learning practices by looking at teachers' perspectives, examining how creative thinking evolves, analyzing teachers' responses, exploring FDK planning, and looking at the implementation of play-based activities in Ontario's FDK classrooms. The teachers' perspectives provide invaluable insight for policy-makers, scholars, administrators, and educators. By sharing teachers' examples of lived experiences in the FDK classroom, their opinions and ideas, their interpretations of policy, and their understanding of improvements for FDK, this research study will guide future Kindergarten classroom practice at a global level.

The Research Focus

In formulating and developing the research study, I reviewed early years education literature and incorporated educational theories. As a result of this research, I also designed and developed a conceptual framework that included models (i.e., the Integrated Child Development—PIE Model and the Five Key Elements in the FDK program—The PIECE model). At the end, after data analysis, I modified the PIE model, merged it with the PIECE model, and created the EYE (Early Years Education) Model—a comprehensive integrated child development model. *Fostering Creativity* focuses on the following questions:

1. What kinds of teaching practices are evident in Ontario's Full Day Kindergarten (FDK) 'play-based' learning classroom?
2. What are the key elements for consideration in setting up of the FDK classroom?
3. What are teachers' perspectives of and challenges with the implementation of the FDK program in Ontario?

In Ontario, the phased-in implementation plan for FDK meant some schools were moving to FDK earlier than others. In accordance with Bill 242, by 2015/16 all schools in Ontario should be providing FDK learning. In this study, teachers share their FDK experiences, which will inform others who are still planning, and developing Full-Day Kindergarten learning and programs in schools. Furthermore, teachers' insight and perspectives give us a better understanding of the reality of the classroom. Teachers who directly experience the policy change may have a different perspective than the policy-makers who plan for it. This current research study seeks to highlight the different perspectives of Kindergarten teachers and share various real-life classroom experiences.

Situating Myself

Deciding on activities and lessons, planning, creating and managing a classroom of young inquisitive minds was always fascinating. As a teacher it always was the joy of children's perspectives that made me smile. It was the love for learning and making learning fun that made my work play. I often explored educational practices in my own classroom, shifting towards constructivist teaching approaches and building learning centres with a holistic perspective in mind. I had the privilege of working with many different elementary schools and recognized different learning and teaching styles, embracing the unique diversity of each community and the varying school cultures. I really enjoyed what I was doing every day. It was the creative aspects as a teacher that was exciting and always evolving in my teaching and learning approaches. Over the past ten years of being a classroom teacher in many different elementary schools, the breadth of knowledge and experience has shaped my thinking and understanding. I believe the more a teacher can allow the child to understand who they truly are they are unravelling a deeper awareness of what makes them unique and special.

Born in England and having been taught in my kindergarten years in a British school system sparked curiosities to look closer at European educational approaches. During my visits to England, Italy, Germany and Switzerland I learned about schooling in towns that I visited. In particular the Reggio-Emilia model brought great impact and influence in developing my educational philosophy and classroom practices when I came back to my own classroom. The memories of travel and connecting deeply and building understanding of best practices globally really got me reflecting and thinking of all the important things I observed and learned. In United States of America the 'high scope' practice I observed focused learning by promoting decision-making and problem-solving. I often visited schools and observed active participatory learning with both small and large groups. It was evident to me that what mattered more was not how much was covered in Kindergarten learning, but how deeply one explored an area of interest. With all the senses and a sense of full awareness a moment of discovery could leave an impression for a lifetime.'

I was fortunate enough to have the opportunity to see different types of schools and educational programs in many countries. It was during my travels to India that I started to take further interest in educational projects and explore international systems of education more closely. This led me to join various educational project committees, and since 2006, I have been supporting educational school development through charitable projects, raising money to help educate the poor in India. During my visits to India in 2006 and 2013, I learned how even schools abroad were honing in on best practices in the early years, and how child-centered learning approaches were evident in these schools.

I expanded my understanding of education at a global level broadening my perspectives and understanding. In India, many children were taught under trees at times. They were often involved in planting fruits and vegetables to build self-sustaining and self-regulating lifestyles. Children also engaged in the daily practices of yoga and meditation. At a very young age, children were taught the power of settling within, building strength, and improving flexibility. Meditation and yoga was a part of the school day. My experiences in India broadened my perspectives, encouraged me to look deeper at Gandhi's philosophies (Gandhi, 1929, 1938) on the power of human intellect, and allowed me to compare educational approaches on a more global level. It was a way of knowing and learning at a global level as well as appreciating simple traditions as effective practices. Sometimes we get lost in the new and forget to go back to the old. Thereafter, as a teacher, during my visits to places around the world, I would look for opportunities to observe educational systems. This became a very interesting and enlightening undertaking. Seeing an international perspective brought me to a more global level. I also began to appreciate the traditional as well as the modern ways of knowing, both Eastern and Western educational philosophies and approaches. As a contemplative practitioner, I could see how all these experiences informed my way of knowing.

Since 2007, as a teacher and researcher, I have continually shifted my approach by re-evaluating and re-examining my work. In the process, I have discovered that it is valuable to have experiences in both teaching and research as one informs the other. I have created a balance between my academic work and my classroom work. This is important to me. Over the years, during the process of questioning and discovering, I began to make meaning of what I observed. Having teaching experience informed my perspectives on how children learn. I also divided the role of teacher and researcher. Starting to wear the hat of an academic researcher challenged me to yet another perspective, and I focused on my researcher role for the purpose of this study.

In addition, as a mother of two children, the parent perspective informed my work. During the time of making decisions for educating my own children in the early years, I began to evaluate different educational approaches. I began to examine the way that classrooms were managed, the opportunities the children had, and the best methods of teaching and learning for 3–6-year-olds. I considered the deeply-rooted moral and philosophical orientations when choosing a school for my children. It was insightful to have the parent perspective and see first-hand the value and importance of investing in quality early childhood education programs in the formative years. The importance of presence in learning and the significance of mindfulness as a foundation of learning cultivated in my mind. At that time, I was on the path to observe, compare, research, and read more about educational philosophies.

Over the years with children and as an adult I realized the importance of opportunities for developing creative energies and how much I even built my confidence when given opportunities to share my thinking and ideas. Fostering creativity became more and more important, in my mind, at any age. Ideally every classroom in elementary school could have a creative corner and not only structured art class once or twice a week. There could be building and art materials, problem-solving challenges, journals and music with greater access for students through out the day. From the early years to adulthood we can achieve excellence with more experiential learning as well as develop critical thinking skills. Cultivating innovators, creative talents, and entrepreneurship will build vibrant leaders for the future. As I followed my curiosities and passion there were multiple avenues for higher-order thinking and personal development.

I learned that as human beings we have the unique capacity to be aware of our internal and external worlds and the interactions between the two. We have the ability to pay attention to our innate human capacity. As educators and parents we need to teach children how to pay attention and not only ask students to - pay attention! Being mindful, empathetic and sensitive can improve the clarity and effectiveness of communication. For me and my children it was a daily practice to find a still and quiet place in the physical, mental and emotional sense to deepen and strengthen connections. A quiet still place was a space to reflect and deepen understanding.

Teaching was not only a job for me but also a personal interest and a journey for defining best teaching practices, as I deeply embedded myself in finding the optimum approaches for child development through study and practice. The inner desire and search for the ideal educational system continued to resonate with me, and the yearning to learn about different educational philosophies incubated within me for years. There often seemed to be something unique that each had to offer, but finding the one ideal educational philosophy was not easy. Looking at both theory and practice was insightful. Raising my own children and working as a classroom teacher in Kindergarten allowed me to deepen my understanding of child development. Both my teacher role and parental role informed my researcher role. This led to my doctoral journey of learning more about the early years educational movement and exploring integrated child development approaches. Then I realized how this research was taking shape before my eyes. *Fostering Creativity* was the accumulation of years of work.

The relationships and connections I have with others and the personal feelings I have for the people around me help define who I am. Therefore, through my journey as an elementary schoolteacher, I met different teachers and educators and worked in five different schools. I learned a lot by working with so many wonderful professionals, and connecting with others really inspired me to begin and continue my passion for writing *Fostering Creativity*. It was the connections with students and seeing them develop that inspired me the most. The quality of early years practices made a difference in childhood development. Educational experiences before the age of six set a foundation for life-long learning abilities (Mustard, 2006; Pascal, 2009a, 2009b; Shonkoff & Phillips, 2000); this fact also reinforces the importance of honing on the quality of programs.

The young minds in front of me each day in my Kindergarten classroom were forming, and I felt a greater sense of responsibility for the search and development of best Kindergarten teaching practices. Thereafter, the importance and calibre of my work took on a new meaning. Finally, the governmental shifts and the introduction of FDK were also emerging, and I began to hear more about Ontario's plans to shift to FDK. Having taught Kindergarten for over eight years I could directly relate to the way things were and the way things were going. The changes, the progressive thinking, the new focus, the shifts and emerging direction of learning for young children brightened the new path of thinking in my own mind.

With the educational policy changes that were happening around me, I could feel the importance and need to map out a clearer path moving forward. I wanted to connect more deeply with teachers and find out more about their thinking on such topics as early years education. Taking on the researcher role began to take priority. Professionally, I felt the desire and responsibility to learn about the new trends and shifts in Kindergarten teaching philosophies and practices, make sense of the new FDK curriculum, and then share my findings.

Laying the Framework

This research study connects what is important to me, and that is giving teachers a voice. Building awareness of what teachers actually do in the classroom and observing different teaching styles gives one a chance to gain insight into areas that we often do not share. Nowadays, children are sent off at an earlier age to a learning environment for many hours of the day, thus, it is vital to give teachers a voice to determine how best to foster learning for children.

In *Fostering Creativity* there is a focus on understanding the Kindergarten program in public schools in Ontario since the implementation of FDK. By having conversations with the different Kindergarten teachers and gathering information from them during interviews, I gained much insight on how teachers were adapting and implementing the FDK model. This was informative and enlightening. At this time, five years into the FDK model there is a lot that has been learned in the implementation phase of policy change. Educators have gained experiences and knowledge as they embarked on this shift in Kindergarten teaching and learning practices.

The outline below provides an overview of the various chapters of this book. The introduction in Chapter One has provided the background information, including a brief history of Kindergarten in Ontario; the context of the research, with some details on the general focus of this research study; the research goals; the framework; and most importantly, the direction of emerging curriculum for the early years.

Chapter Two develops a literature review and theoretical framework for this research. This chapter will explore the body of literature that speaks to my topic of research. The literature review focuses on seminal scholars and theorists on child development, educational philosophies, and play. This research inspired the design of three models: i) PIE Model (Play, Inquiry, Experiential Learning), ii) PIECE Model (Play, Inquiry, Experiential, Child-Centered, Environmental Education), and later the iii) EYE (Early Years Education) Model was created. The three models identify key elements and guide teaching practice with the emerging curriculum in the Kindergarten years.

Chapter Three highlights the qualitative methodology employed to collect data for this study. I explore the literature on qualitative research, in particular the case study approach. I describe the design of the research, data collection methods, and data analysis. I also discuss some of the ethical considerations and limitations of the study, Furthermore, there are details on the teacher participant profiles as well as each teacher's classroom demographics and routines provide rich details for the stories that follow.

Chapter Four identifies the key findings from the research study. It identifies specific quotes, teaching practices, and opinions from different teacher participants. There are more specific details from each teacher participant's classroom practices and a summary of teaching styles. I also highlight the significance and implications of the key findings according to identified themes derived from the coded data. Overall, data results are summarized in this chapter. The stories reveal real-life examples of how teachers are fostering creativity and implementing emerging teaching and curriculum practices.

Chapter Five makes connections to the data findings, with discussion and data analysis. The key themes are identified, and the weaving of data findings with the literature review ties the research to the key research questions. I present and analyze the experiences of the teacher participants in the FDK classroom, their teaching styles, and specific classroom practices. I connect the scholarly theories and concepts with classroom practices, examining it as a researcher and reporting on how it connects with the Integrated

Child Development Model and the development of the EYE (Early Years Education) Model. Key elements of FDK teaching practices and the integrated approach in the Kindergarten classrooms are highlighted. Finally, I discuss the overall teachers' perspectives and the research process itself; I also present the various implications and limitations of the study, along with some thoughts on future direction for research. Overall, this personal journey as a researcher inspired me to build a breadth of knowledge, awareness, and insight into teaching practices, as I pieced together thoughts, data, and scholarly work I embraced my work and documented my finding to provide insight for educators. A teachers' voice provides a unique perspective, a glimpse into the classroom and a deeper understanding of the teaching and learning process.

Chapter 2

EDUCATIONAL PHILOSOPHIES

"Children are not shaped by experience, but are the ones who give shape to it"

(Loris Malaguzzi, 1989, p.86)

Introduction

This literature review summarizes various educational philosophies, theories, and concepts that guided my research work on FDK. While conceptual theories guide the research and establish a base to look at child development theories, some thoughts on creating a new model to directly address the needs of children as learners is developed. By reviewing schools of thought on child development and deepening the meaning and understanding of Kindergarten pedagogical approaches, this chapter brings awareness to key elements in the FDK program.

There are many seminal and influential early childhood education scholars whose works have informed this research study. For instance, this literature review examines the works of Froebel

(1887, 1889), Dewey (1916, 1929), and cognitive development theorists such as Piaget (1950, 1962, 1969), Vygotsky (1934, 1978), and Bruner (1961, 1967, 1976), who further researched the power of play for child developmental stages. The literature review also examines the research undertaken by play theorist such as Sutton-Smith (1966, 1976, 1997). In addition, educational philosophies, including Montessori (1967/1973, 1995) and Waldorf, inspired by Steiner (1994), as well as Reggio-Emilia's emergent curriculum, developed by Malaguzzi (1993) were later influential schools of thoughts in early years education. Lastly, more contemporary holistic education practitioners such as R. Miller (1991, 1992, 1995, 2000, 2002, 2006), J. P. Miller (1993, 1996, 2000, 2006, 2007, 2010, 2011), and P. J. Palmer (1993, 2004, 2007) are discussed. The scholarly work on schooling and individual identity by Gardner (1987 1987), Wane (2007, 2010, 2011), and Binder (2008, 2011) also informed the research.

The key elements of FDK learning are discussed and identified in the PIECE (Play, Inquiry-based learning, "Experiential" learning, Child-centred learning and "Environmental" education) Model. The new FDK curriculum showed evidence of more constructivist teaching approaches and the FDK practices have shifted from traditional teaching approaches to more contemporary ones as teachers open up to new pedagogical paradigms. There was a greater sense of experimentation with combining pedagogical approaches in classrooms today. Therefore, understanding the different teaching practices, FDK focus in Ontario schools, and early learning philosophies informed this research study. The identification of specific scholars and their works on early years development shed light on and guided the discussion. Understanding the background and various details related to concepts, ideologies, and theories gave more insight into this research study. In the next section, I begin to elaborate on literature of Froebel (1887, 1889), the 'Father of Kindergarten,' and then follow with an examination of influential child development theorists.

Froebel as the 'Father of Kindergarten.' Friedrich Froebel, known as the 'Father of Kindergarten,' was a German educationalist who believed that humans are essentially productive and creative. Froebel (1887, 1889) thought it was important to encourage creativity, free self-activity, motor expression, and social participation in the educational setting through the direct use of materials. He also believed that it is through engaging in the world that understanding and learning unfolds, hence the significance of play as both a creative activity and a means through which children become aware of their place in the world. Children would develop creativity if they were given proper play materials and were instructed on their use. A rich environment that provided a variety of learning materials and equipment would contribute to the development of children's intellect.

Froebel (1887) advocated for 'free play' in childhood using special 'gifts' and 'occupations,' which demonstrated certain relationships and led children to compare, test, and explore. According to Froebel, each 'gift' (or Gabe) given to a child was designed to provide material for the child's self-directed activity (1887, p. 285). The 'gifts,' or special materials, consisted of a series of natural wood play materials. Two examples of 'gifts' included four geometric wooden blocks and six crocheted woolen balls consisting of 3 primary and 3 secondary colors. Three common solids (sphere, cube, and cylinder), suspended in such a way that children could examine their different properties by rotating, spinning, and touching, were also a common gift. In total, there were over twenty types of 'gifts.' "The 'gifts' led to discovery…the 'gift' gives insight" (1887, p. 287). 'Occupations,' according to Froebel, move from three-dimensional to two-dimensional surfaces and are more activity-based. 'Occupations' consist of weaving, drawing, and clay modeling, which recognized as traditional components of a Kindergarten program. Initially, Froebel (1889) thought both 'gifts' and 'occupations' were taught through educational games in the family, and later in his life, his work was linked to provisions in educational centers for the care and development of children outside of the home.

Froebel's (1887) philosophy of educational play rested on four basic components: (a) free self-activity; (b) creativity; (c) social participation; and (d) motor expression. As Froebel (1887, 1889) asserts, Kindergarten signifies a 'garden' for children; it signifies a location where they can observe and interact and where they themselves can grow and develop in freedom. In the 1880s, when the Froebelian approaches to Kindergarten were first introduced in Canada, only Senior Kindergarten (SK) was established, as many believed the younger children (under 5 years old) should be at home with their mothers. Moving forward through the 1900s, European influences on education continued in Canada and then eventually more awareness of world-wide philosophies in early years education brought a more global realm of approaches. In Canada it was not until the 1940s that the Kindergarten began to extend to include three- and four-year-old children, which came to be known as Junior Kindergarten (JK).

The Kindergarten classroom in public schools began to become more widely accepted and developed based on the Froebel philosophy. Froebel's (1887) main methods included circles, singing games, art activities, and child development through play. We are fortunate to have had Froebel's Kindergarten ideas in our heritage as, once it took root, it grew and flourished. The Froebel 'play-based' learning was grounded from centuries ago and this approach nurtured and cultivated thousands of young minds. This continues to be a key component in the new FDK model today. Froebel's methods also inspired various schools of thought including the works of Montessori (1973, 1995), Steiner's Waldorf philosophy (1994), and Malaguzzi's Reggio-Emilia curriculum (1993), which were later developed.

Dewey's Principles of Education. Scholars such as John Dewey, one of America's most famous educators and philosophers, believed that one learns by doing and that children's play is a primary vehicle for mental growth. Therefore, child-initiated, child-directed, and teacher-supported play is an essential component of developmentally appropriate practices in the early years (Bredekamp, 1987). Dewey (1929, 1933, 1938) asserts that children learn through experience and that they each have particular individual interests. Dewey, who can be considered more of a philosopher for progressive education than an educational theorist, described educational excellence as helping each child become self-directed and getting children involved in learning. Dewey (1916, 1929) influenced Kindergarten programs (especially from the 1920s to 1950s) and created classrooms where there were many different areas; daily routine was stressed, but formal reading and math were not taught as an isolated skill. Dewey (1929, 1933, 1938) believed that children should be engaged in scientific inquiry in all subject areas in order to develop into good communicators and thinkers, and he created an atmosphere that was more relaxed to make children comfortable in the school environment. Whether traditional or progressive, Dewey's (1929, 1938) principles of carefully developed philosophy of experience examined a true learning situation as orderly and dynamic, and as employing a progressive organization of subject matter. It is important to look at the present experience. Dewey (1938), in his book, *Experience and Education*, states:

> Give the pupils something to do, not something to learn; and the doing is of such a nature as to demand thinking; learning naturally results... experience arouses curiosity, strengthens initiative, and sets up desires and purposes that are sufficiently intense to carry a person over dead places in the future, continuity works in a very different way. Every experience is a moving force. (p. 38)

Dewey (1929, 1933, 1938) believed that education is a process of living and advocated that curriculum should be connecting the child's past experiences and interests to develop the present experience to greater satisfaction. The environment and the social actions, dialogue between teacher and learner were important. The child is credited for bringing prior knowledge to the world of learning and the teacher encourages reflective capabilities as a way of fostering understanding. Dewey's work (1938) has influenced Piaget's work (1950, 1969) and has reinforced the importance of the social aspect of education and the necessity to connect home life with school life, in order to enrich the overall learning experience. Furthermore, these works raised awareness that children's learning does not occur in narrowly defined subject areas. The process of interacting with materials and people results in learning. Education, as Dewey describes, must be focused on enabling individuals to build a love for learning. Dewey clarifies, "The aim of education is to enable individuals to continue their education ... [and] the object and reward of learning is the continued capacity for growth." (Dewey, 1916, p.117). This starts with giving children the best possible childhood and early years education.

Child Development Theories

Piaget's Constructivist Theory and thoughts on play. Jean Piaget, Swiss Psychologist, was interested in the 'cognitive developmental theory.' Piaget (1927, 1950) believed that children think differently from adults, and he opened the way for educators to explore how children come to learn new knowledge. He unveiled that cognitive behaviors evolved through stages of mental development called 'cognitive schemes,' and he focused more on individual contact with objects than with people. Piaget (1950, 1952) also viewed language and thought as significant cognitive processes. He theorized that mental development took place through three periods from birth to pre-adolescence. Overall, Piaget (1950) set many developmental milestones and developmentally-appropriate practices in early years.

Piaget (1962) reinforced that adults can facilitate a child's learning schema by verbal encouragement, physical proximity, and focused attention as well as by opportunities for social interaction and trial and error. Piaget (1962, 1969) also thought it was important to provide activities and an environment to support growth corresponding to the developmental level of the child. Piaget (1972) believed that the social support and opportunities for interactions and communication enriched the overall learning experience.

Piaget's Theory of Cognitive Development (1950, 1972) is a cornerstone for understanding how children think and learn. During the preoperational stage (2 to 6 years of age), children develop the ability to think in 'symbolic form' and use language to name symbolic representation or to make meaning of objects. At this stage, children are developing proficiency in the use of language, and are able to think logically and reason in one direction. They also have a sense of adaptation or ongoing interaction with the environment and new experiences add to the child's organization schema. Thus, it is important to allow children to explore objects and learn by interacting with their environment as they make sense of the world by feeling, seeing, and categorizing objects.

Within the Theory of Cognitive Development (Piaget, 1950, 1952) lie four stages, each one containing the processes to adapt assimilation (transform the environment) and accommodation (change thought process and accept something in the environment). Piaget's (1950, 1972) four cognitive development stages are as follows: i) Sensorimotor stage (birth to age two), ii) Pre-operational stage (ages 2-7), iii) Concrete operational stage (ages 7-11), and iv) Formal operational stage (age 11+). It is the 'Pre-operational' stage that affects the Kindergarten years and this is when children start to use mental imagery and language. Children are very egocentric and view things around them with one point of view—theirs. Only in the 'Concrete operational' stage are children capable of taking another person's point of view and reasoning with concrete knowledge as the egocentric stage diminishes. During the 'Formal operational' stage, children can think logically, abstractly and theoretically. Understanding these child developmental stages informs classroom practice.

Piaget (1969, 1972) studied the mental processes of perception, memory, judgment, and reasoning and the stages a child moves through in order to acquire this ability. Piaget's contributions in understanding children's cognitive development and the different stages outlined major windows of opportunities. Piaget's ideas are utilized today in the set-up of Kindergarten and his theories of thought and cognitive development have no doubt influenced the philosophers who followed in his footsteps.

Vygotsky's Social Constructivist Learning Theory. Lev Vygotsky (1934, 1978) took the omission of social world of the child from Piaget and paved the social constructivist theory of child development. Learning and schooling have a highly complex and dynamic relation with social development. Vygotsky's (1934, 1978) main concept, referred to as the Zone of Proximal Development (ZPD), paved a new road in working with the child as a learner and understanding that each child has areas for potential development. Vygotsky's (1978) emphasis on the historical, social, and cultural aspects of development and learning supported a more meaningful involvement of the child, teacher, school, and community. The child is a social being, and Vygotsky's work (1934) looked closer at how we, as humans, naturally engage in our world. The relationship between play and cognitive development is described differently in Piaget's cognitive development theory and Vygotsky's social constructivist theory which dominate early childhood education. Piaget and Vygotsky both proposed an ideology that shaped the early years movement. The differences will be explored below by examining play and cognitive development.

Vygotsky's (1934, 1978) thinking and approach had holistic elements in that he rejected the view that what is to be learned can be broken down into small subcomponents and taught as discrete items and skills. Instead, Vygotsky argued that meaning should constitute the central aspect of learning. The notion of ZDP enables cooperation and positive interdependence. Rather than rote learning and paper-and-pencil approaches, there is an awareness and appreciation for the use of other forms of learning, including the incorporation of a variety of activities involving music, anxiety-reducing techniques, risk-taking, interpersonal relations, storytelling, role-play, drama, humor, and games in the classroom. These are known to facilitate the deep engagement among students and the transformation that is essential for the achievement of higher potential in teaching and learning. The Vygotskian 'Developmental Path to Play' defined age-related descriptions of play and fostered quality play experiences using props, imagination, defined roles, effective use of language, and dramatization.

In recent decades, the cognitive theories of Lev Vygotsky (1987, 1998) became more influential as he described children as learning, first interpersonally in relation with the minds of others, and then intra-personally within the individual child's own mind. In consequence, mental development is seen as a process in which children first borrow the ideas and language of others while playing, then transform them into mental structures that they can use and apply independently. Vygotsky (1978, 1998) viewed play as having a key role in children's learning, arguing that play is a social and cultural activity. The work of Piaget (1950, 1969, 1972) andthe published works of Vygotsky (1978, 1987, 1998)have demonstrated that learning is a complex process that results in the interaction of children's own thinking and their experiences in the external world. As children get older, they acquire new skills and experiences that facilitate the learning process. Children learn by doing, and play stimulates self-regulation, self-awareness, and self-confidence in children.

Bruner's Discovery Learning. Psychologist and cognitive learning theorist Jerome Bruner, born in New York and a Professor of Psychology at Harvard, published books such as *The Process of Education* (1960), *Acts of Meaning* (1991), and *The Culture of*

Education (1996). Bruner et al. (1976) first outlined the principles of discovery learning about how people construct knowledge based on prior experiences and then classified information and knowledge under three modes: enactive skills (manipulating objects, spatial awareness), iconic skills (visual recognition, the ability to compare and contrast), and symbolic skills (abstract reasoning). Bruner (1976) also examined the role of play in problem-solving skill development. Bruner (1967, 1976) initiated curriculum change based on the notion that learning is an active, social process in which students construct new ideas or concepts based on their current knowledge, and his work in childhood learning and perception has made him a key figure in educational reform. According to constructivist theory, we don't just absorb understanding; instead, we build it.

Bruner, Sylva, and Genova contend that "play enables a child to sustain his activity over a long period of time" (1976, p. 244). Play also contributes to problem-solving. Bruner et al. (1976), discovered that those who have had prior opportunities to play "are better equipped to solve problems and that they encounter frustration better than those who did not" (p. 245). In addition, Bruner et al. (1976) described how play influences the ability of the child to speak, listen, read, and write. Thus, it has been established that there is a connection between play and language development.

Understanding Individual Identity

Gardner's Multiple Intelligences and the importance of individual learning styles.

Howard Earl Gardner (2009, 2011), born in Pennsylvania in 1943, and co-founder with Nelson Goodman of 'Project Zero,' focused on studies of artistic thought and creativity and human potential. Gardner's ideas were published in the books *The Shattered Mind* and *Frames of Mind*. Gardner felt strongly that teachers should take individual differences among children seriously. Gardner (1999) emphasized that the bottom line is a deep interest in understanding how children's minds are different from one another's, and in helping them use their minds well in order to successfully participate in classroom learning.

Gardner's (1999, 2011) Multiple Intelligences (MI) theory raised awareness of the importance of honouring individual learning styles, particularly given students' diverse backgrounds and lived experiences; the student was no longer seen as an empty vessel that needed to be filled. Connecting learning to students' lived experiences had a very meaningful role in the learning process. The need for learners to take more responsibility (Gardner, 1975) led to a changing relationship between the student and the teacher. As children were encouraged to question and think, and teachers were required not to give answers, the teacher's role inevitably became more of a facilitator, and the students' participation and engagement became priorities.

Understanding that children learn in different ways and there is more than one type of intelligence opened the eyes of educators to look at various teaching approaches and differentiated learning practices. Gardner defined intelligence as the "ability to solve problems or create products that are valued within one or more cultural settings" (Gardner, 1999, 33–34). Not only did he define mathematical or linguistic intelligences, but with his new outlook, Gardner also defined many more types of intelligences that looked at other areas such as music, movement, visual, and personal. He conceived of 'seven intelligences': verbal-linguistic, musical-rhythmic, logical-mathematical, visual-spatial, bodily-kinesthetic, and personal (interpersonal and intrapersonal). Two decades later, Gardner added two more potentialities: naturalistic and existential intelligences. Implicit in his theory is the overlap of the intelligences (Gardner, 1999). His focus was more on how children learn in different ways.

Wane on defining spirituality in education: Cultural and gender identities.

Individual identity should not be marginalized in the classroom. Wane et al. (2005, 2011) argued that we need to appreciate individuals' spiritual and cultural identities. By defining what spirituality means to individuals, one can also see what influences someone's thinking. The transformative power of a spiritual vision engages the whole self and encourages sharing of sacred moments and practices. Wane (2011) reinforces how individual identity cannot be ignored in education. Rather, we need to appreciate that knowledge is not constant but is in constant flux and recreating itself, and reality is therefore an unfolding process determined by our own thoughts, words, and actions. Wane (2008, 2010) highlights that within this ongoing, unfolding process, appreciative inquiry entails having a conscious awareness of one's own spiritual way of knowing as well as that of others.

Optimal classroom experiences develop and focus learning in an effective way that considers inclusion, student voice, respect, and uniqueness. Making learning enjoyable for children and connecting it to individual learning experiences brings a natural flow to the process of discovery. In Kindergarten, the FDK model allows for a better flow and deeper engagement. There are opportunities for making personal connections, and children's voices and thinking are given more priority. Furthermore, personal enjoyment, choice, and self-expression in the tasks are encouraged. With opportunities for inquiry, children have an increased amount of time to just explore, discuss, and make connections.

Wane (Wane, 2010; Wane, N., Maryimo, E., & Ritskes, E. 2011) discusses spirituality and schooling while taking the following into consideration: sociological implications, nurturing self-awareness, identity, ancestral roots, and inner beings. These essential components are required in order to feel complete. Weaving spirituality into the learning environment can strengthen connections between the learner, knowledge, and process of schooling and also build awareness of hidden biases that may interfere with one's learning. The cultural aspects that affect the interpretation, life experiences, and intellectual journey are important as we cannot just focus on the academic aspect of schooling. This is because integrated approaches, empowered with cultural knowledge, build identity and awareness of ourselves and our environment. As Wane emphasizes, without this acknowledgement and awareness, we are silencing a part of us. Seeing people in their entirety, regardless of race, gender, or creed, and seeing what makes individuals' perspectives different builds for better interpretation and understanding. Kimani and Wanjiku (2004, 2012) also identified gender as an important aspect of diversity and the developmental process. Considering gender identities and gender dynamics (Kimani & Mwikamba, 2010) in the classroom means teachers must be aware of the difference of developmental domains and personal interests among boys and girls. In other words, the increasing percentage of the ESL population in schools, which often implies varying spiritual beliefs, and the knowledge that boys and girls may learn differently, means educators and administrators are required to be aware and adapt teaching and learning practices to the diverse needs of learners.

Spirituality in schooling is also connected to social justice in our environment. Social justice issues are emerging and continue to be a part of twenty-first century learning environments even from the Kindergarten years. Anti-bullying programs and teaching children how to respect differences in people, share materials, not make fun of others and including others in play are part of the daily lessons in the Kindergarten classroom. Educators can also pay more attention to nurturing the inner being and the inner voice of students in order to develop critical and higher level thinkers. Genderized (Kimani & Mwikamba, 2010) and racialized (Wane, 2008; Wane& Chandler, 2002) systemic barriers in educational teaching and learning practices (Wane, 2007, 2010) need to be continually examined. Equality and equity in classroom practices, activities, and learning opportunities as well as accessibility considerations for those with developmental challenges are part of building an inclusive classroom environment. Inclusive classroom environment is linked to holistic learning approaches.

Binder's use of arts for understanding identity in children.

Marni Binder (2008, 2011, 2012) validates the importance of the arts in Kindergarten. Binder argues that "the learning environment must engage children in experiences that empower them to make their thoughts public" (Binder, 2011a, p. 339). The way children think and how they see themselves, their peers, and others in the community can be expressed further in personal drawings and artwork. Each child has his / her own identity and views of the world. Therefore, educators can make meaning of their children's thinking by looking closer at their use of imagination and what they represent in their artwork. Binder and Kotsopoulos (2011) discuss multimodalities and multiple literacies in their research study on Kindergarten children and discuss further how young children's identity can be revealed through the arts.

Binder (2012) also reinforces the value of story-telling and brought awareness to teacher identity and the role of the teachers as researchers, explorers, and ethnographers themselves. In her article, "Teaching as Lived Research," Binder (2012) reflects on her own journey to explore and recognize teacher voice whereby she shares, "everyday classroom experiences open a critical space for making teacher voice visible through educational inquiry" (p. 118). Binder (2011), in her article "Remembering Why: The Role of Story in Educational Research," further elaborates on the value of teacher and student stories in educational research and shares that being observant and aware enables us to explore and reflect on personal stories and knowledge as valuable contributions in the teaching and learning journey. Personal identity and voice cannot be ignored in education.

Understanding Child-Centered Learning

The Reggio Emilia Inspired Curriculum.

The emergent curriculum inspired by the Reggio Emilia approaches (Cadwell, 2003) is also another form of alternative learning that has been drawing more attention in recent years. In the Reggio Emilia-inspired pedagogy (Wien, 1995), the focus is on the arts. Whether it be through drawing, sculpture, music or drama, Reggio Emilia schools have helped very young children to develop their skills in visual representation (Edwards, Gandini, & Forman, 1993). This focus on the arts is important because it provides another voice for children to express themselves and another vehicle for them to develop their ideas.

Reggio Emilia is often synonymous with the concept of the *Hundred Languages of Children* (Edwards, Gandini, & Forman, 1993). Young children are encouraged to explore their environment and express themselves through all of their natural languages or modes of expression, including words, movement, drawing, painting, building, sculpture, shadow play, collage, dramatic play, and music. Sobel (1996) has also recognized the arts as a means for young children to deepen their learning and express their ideas about nature. Finding ways to bring in a variety of materials into the classroom, teaching children to be creative and individualistic in their design/thinking, and letting children express themselves in their artwork became a focus in the Reggio Emilia inspired curriculum.

Loris Malaguzzi (1993), who is credited with founding the Reggio Emilia approach, referred to it as an "education based on relationship and participation bringing together the voices of children and teachers" (p. 75). Rebecca New (1993) suggested that the Reggio- Emilia curriculum might be described as both child-centered and teacher-directed. The emergent curriculum relies on teachers' complex and intricate dialogues with children, in interaction with the indoor and /or outdoor environment, to draw out and expand on their interests, ideas, and theories, and scaffold children to go more deeply into projects and investigations than they would be able to do on their own (Jones & Nimmo, 1994; Malaguzzi, 1993). According to Malaguzzi (1993), "the central act of adults, therefore, is to activate, especially indirectly, the meaning-making competencies of children as a basis of all learning" (p. 75).

Steiner's Waldorf educational philosophy.

Learning in general is moving more toward child-centered approaches rather than teacher-directed learning. The shift toward child-centered learning has been part of the constructivist theories development. Piaget, founder of constructivism, argued that humans generate knowledge and meaning from interactions between their experiences and their ideas (Piaget, 1950, 1972). Given the value placed on the children themselves and being mindful of their ways means that teachers are also learning more about their students. Various pedagogical schools of thought are also based more on child-centered learning.

Rudolf Steiner (1965, 1994), Austrian philosopher and scientist, knew intuitively that the whole person must be touched by the educational process. From the very beginning, when Steiner's (1965, 1994) Waldorf schools began in Germany in 1919, he turned toward understanding the whole child at an early age, seeking an interconnecting ground for the teaching of art and science. After visiting the Waldorf school and researching Waldorf philosophy (1965, 1996, 1997, 2004), I understood more about how Waldorf philosophy builds upon holistic approaches. The Waldorf educational philosophy nurtures the soul and inner spirit of a child by building on individual learning plans, nurturing a strong sense of community, integrating tradition and simplifying the environment to a home life atmosphere.

Steiner (1973) believed that a greater sense of individual and personal freedom could enhance perception. By weaving these into the teaching methods and concepts of his 'anthroposophy theory,' Steiner (1996, 1997, 2004) hoped to create a seminal model of education that concentrated on 'inner experience' and the spiritual domain in education. Focusing on humanity and on body, mind, and spirit, he looked closely at each individual as he developed his spiritual philosophy of education. Steiner's (1965, 1994) resulting educational system is designed to foster emotional intelligence, nurturing a lasting sense of self-esteem and creativity to develop problem-solving skills. The strong relationship between teachers and children builds security and comfort for children. Often the same teacher who teaches math in Grade One will teach math to students in higher grades.

Waldorf pedagogy, developed by Steiner (1965, 1996, 1997), identifies three broad stages in child development, each lasting approximately seven years. The early years education focuses on providing practical, hands-on activities and environments that encourage creative play and foster imagination. In elementary school, the emphasis is on developing pupils' artistic expression and social capacities, fostering both creative and analytical modes of understanding. Secondary education focuses on developing critical understanding and fostering ideals. Throughout, the approach stresses the role of the imagination in learning and places a strong value on integrating academic, practical, and artistic pursuits. In addition, the teacher plays an important element as the one who orchestrates and choreographs the rhythms of each day. The outdoor education program is also strong at Waldorf schools.

Rudolf Steiner's (1965) discussed in his book, *Education of the Child in Light of Anthroposophy,* the importance of spirituality and having a sense of sacredness, and not just physical and social interconnections. There is a greater vision, which not only focuses on teaching techniques and assessment strategies, but also on nurturing individuals in their entirety. Steiner's investigation and development of approaches for Waldorf education began in 1919 and has become the fastest growing independent school movement in the world. It is important to look at "body, mind, and spirit" (Steiner, 1994, p.13). Steiner's (1994, 1996, 2004) advice to teachers was to be creative and flexible, to use humor and surprise in the classroom, and to teach with enthusiasm rather than a rigid schedule. According to Steiner (2004), it is important to build on curiosities by creating wonder and awe in the program and integrating the arts into all subject areas.

Montessori methods.

Maria Montessori developed early years programs (1936, 1946) where classrooms were set up with small furniture, low-leveled shelving, and natural materials; the focus was on meeting the needs of children and on the development of life skills. To build a foundation for learning, children needed to have various pre-writing experiences and opportunities to develop fine motor skills. The Montessori philosophy resonated with the voices of educators who pleaded for a deeper education where the spirit of all involved could be nurtured. Montessori (1946, 1949) envisioned a perennial approach to education also called a 'cosmic curriculum' that would nurture the 'whole child' in relation to the rest of existence. Montessori (1973) believed that all things are part of the universe and are connected with each other to form one whole unity. The teacher needs to respect and gain a deeper appreciation of the child and let the child feel that he/ she is a part of the universe. The shift toward more child-centered learning was emerging; thus, learning was allowed to occur naturally and on an individual basis. This meant that children were free to participate in different types of activities and that they were not all expected to do the same thing at the same time. Montessori's ideas (Crain, 2000, 2004) of looking at learning with a more individualized perspective opened doors to alternative educational pedagogical systems that were deeply rooted in considering the developmental needs of each child.

Schools of thought on Montessori (1973, 1995) play have historically focused on meeting the goals of the Montessori philosophy. In a Montessori school, children are encouraged to have some free choice in activities; however, they also have activities where they are required to use the materials in a particular way and only when ready are they shown how to properly use them. For example, cylinders were designed to teach spatial dimensions. Therefore, a child is expected to place each cylinder in the proper hole rather than use the cylinder for any other purpose (e.g., rolling or stacking). Children at work in a Montessori environment spend part of the day practicing daily living skills. For example, a 4-year old may cut vegetables to develop perceptual-motor skills. Montessori also looked deeply into the world of nature and believed in connecting it to the curriculum. For example, "a rich contact with nature and the outdoors is vital. The sight of a flower, an insect, or an animal fills the child with joy and wonder" (Crain, 2004, p. 79).

Montessori (1973) supported the idea of an artist's creative imagination because it was tied more closely to reality. In her book, *Absorbent Mind,* Montessori (1995) refers to how an artist is made aware of form, color, harmony, and contrasts. Thus, children must refine such powers of discrimination to become more creative. Free drawing is limited and again the focus is on having the child discriminate among forms by doing activities such as coloring shapes after tracing them or cutting colored paper. During my visits to Montessori schools, I could see how there were specific structured art activities connected to themes they were covering but few dramatic play areas in the classroom. For example, during International Day children made flags; when studying parts of a spider, they did a craft related to spiders. Classroom materials included maps, flags, and understanding the world around them. History, art, culture, geography, and social studies were a part of the Montessori curriculum in the early years of schooling.

Montessori's (1967) 'cosmic education' differs from traditional education in that it discusses the importance of going beyond the acquisition of knowledge to encompass the development of the whole person. With a 'cosmic education' children are developing from the inside out and have a clearer understanding of the natural world. Therefore, they are better balanced and more responsible, and are physically, intellectually, emotionally, and socially better prepared as independent and confident learners. Montessori (1995) concludes that in the early formative years (from birth to age of 3), the 'spiritual embryo' is developing and the child has a mind that is capable of incredible powers of absorption. The child's personality is forming at this sensitive period. Nurturing the 'spiritual development' of the child brings inner peace, focus, and concentration. The child's soul and spirit was recognized by Montessori, and she had a unique perspective for early years education. Montessori argued that: "All things are part of the universe, and are connected with each other to form one whole unity" (1973, p. 8). Montessori (1967) believed in harmony, humanity, and finding inner peace.

Principles of Holistic Education

R. Miller's basic principles of holistic education.

Ron Miller, is a historian of alternative education and was the founding publisher of Holistic Education Review. In books such as *What are Schools for?*, *Holistic Education in American Culture* (1992), *New Directions in Education* (1991), and *Educational Freedom for a Democratic Society* (1995), R. Miller discusses the gentleness, humility, and compassion that need to be embedded in holistic education. This is the spiritual aspect of education, which is not necessarily related to religion. Spirituality in education is another way of considering what constitutes a holistic approach. A holistic way of thinking tries to encompass and integrate multiple layers of meaning rather than narrowly defining human experience.

R. Miller (1991, 1992, 1995) identifies four basic principles of holistic education. First, holistic educators believe that the human being is a complex, existential entity, made up of several different layers of meaning. R. Miller (1991) argues that humans are complex creatures because of the interplay and interactions of all of these different layers (biological, ecological, psychological, and emotional) and because of the different environments we live in (ideological, social, cultural, and spiritual). R. Miller (1992, 1995) acknowledges the complexity of humans and finds holism is a point of view that also recognizes these interrelations.

Then, R. Miller (1992, 1995) points out that human development occurs at a personal level. Good educators recognize the stages of a child's development. This includes knowing how the child thinks and feels and the way the child relates to the world. They also recognize that each child develops at a different rate. Educators also have to keep in mind that the development of the child has a spiritual dimension. Children are connected in different ways to the world around them, and seeing how they relate to the world around them is tremendously important.

Next, R. Miller (2000, 2002, 2006) states that part of the spiritual nature is understanding the social and cultural reality and identity of a student. The spiritual domain is a tremendously important part of one's identity, and educators have to be aware of it, acknowledge it, and address it directly. Holistic education (Palmer, 2004) has cultural, historical, and political grounding. We need to honour the individual spirit of our children. This may include paying attention to the cultural and social identities, and avoiding mechanization and standardization when it comes to views of children's identity. All beings are not the same.

Finally, R. Miller (1995, 2000) argues that holistic education cannot be reduced to a single technique. Holistic education is about the art of cultivating meaningful human relationships. It is a dialogue between the teacher and student within a community of learners. It is interconnected, authentic, and complex. There is a sense of bonding and attachment that occurs between students and teachers through the course of the school year. A sense of security is created via the support of others around children. The dynamics of a class are cultivated by the individual relationships nurtured within the classroom. Children remember the teacher who may have impacted their lives, and in the early years, that bond is even stronger and more impressionable. Therefore, the quality of this relationship is even more important.

As discussed above, we recognized the importance of acknowledging the inner voice (Herry, 1989) of a child. This is also true for the teacher. The inner life or holistic curriculum, as R. Miller (1992, 1995, 2002) explains, needs to be embedded in the consciousness of teachers who, through their own authentic way of being and caring, bring their own inner way of knowing into the classroom. Teachers need to be in touch with, and able to listen to, their own inner being in order to facilitate learning. A teacher who is in touch with his / her own center realizes that there is a link between one's consciousness or inner life and other beings. R. Miller affirms:

> To be fully authentic there must then be a fundamental awakening to our inner life —our thoughts and images and their connection to other beings. By being aware of how thoughts arise in our consciousness we can sense our connectedness to others and to what Emerson called the 'Oversoul.' (2002, p. 178)

J. P. Miller's whole child education and holistic curriculum.

J. P. Miller (2010) in his book, *Whole Child Education*, discusses how many mainstream schools in the past were focused on standardized testing and student academic achievement. He also discusses that since the holistic movement, there is an increased awareness around the world of the need to focus on the whole child in teaching and learning. With this focus, as children mature, they can become critical thinkers. J. P. Miller (2010) states:

> As children mature, they need to be able to think critically and creatively. They can solve problems that they face in their lives; they can investigate and inquire. It is often observed how the young child tends to have a natural curiosity about the world. This curiosity should be nurtured throughout a child's education. (p. 8)

The intimate relationships and deep connections that children develop with the adults and children around them foster a strong sense of self-awareness and a better understanding of their surroundings. J. P. Miller (2010) distinguishes between learning environments based on 'transaction, transmission and transformation' teaching practices in his 3T Model. The 3T model identifies 'transaction' (T1) with the teacher imparting information; the relationship here is one directional. 'Transmission' (T2) is two-way interaction, but the focus is information sharing. The higher level learning is based on transformational practices and transformation (T3), which synthesizes and allows multiple interactions and can lead to change. Holistic educators aim for transformational classroom practices. J. P. Miller and Seller (1990) present holistic perspectives and practices and discuss ways to shift teaching approaches to engender transformational learning.

Understanding thoughts from early childhood philosophers and holistic educators allows one to explore the different schools of thoughts specific to Kindergarten education. The holistic approach in Kindergarten can be more transformative, and it can push the boundaries of the present-day educational system. J. P. Miller's concept of 'timeless learning' clarifies what whole-child education should focus on and states that timeless learning should be "... moments when powerful learning occurs." (p. 4). As J. P. Miller (2006) emphasizes, timeless learning is not limited to the intellect; it also is connected to the emotions, the body, and the soul. All elements are linked interdependently and 'timeless learning' does not just remain in the head; it becomes embodied. Moreover, J. P. Miller (2006, 2007, 2010) discusses holistic principles such as balance, inclusion, and connection.

It is through stronger relationships that learning can be more authentic and meaningful. Deeper connections in education are possible if we are using the hand, heart, and head as well as key elements of holistic learning. This vision is further explained by J. P. Miller (2007) in his book, *The Holistic Curriculum,* where he identifies the following six connections as essential to education: Earth, Subject, Intellect, Intuition, Individual, Community, Mind / Body Connections, and Soul Connections. J. P. Miller states:

> Whole teaching also attempts to avoid fragmentation by making connections. It explores the relationship between linear thinking and intuition, the relationship between mind and body, the relationships among academic subjects, the relationship between individual and community, the relationship between human beings and the earth, and each person's relationship to his or her deeper sense of self, or soul. In such instructional approaches as theme-based learning and curriculum integration, students not only become aware of these

relationships, but also develop the skills necessary to transform the relationships when appropriate. (2007, p. 13)

As educators such as J. P. Miller (2010, 2011) advocate, holistic education honors balance, inclusion, and connection. In fact, we are all different, which educators need to acknowledge and address in the classroom environment. In addition, J. P. Miller (2000, 2006) argues that the focus on relationships, the sense of engagement with the world, and belongingness will foster connectedness and community. Good teachers thrive on the ability to deepen the connections for the learners.

Understanding Spiritual Domain of Development

This idea of spirituality was also discussed by Montessori (1973, 1995) when she introduced principles of natural laws and the 'spiritual embryo' of a child. Steiner reinforced this notion by identifying that spirituality can be found in each child. There are connections to spiritual development by pursuing art and creative approaches in learning. The 'spiritual domain' encompasses a wide range of pedagogical practices that develop the child's individuality, morality, and identity. The focus is on wholeness, and it attempts to avoid excluding any significant aspects of the human experience. Having emerged as an educational approach (Forbes, 2003; Glazer, 1999) through an eclectic and inclusive movement, the main characteristic of holistic learning is the idea that educational experiences foster a less materialistic and more spiritual worldview. It also proposes that educational experience should promote a more balanced type of child development.

According to the United Nations Educational, Scientific and Cultural Organization (UNESCO, 2004), holistic education strives to cultivate the relationships among the different aspects of the individual (intellectual, physical, spiritual, emotional, social, and aesthetic) as well as the relationships between the individual and other people, the individual and the natural environment, the inner-self of students, and the external world. Therefore, holistic education (R. Miller, 2000, 2002; J. P. Miller, 2006, 2010) is also concerned with emotional regulation and spiritual development, different forms of knowing, and understanding life experiences, rather than just with narrowly defined basic academic skills.

Furthermore, through holistic approaches there is a deeper understanding and a capacity to lead students into new areas of thinking—a higher level of thinking. Students can broaden their personal and critical thinking even at an early age, and they are capable of developing an appreciation and understanding of the world around them. Teachers can empower students to think differently, to think creatively, and to reflect on their own values. The idea is that the children themselves have a lot to share through their own experiences with the environment and world around them. Therefore, acknowledging festivals and celebrations, encouraging personal opinions and voice, sharing ideas and beliefs, and fostering creativity are predominately parts of the spiritual domain of development.

According to holistic educators (R. Miller, 2000, 2006; J. P. Miller, 1993, 2007, 2010), the cognitive, physical, emotional, social, and spiritual parts of the child are all equally valued and therefore given equal importance. It is important to balance all aspects and allow for the natural connections between these domains. Education should reach far beyond a solely academic curriculum. Educators' goal is to make meaningful connections between children and all aspects of the world around them. Holistic education is a student-centered approach to teaching and learning in which students learn to see relationships between themselves and their environment. According to R. Miller (2006), the emphasis is on the whole student as the teacher recognizes that intellectual development cannot be isolated from emotional, social, physical, and moral development.

J. P. Miller (2010, 2011) recognizes that students do not simply learn through their intellects but also learn through their feelings and concerns, their imaginations, and their bodies. Therefore, in planning and implementing curriculum play-based pedagogy, along with inquiry-based learning, environmental education, and arts-based curriculum goals, teachers can aim to engage the learner in many ways and support constructivist learning in the classroom.

Play as a Pedagogy in the Kindergarten Classroom

Play enables children to progress along developmentally appropriate practices. It has a role for cognitive development, but also serves an important function in children's physical, emotional, and social development (Piaget, 1952; Herron & Sutton, 1974). Learning materials that are concrete, real, and relevant to children's lives also make a difference (Piaget, 1972). With children's active participation in play involving sand, water, clay, blocks, puzzles, and games, the learning becomes more appropriate and meaningful to their lives. Therefore, adult-made materials such as workbooks, worksheets, and coloring books are not the most appropriate for daily activities. Activities with more open-ended options, a variety of levels of difficulty and complexity as well as a wider range of developmental interests may better meet the needs of children (Greenburg, 1976; Smith, 1982). Providing a wide variety of multicultural, non-stereotyping materials and activities (Chaillé & Silver, 1996) also helps to ensure individual appropriateness of the curriculum, as it enhances self-concept, self-esteem, and supports the integrity of the family as well as enriches lives of all participants (Ramsey, 1979, 1982; Saracho & Spodek, 1983; Sprung, 1978).

Froebel's and Dewey's educational philosophies and principles were the starting point for many 19th and 20th century early years pioneers, including Montessori. In particularly, Froebel maintains that young children's learning needs to be 'hands-on,' enjoyable, and self-directed. It should include such activities as building with blocks, exploring sand and water, listening to stories, engaging in pretend play, singing, dancing, and movement. In the 20th century, Piaget and Vygotsky were explaining more about how play functions to develop children's skills and development.

The work of Piaget (1950, 1962) and Froebel (1887, 1889) emphasizes that play is child-focused. The child enters into the play because it is freely chosen and intrinsically motivating, and because the child feels that she has some degree of control over it. Therefore, to make learning most meaningful and enable it to be truly assimilated, it must be integrated, interesting to the child, experimental, hands-on, and authentic. In other words, if the child is involved with excitement and enthusiasm, then he/she will remember and learn at a deeper level. For Piaget (1962), play was also an important activity because it contributed to the development of a child's cognitive abilities. Eminent researchers such as Bruner (1976) and Sutton-Smith (1997), who supported Piaget's work, have also linked play to enhancing children's problem-solving abilities. For Piaget and his followers, play was important, but only because it contributed to a child's intellect and not because of its intrinsic value. Piaget enhanced the cause of education incalculably (1962) because of his emphasis on the use of manipulatives during the stage of concrete operations as a prerequisite to abstract thinking.

Piaget (1962) defined play as assimilation, or the child's efforts to make environmental stimuli match his or her own concepts. Piagetian theory holds that play, in and of itself, does not necessarily result in the formation of "new" cognitive structures. Piaget claimed that play was just for pleasure, and while it allowed children to practice things they had previously learned, it did not necessarily result in acquiring new knowledge. In other words, play reflects what the child has already learned but does not necessarily teach the child anything new. In this view, play is seen as a "process reflective of emerging symbolic development, but contributing little to it" (Johnsen & Christie, 1986, p. 51).

In contrast, Vygotskian theory states that play actually facilitates cognitive development. Children not only practice what they already know; they also learn new things. In discussing Vygotsky's theory, Vandenberg (1986) remarks that, "play does not so much reflect thought (as Piaget suggests) as it creates thought" (p. 21). Piaget's theory of development states that children develop as they grow, and they get to understand things as they increase their age. Vygotsky's theory adds that a child develops through learning and interacting with other children.

Observations of children at play yield examples to support both Piagetian and Vygotskian theories of play. A child who puts on a raincoat and a firefighter's hat and rushes to rescue his teddy bear from the pretend flames in his play house is practicing what he has previously learned about fire fighters. This scenario supports Piaget's theory. On the other hand, a child in the block center who announces to his teacher, "Look! When I put these two square blocks together, I get a rectangle!" has constructed new knowledge through his / her play. This supports Vygotsky's theory. Whether children are practicing what they have learned in other settings or are constructing new knowledge, it is clear that play occupies a valuable role in the early childhood classroom.

As many scholars (Sutton-Smith, 1966, 1976; Piaget, 1962, Vygotsky, 1978, 1986) have argued, play is a significant component of the early years education program and it is defined in a broad context as it integrates many types of activities. Play contributes to emotional health because it facilitates self-discovery. "It is by means of play that children are discovering what they feel, what they know and what they want" (Slade, 1994, p. 91). In the same way that adults tell their understandings of events in a way that "is classifying and ultimately curative, children create play narratives that, because they express difficult emotions in a coherent and fundamentally communicative fashion" (Slade, 1994, p. 91). Play also serves as a vehicle which enables the child "to make sense out of the world" (Chaillé & Silvern, 1996, p. 277). Different scholars have greatly influenced the way educators have developed play in education. Play is a vehicle for mental growth, development of language, social and cultural awareness, and for scaffolding ideas and concepts in the understanding of child development in early years learning. Understanding play means looking closer at play theory.

Adults can extend and enrich play. For example, the teacher can provide props and a variety and range of materials, organize time, space, and support, and be aware of the many different types of play. Integrating critical thinking, problem-solving, and emotional regulation into play often stems naturally if the teacher observes and asks a few questions at the appropriate time. Malaguzzi (1993) describes the child's play and the adult intervention as a table tennis match where the child hits the ball, and the adult returns it but keeps it in play extending and enriching the learning. Malaguzzi (1993) explains playful teaching as a way of weaving adult teaching with children's learning. The adult acknowledges the child's idea but the important part is to add a little challenge to the game so the child will develop new thinking.

Malaguzzi (1993) believed the natural flow of play is important. Teachers had to be aware not to control the play completely, but to let the child lead the play, based on their interest to develop the play in a deeper way. If the child centered into the play either unwillingly or was uninterested, then the information that entered his / her head would be quickly forgotten or rendered meaningless. "If it cannot be assimilated and integrated into what is important or useful to him, it is not likely to be retained" (Weininger, 1979, p. 29). Children's active engagement in their play ensures meaningfulness (Wien, 1995). Educators should focus on encouraging children to experiment and figure things out rather than be told what is right or wrong. We need to provide children with the tools for thinking and for understanding the world around them, not always give them the answers. A peak period for creative self-expression occurs between the ages of 4 and 6 (Schirrmacher, 1998).

Sutton-Smith's play theory. Brian Sutton-Smith, prominent play theorist, was born in New Zealand in 1924 and developed his academic career in the U.S. with a focus on children's games, drama, and play. Sutton-Smith (1966, 1976, 1997) is of the view that play is as much a quest for excitement, uncertainty, and disorder, as it is a search for order, control, and cognitive harmony. Citing his own research with children's rhymes and stories, Sutton-Smith (1997) emphasized how children often produce outrageous accounts filled with harrowing adventures, fantastically improbable situations, gigantic bodies (and body parts), and naughty words and behaviors (Henricks, 2009, p. 13). Play is more interest–based and pleasure-seeking. Furthermore, Sutton-Smith (1997) defined play as a "facsimilization of the struggle for survival [which] increases the organism's variability in the face of rigidifications" (p. 223). Furthermore, Sutton-Smith considered play as a fundamental act of emotional survival, stating that:

> Play is a consultation with deep-seated, evolutionary emotions. When we play, we prod the world—and ourselves—to discover our limits. We willfully put ourselves in precarious situations so that we can experience the emotions that attend success and failure, danger and security. In so doing, we see more clearly the spectrum of our own possibilities. We pursue experiences that enhance our capabilities and prepare us for the numerous, unforeseen difficulties that lie ahead (1997, p. 227).

Sutton-Smith (1997) focused his play theories on seven distinct rhetorics—Fate, Power, Identity, Frivolity, Progress, Imaginary, and Self that were culturally derived. The ideologies or themes about play and its purpose were further elaborated on by Sutton-Smith (1997) in his book, *The Ambiguity of Play,* where the challenges of defining play are further explored.

Research Studies on Play

Perlmutter and Burrell (1995) maintain that play and language are intimately linked. Cooperative play provides constant opportunities for oral language to develop. "Two children building a fort or playing store must discuss and organize their efforts with words as well as actions" (Perlmutter & Burrell, 1995, p. 17). Cazden's (1972) and Pellegrini's (1976) express the conviction that the more children play, the more likely they are to read early, to write well, and to have advanced language skills. Play influences language development because it is an essential form of communication. In play, children express their ideas and feelings in verbal and non-verbal ways. "When they speak, children practice their vocabulary and concepts" (Weininger, 1979, p. 31). Moreover, their "language development is facilitated and enhanced by the fact that they communicate with one another without the fear of correction or constraint" (Chaillé & Silvern, 1996, p. 276). It is evident that play experiences enhance learning and ensure a multitude of purposes in child development.

In the book *Pretending at Home: Early Development in a Sociocultural Context*, researchers Haiget W. and Miller (1993) prove that by the age of four, children are "prolific pretenders," spending an average of 12.4 minutes per hour pretending (p.118). Up to the age of three, children play partners were primarily mothers, but after three years of age, more attempts should be made to allow pretend play opportunities with other children (siblings, friends) because this provides good learning and language development in the early years. The study showed that at the age of four, pretend play episodes with peers were twice as long as solo episodes, which in turn were twice as long as episodes with mothers.

The main purpose of observing pretend play according to Piaget, is to get a glimpse of the child's mind. Observations in Haiget, W. and Miller, P. (1993) longitudinal study of children between two and four years of age corroborates Piaget's claim that pretend play increases in frequency during the preschool years. W.

61

Hiaget and P. Miller conclude that "as they got older, the children not only engaged in more pretending but produced longer episodes, suggesting an increase both in the inclination to pretend and in the complexity and elaboration of episodes" (1993, p. 119).

Chaillé and Silvern (1996) also appreciate the significance of the active component to child's play when they say that, "understanding [through play] is created by doing, by doing with others, and by completely being involved in that doing" (p. 277). Play is difficult to identify and with the different meanings of play and various theorists and educational philosophies learning is more complex. There are also many different types of play. Kindergarten programs should provide adequate opportunities for all different types of play. Greenburg (1976) also conducted a research study on music in early childhood education and found that play with a musical focus is also important.

In defining play, researchers such as E. Miller and J. Almon (2009) in the report, *Crisis in the Kindergarten: Why children need to play in school*, discuss twelve types of play in a transformational Kindergarten classroom:

> The play-based approach calls for teachers to know each child well and to differentiate their teaching methods to meet individual needs. It is the antithesis of one-size fits-all model of education…. Play has many faces…Twelve key types of play are: large motor, small motor, mastery play, rules-based, construction, make-believe, symbolic, language, play with the arts, sensory, rough and tumble, and risk-taking play. (2009, p. 53)

E. Miller and J. Almon (2009) reinforce the importance of 'free play' and uninterrupted play periods of sixty to ninety minutes long. They further state that it is ideal to have three periods of play with one period outdoors and in a six-hour Full-Day Kindergarten program. Exploring the different types of play and the different educational theorist's views on play is insightful. The complexity of defining play is further examined.

The dynamics of defining play. The different pedagogical approaches and educational philosophies see play differently. Montessori philosophy has a program to teach children in the Kindergarten years, but it uses specific Montessori approaches and materials. For example, in Montessori, methods are based on different types of play, and on a different variety of materials. The children are self-directed to use geometrical solids, metal insets, tracing materials, natural wood materials and less plastic toys. Music and French along with math, language, social studies, and science are the types of subjects taught in many Montessori schools. The potential of the child is not just mental; it is revealed only when the complete Montessori Method is understood and followed. The child's choice, practical work, care of others and the environment, and above all, the high levels of concentration reached when work is respected and not interrupted is are of value. A child who cares deeply about other people and the world, and who works to discover a unique and individual way to contribute his thinking, is deeply connected from an early age. Awareness of the critical life stages of a child is the essence of Montessori's philosophy as discussed in *The Absorbent Mind* (Montessori, 1995).

Steiner (1994), in his Waldorf pedagogical approaches, believes in letting children play and build their imagination in play. By making crafts out of natural materials, doll-making, sewing, knitting, and felting techniques, children were allowed to develop fine motor skills. For Steiner, less finished toys had greater educational value as they allowed for more open-ended imaginative play. Children in Waldorf schools engage in the arts as a method of learning with a greater focus on drawing, movement, singing, and games. In Waldorf philosophy play is viewed as the 'work' of the young child. The magic of fantasy, which is so alive in every young child, is an integral part of how the teacher works with the child. Unlike Montessori

(1995), where the mind is seen as a sponge and knowledge and experience should be embedded early to develop the intellectual mind, the Waldorf curriculum is not driven by early intellectual focus, but more by child-interest activities. Rather than intellectual tasks, the Waldorf teacher incorporates storytelling and fantasy into the curriculum. Overall, where Montessori emphasizes reality, the Waldorf classroom enhances the world of child's fantasy.

Piaget saw play as simply a manipulative exercise, primarily focusing on the relationship between an individual and his or her environment. Play theorist Brian Sutton-Smith (1966) looked at play in a broader interpretation for its cognitive and emotional contributions. Sutton-Smith (1976, 1996, 1997) recognized play for its social and cultural relationships integrating the great diversity in the play phenomena. Brian Sutton-Smith describes a list of some examples of play (1997) in his book, *The Ambiguity of Play*, in which Sutton-Smith describes the cultural significance of play for survival from childhood to adulthood. Sutton-Smith (1997) identifies 308 forms of play and categorizes them into seven rhetorics, as follows: *mind or subjective play* (dreams, fantasy, imagination); *solitary play* (hobbies, collections, art projects, computers, music); *informal social play* (jokes, tricks, parties, potlucks and parks); *vicarious audience play* (television, concerts, theatre, museums); *performance play* (piano, musical instruments, acting); *celebrations play* (birthdays, gifting); *contests* (sports, games, board games); *deep or risky play* (kayaking, rafting, skiing, racing). Lev Vygotsky suggests that play is an arena for language, social and cultural acquisition.

According to Vygotsky (1978, 1986, 1987), pretending helps children to explore everyday situations and social roles. It also develops the imagination. Vygotsky (1978) also supported make-believe play because it contributes to cognitive and social development. Vygotsky's focus was on more socio-dramatic play experiences than non-pretend activities such as drawing or puzzles. Vygotsky's studies (1934, 1978) showed that preschoolers' play lasted longer, showing more involvement and drawing more interest, if it was pretend play. Vygotsky's findings (1978) showed that teachers see preschoolers who spend more time at dramatic play as more socially competent. Make-believe play (Vygotsky, 1978, 1986) strengthens a wide variety of mental abilities, including sustained attention, memory, logical reasoning, language and literacy, imagination, creativity, and the ability to reflect on one's own thinking and take another's perspective.

Outdoor play and the focus on the environment of learning are deeply embedded in Dewey's principles and the Reggio Emilia approach to learning. Dewey (1929) argued that children learn best in real-life settings. In the literature on the Reggio Emilia-inspired emergent curriculum, much attention is also given to the role of the environment—or more generally, space, both natural and structured—in establishing the implicit curriculum, in providing opportunities for different kinds of play and for social interaction (Edwards, Gandini, & Forman, 1993; Lewin-Benham, 2006; Wien, 2008). The Reggio Emilia approach is deeply embedded in place, in the sense of the socio-cultural place of the region of Italy in which it occurs. Schools are constructed, set up, and designed to reflect cultural values. Topics for investigation are selected from children's experiences and areas of interest. This is an intentional decision, because when the topic of a project is very familiar to the children, they can contribute to the project from their own experiences and knowledge. More questions, ideas, information, thinking, and planning come right from the children themselves.

Looking at play from other theorists during different time periods will also highlight how different scholars define play. Montessori (1949, 1973), however, believed strongly in the richness of nature, focused play, intellectual activities on practical life skills. Montessori was not convinced of the value of fairy tales, which she thought blurred reality for the child. Montessori (1995) also viewed art activities focused more on developing the skills of discrimination and judgment. Free drawing was not encouraged. Therefore, play and art can mean different things in different educational philosophies.

Play is also dynamic and defined differently among the different educational philosophies and child development and play theorists.

Building Quality Early Years Programs

Good quality education early in life sets a good foundation. Similar to Montessori's (1936, 1946) philosophy where children are mixed with different ages, dual-age Kindergarten also has both JK and SK students mixed in one class (i.e., JK—aged 3 or 4 years old, and SK—aged 5). Kindergarten encourages consistency and stability, and fosters comfort with a two-year program. Furthermore, in Kindergarten, learning through the use of concrete materials (Piaget, 1969) is evident. For example, children develop an understanding of mathematical skills and concepts by working with concrete materials. Also, talking is important for literacy (Vygotsky, 1978), for thinking, and for socializing with others. Language development is supported by reading and by other forms of expression, such as drawing, painting, building, and writing.

According to Ross A. Thompson (2006), there are 'windows of opportunity' and key experiences occurring during sensitive and critical early periods that are crucial to shaping and pruning neural systems in the developing brain (p. 48). For example, the social cognitive development in early years affects socio-emotional competence in later years. Thompson suggested:

> If early childhood establishes the foundations for the development of social cognition, moral judgment, and self-understanding of the years that follow, then relationships and other influences experienced in the early years set the context for the growth of an empathic, humanistic orientation toward others, balanced self-concept, capacities for relational intimacy, social sensitivity, and other capacities

conventionally viewed as achievements of middle childhood and adolescence. (2006, p.25)

The social and emotional interactions of children at an early age, among peers and with adults can contribute to social cognitive understanding of relationships. In other words, as Thompson(2006) explains, the development of the person—social understanding, relationships, self, conscience—highlights the importance of a child having the ability to share feelings and thoughts at an early age and working toward self-regulation, as this can aid later in life. Developing social and emotional management competencies are needed from the child's early years of life.

In addition, in a Harvard University study (2007) by the National Scientific Council on the Developing Child, it was reported that the timing and quality of early years education makes significant differences in the development of the brain architecture. Research (Thompson, 2006; Thompson & Lagatutta, 2006; Thompson, Goodwin, & Meyer, 2006) continues to support the benefits of quality early years education. The Harvard report stated:

> [T]he quality of a child's early environment and the availability of appropriate experiences at the right stages of development are crucial in determining the strength or weakness of the brain's architecture, which, in turn, determines how well he or she will be able to think and to regulate emotions. (National Scientific Council on the Developing Child, 2007, p. 1)

The term 'quality educational programs' also implies consideration for class sizes. Ideally, smaller class sizes are also beneficial in the primary years. Bascia's (2009) research studies have shown that reducing class size does provide an environment where teachers can teach differently and provide a variety of instructional methods; this also allows increased opportunities for higher order co-construction and more interaction with students. Indicators used to measure quality in educational programs, in particular early years educational environments, include class size, child-teacher ratio, material availability, and teacher training (UNESCO, 2004). Therefore, optimal class size, such as keeping the class-size to 20 students or less, is an important indicator of quality educational programs and would be beneficial to improving the quality of FDK in Ontario.

Barbarin, Downer, Odom, and Head (2010) showed that self-regulation and school readiness are linked to academic competencies. Teachers agree the social and emotional state of self-regulation is a priority in the school setting. Self-regulation, as an essential ingredient for school readiness is important in the Montessori program as well. The successful social adjustments in the classroom setting build security in the child. Obedience and adherence to rules are important, but so is the autonomy of making choices. Learning is self-directed in the Montessori philosophy, and center-based learning is very important.

The field of early childhood education has a noble history that has resulted in a proliferation of program designs and research studies. In the past decade, there have emerged more scientific investigations of brain development and the number of findings that support the significance of good early childhood education have increased (Mustard, 2006; Rushton & Larkin, 2001; Rutledge, 2000; R. Shore, 1997; Washington, 2002). Developmentally Appropriate Practice (DAP) means learning activities are planned for children at the correct level considering age, interests, abilities, and cultures. DAP guidelines were also developed by the National Association for the Education of Young Children (NAEYC). The use of DAP has been controversial as children develop differently and such pigeonholed developmental practice may go against holistic educational philosophy. It compartmentalizes abilities, knowledge, and skills based on age. Therefore, some debate about whether or not developmentally appropriate practices are considered holistic educational philosophy. Many educational experts such as Steiner (1994) and Malaguzzi (1993) insist on more 'free play' and fewer structured activities for children. Article 31 of the United Nations Convention of the Rights of Children states that children have the right to rest and leisure, to engage in play, and to participate in recreational, cultural, and artistic activities (United Nations, 1989).

Inquiry-based Learning as an Integrated Approach

Inquiry-based learning is primarily a pedagogical method, developed during the discovery learning movement of the 1960s. The philosophy of inquiry-based learning finds its antecedents in constructivist learning theories, such as the work of Piaget (1962), Vygotsky (1934, 1978), Bruner (1961), and Dewey (1938). Inquiry-based learning emphasizes constructivist ideas such as knowledge being built from experience and process, especially socially based experiences. Under this premise, learning develops best in group situations, with field work, case studies, and through investigation and research. Progress and outcomes are generally assessed by how well people develop experimental, analytical, and questioning skills. In the Kindergarten years, this can be introduced through nature walks, field trips, indoor or outdoor play situations, individual and group investigations as well as through paying attention to what children are curious about in their environment. Children will explore questions they may have, look into different scenarios, or look at a specific problem. Although a teacher or facilitator may assist the process, the discoveries and interests of the children themselves primarily lead it.

Heather Banchi and Randy Bell (2008) suggest that there are four levels of inquiry-based learning in science education: i) confirmation inquiry, ii) structured inquiry, iii) guided inquiry, and iv) open inquiry. The progression seen from level one through four provides an excellent guide for how to scaffold inquiry-learning skills for your students. Each type of inquiry is unique and the definitions of the four levels of inquiry are outlined below.

According to Banchi and Bell (2008), the four levels of inquiry have a specific focus. In confirmation inquiry, students are provided with the question and procedure (method) where the results are known in advance, and confirmation of the results is the object of the inquiry. Confirmation inquiry is useful to reinforce a previously learned idea; to experience investigation processes; or to practice a specific inquiry skill, such as collecting and recording data. In structured inquiry, students are provided with the question and procedure (method), however the task is to generate an explanation that is supported by the evidence collected in the procedure through evaluating and analyzing the data that they collect. In guided inquiry, students are provided with only the research question, and the task is to design the procedure and to test the question and the resulting explanations. Because this kind of inquiry is more open than a confirmation or structured inquiry, it is most successful when people have had numerous opportunities to learn and practice different ways to plan experiments and record data. In open inquiry, students form questions, design procedures for carrying out an inquiry, and communicate their findings and results. This type of inquiry is often seen in science fair contexts where students drive their own investigative questions. In the Kindergarten classroom, the level of inquiry most often employed is guided inquiry.

Vygotsky (1934), Dewey (1938), Piaget (1962), and Bruner (1961) advocated for discovery learning and demonstrated an understanding that open inquiry motivated student learning. Furthermore, Banchi and Bell (2008) explained that teachers should begin their inquiry instruction at the lower levels and work their way to open inquiry in order to effectively develop students' inquiry skills. Open inquiry activities are only successful if students are intrinsically motivated and if they are equipped with the skills to conduct their own research study. Teachers facilitating this type of learning also need to have a deep understanding of how to appropriately conduct experiments or research so that students can be guided and re-directed throughout their own studies. Inquiry-based learning is fundamental for the development of higher order thinking skills.

In the book *Natural Curiosities: Building Children's Understanding of the World*, environmental inquiry as a pedagogical framework was developed by the Dr. Eric Jackman Institute of Child Study at the University of Toronto (The Laboratory School at the Dr. Eric Jackman Institute for Child Study, 2011). A couple of teachers interviewed for this research study were also aware of this resource as it guided practice in their classroom. In the following section, environmental inquiry as a pedagogical approach will be discussed.

Understanding the Importance of Environmental Education

According to UNESCO (1978) in the Tbilisi Declaration, environmental education is a learning process that increases people's knowledge and awareness about the environment and associated challenges, helps them develop the necessary skills and expertise to address the challenges, and fosters attitudes, motivations, and commitments to make informed decisions and take responsible action. The roots of environmental education can be traced back as early as the 18th century. Jean-Jacques Rousseau (1979) stressed the importance of an education that focuses on the environment, the understanding that humans are good by nature, and the notion that learning should focus on emotion, not reason, in early years. Rousseau also believed that children should be raised close to nature and not in the city. Louis Agassiz, a Swiss-born naturalist, echoed Rousseau's philosophy as he encouraged students to "study nature, not books." These two influential scholars helped lay the foundation for a concrete environmental education program, known as 'nature study,' which took place in the late 19ᵗʰ century and early 20ᵗʰ century.

J. A. Palmer (1998), in the book *Environmental Education in the twenty-first Century: Theory, Practice, Progress and Promise,* shares a model for ecological thinking in which she defines the development of environmental understanding, awareness, and concern as well as which action needs to be developed in the Kindergarten years. In addition, the educational philosophies of Reggio Emilia, Waldorf, and Maria Montessori also encourage the integration of environmental education awareness and outdoor play in their program. Gardening, inquiry, and experiential learning connect with environmental education. As discussed in this study, it is clear that connecting to nature in the early years is important and emphasized in many different educational philosophies as it is an integral part of child development.

Aasen, Grindheim, and Waters (2009), and Nimmo and Hallett (2008) suggest that young children already have an orientation toward each other and the natural world; it is the responsibility of schools to strengthen and sustain this orientation. An important focus in early years education, and particularly in Ontario Kindergartens, is helping young children develop a love and respect for nature, building play around natural materials and bringing the concept of the outdoor classroom into FDK programs. Integrating the natural world into different subject areas is also possible. For example, the connections between literacy, literature, and nature is receiving increasing attention, even in the educational mainstream. *A Place for Wonder,* a recent book by Georgia Heard and Jennifer McDonough (2009), taps into the potential to enhance both the development of young children's writing skills and their sense of wonder about the natural world. Heard and McDonough (2009) described how they established opportunities in a Kindergarten class for wondering and pondering about questions in nature. Gardening offers an opportunity for taking action in the local natural environment (Sauvé, 2005).

David Orr (2004), ecologist and scholar, emphasizes in his book, *Earth in Mind: On Education, Environment, and the Human Prospect,* that our ability to restore planet Earth rests primarily on the decisions we make about education. Orr (2004) further discusses environmental inquiry initiatives that build on four pillars: inquiry-based learning, integrated learning, experiential learning, and stewardship. Getting children to build a growing commitment to protect water, air, plants, and wildlife builds a sense of care and responsibility that is important. In the book, *Natural Curiosity,* Orr states:

> Education that nurtures children's innate curiosity about the natural world, that fosters their understanding of the interconnectedness of all living and non-living things, and instills in them an abiding sense of care and responsibility for the well-being of their communities and planet Earth.
>
> (The Laboratory School at the
> Dr. Eric Jackman Institute
> of Child Study, 2008, p.1)

The book *Natural Curiosity* highlights ways of building children's understanding of the world through environmental inquiry. Knowledge Building (KB) circles and discourse can be ways of engaging children in the Kindergarten classroom. There are many things teachers can do to facilitate building and extending upon natural curiosities. As teachers facilitate rather than transmit knowledge, they engage students in multiple and diverse ways. Students' questions and ideas are placed at the center and teachers are required to be responsive, flexible, and reflective. Teachers often observe and document as well as model the inquiry-based process. A summary was presented by the Dr. Eric Jackman Institute of Child Studies "Concept Map of the Teacher's Key Role in an Inquiry-based

Learning Environment." The more student-directed the learning, the more open the inquiry, the more teacher directed the learning, the more closed the inquiry (The Laboratory School at the Dr. Eric Jackman Institute of Child Study, 2008). There are different ways teachers can support inquiry-based learning and build it into FDK curriculum and play-based learning.

In 2009, the Ontario Ministry of Education released a policy document, *Policy Framework for Environmental Education in Ontario Schools*, which emphasized fostering children's sense of connection to each other and to the natural world through active participation. It holds within its pages the potential to transform schooling in Ontario from an approach that relegates place to the periphery, to one that recognizes both the potential of place to engage children in learning, and the innate, undeniable value of place if we are to live sustainable, healthy lives. In this century, increased funding and resources from the government support environmental education efforts in schools. Our present investments in building environmental awareness from an early age will lead to long-term improvements in the future.

Studying habitats of animals and the life cycle of a plant along with discussing local and global environmental concerns or projects will build awareness of the world around us. Through active citizenship and stewardship, from a young age we can promote more awareness and make our students environmentally conscious individuals. Scientific inquiry is a great way to build curiosities, awe and wonder. In learning environments, such as the Equinox Alternative Holistic School, children have been part of the PINE and POND projects which are local nature-based marsh, plant, and wildlife areas in the community, where students can study ecosystems, biodiversity, habitats, and the natural cycles of nature. Through sit spots, visualization, journaling, observations, group circles and inquiry, children build an appreciation and curiosity about nature in the Kindergarten years.

There is a greater awareness of how humans impact the environment, and the impact that the environment has on calming and centering humans. Schools are not only involved with eco-friendly recycling activities, but like to build in more field trips to marshes, ponds, forests, and natural habitats. In addition, the creation of outdoor spaces for learning and sitting are a growing concept with the emergence of the outdoor classroom. There is a growing and deeper connection with our earth, nature, and the outdoor environment in integrative and comprehensive approaches in the FDK model in Ontario.

Ontario's pedagogy for the early years more recently (2014) was shaped by a resource called *How Does Learning Happen?* As the government releases new resources and eventually the new FDK curriculum document there is more and more evidence of the importance of understanding the role of children, families and educators in establishing the four foundations of belonging, well-being, engagement and expression. Responsive teaching means we must always think, feel and act in ways that reflect the environment, the circumstances, the family and the child. There is a deep understanding that "families are the experts on their children" (Ministry of Education, 2014, p.7). Another important document is the release of *Think, Feel, Act*: *Lessons from Research about Young Children* (2013c) by the Ontario Ministry of Education and it presents briefs from leading experts in the field of early years childhood education that highlight strategies to put ideas into practice and challenge the status quo and encourage critical reflection of teaching and learning practices.

Research projects (Pelletier, 2012) with the Ontario government and various universities are showing some specific areas of improvements with students' performance after the implementation of FDK. The comparison of the Half-Day Kindergarten student performance and Full-Day Kindergarten student performance continues to be followed by researchers and is measured by the Early Developmental Instrument (EDI). This next section will highlight some relevant findings on FDK research studies in Ontario.

FDK Research Studies

The rich learning experiences in FDK are starting to show some positive outcomes in the later years. Researcher Janice Pelletier, from the University of Toronto, conducted an Ontario longitudinal study (Pelletier, 2012) of the first-year impact of FDK in Ontario and results indicated some benefits, but some comments related to various challenges were also evident. In literacy skill development, vocabulary improved and overall school behaviour and adjustment into Grade One reportedly improved. In another report for Year 3 of FDK, Pelletier (2014) reported that findings on self-regulation were 'cornerstones' of the developmental readiness of children. There are some reported successes with the investment in FDK (Pelletier, 2012, Vanderlee, 2013), but there are still some areas for improvement. In her 2013 Queen's University study, Mary Louise Vanderlee, associate professor and early years expert, reported that the play-based approach needs to be continued in Grade One for there to be greater benefits. There is some discussion at the board level of providing more training to Grade One teachers about play-based learning approaches and less paper-and-pencil teaching practices. Overall, this means that the FDK work is continuing and developing in Ontario. This is promising and shows that FDK is getting more attention and support in Ontario schools.

The Queen's University Study, *Final Report: Evaluation of the Implementation of Ontario Full-Day Early Learning Kindergarten Program,* (Vanderlee, M. L, Youmans, S., Peters, R., & Eastabrook, J., 2012) collected qualitative data on 16 case study schools. The focus of the research was on whether or not the FDK program improves school readiness as indexed by difference in scores in EDI as compared to non-FDK schools. There was also a closer look at whether or not FDK programs help decrease the academic gaps in high needs schools.

The Ministry of Education, Government of Ontario released a report, *The meta-perspective on the evaluation of Full-Day kindergarten during the first two years of implementation (October 2013)* (Ontario Ministry of Education, 2013), that provides some insight into the early measure and impact of FDK on child development and learning. The Early Development Instrument (EDI) is a measure of child development in Kindergarten programs. Teachers are expected to fill in information on each student and this information is gathered on basic literacy and numeracy skill development across the province of Ontario. EDI results have come in the early stages of FDK and some areas of basic literacy are similar to half-day programs such as letter recognition and sound, awareness of rhyming words and writing of one's name; however more advanced literacy skills such as reading have shown some improvement, as did oral communication skills. Numeracy skill development was similar in some areas and improved in others when full-day and Half-Day Kindergarten students were compared. The research on EDI for FDK is detailed in a report (Ontario Ministry of Education, 2013; Pelletier, 2012). The EDI measures developmental domains such as physical, social-emotional, cognitive, language development communication skills, and general knowledge.

This research study focused the knowledge of the educators about FDK classroom practice and teaching approaches. Therefore, the highlights of this report are about what educators are doing rather than on how well the children are learning. Since the FDK in Ontario schools has been in place about five years, understanding the impact of quality FDK and using measures is informative as we move ahead and consider areas for future research. Therefore, with more time and research in the future it is also important to track how students are benefiting with FDK in the long term.

Other recent research (Cleveland et al., 2006; National Research Council, 2001; Sylva et al., 2004) supports the effectiveness of quality early childhood education. It has been found that Kindergarten programs that are developmentally appropriate have academic and behavioural benefits for young children. In full-day programs, less hectic instruction geared to student needs and appropriate assessment of student progress contribute to the effectiveness of the program. While these can also be characteristics of high quality Half-Day Kindergarten programs, many children seem to benefit, academically and behaviourally, from all-day Kindergarten. Of course, the length of the school day is only one dimension of the Kindergarten experience. Other important issues include the nature of the Kindergarten curriculum and the quality of teaching. Curriculum should be evaluated by how well it enables children's full participation (Bernhard, Lefebvre, Chud & Lange, 1997). The Best Start Expert Panel on Early Learning (January, 2007) discussed having a planned curriculum with specific goals for children's holistic development benefits, children's enjoyment, development, and learning.

Research studies (Cryan, Sheehan, Wiechel, & Bandy-Hedden, 1992) do show differences in academic achievement in children enrolled in half-day versus full-day programs. Cryan et al. (1992) conducted a two-phase study that examined the effects of Half-Day and Full-Day Kindergarten programs on children's academic and behavioural success in school. In the first phase of the study, which was retrospective, data were collected on 8,290 children, from 27 school districts, who entered Kindergarten in between 1982–1984. The second phase was a longitudinal study involving nearly 6,000 children who entered Kindergarten in two cohorts, in 1986 and 1987. The researchers found that participation in Full-Day Kindergarten was related positively to subsequent school performance. Children who attended full-day Kindergarten scored higher on standardized tests.

Hough and Bryde (1996) also found that students enrolled in Full-Day Kindergarten programs benefited academically. Student achievement was examined for 511 children enrolled in half-day and all-day Kindergarten programs in 25 classrooms during the 1994–95 school years. Data were collected from: (a) classroom observations; (b) focus groups with children, teachers, and parents; (c) report cards; (d) parent surveys; and (e) achievement test scores. Children in the all-day programs scored higher on an achievement test than those in Half-Day programs.

The McMaster University Study (Janus, M., et al., 2012) on Full-Day Kindergarten in Ontario reported the early impact of FDK and the investigation of developmental outcomes and status on children. There were over 16, 000 children included in this study and they were three groups of children (2 years of FDK, 1 year of FDK and 0 years of FDK) that were compared on developmental domains such as social competence, emotional maturity, language and cognitive development, communication skills and general knowledge and overall physical health and well-being.

Developing a Lens to Examine Kindergarten Learning

Scaffolding is an important part of the learning process, and the illustration of the ZPD in *Figure 1* was designed to reinforce the potential development for a child. It is important to understand where a child is and what the possible areas for development are. The child as a learner is capable of achieving higher potentials.

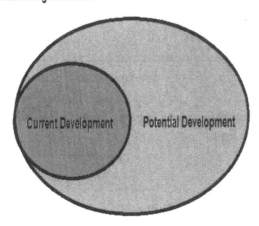

Zone of Proximal Development (ZPD) is the area of potential development where with guidance and encouragement from a knowledgeable person the learner can improve their own knowledge and skills.

Figure 1. **Zone of Proximal Development—(Vygotsky, 1978)**

Maslow's Hierarchy of Needs

Psychologist Abraham Maslow (1943) defined a theory that showed stages of developing personality and personal growth as a human. In his writings in *A Theory of Human Motivation in the Psychological Review*, Maslow (1943) illustrated what motivates human development and he defined it in a pyramid model (see *Figure 2*). The pyramid hierarchy outlines an order that shows—at the bottom—the specific needs of individuals, from basic needs such as food, shelter, and sleep that need to be met, then the need for safety and security. Love, family and social relationships are important in the social needs level and eventually the esteem level considers a sense of belonging, self-esteem, and confidence. Lastly, the top of the triangle is self-actualization needs or higher level needs such as the drive for creativity, morality, and problem-solving at the top tier. Maslow defined levels distinguishing the more basic to more complex needs as one goes up the ladder. It is during certain ages or times in life that one would focus on a specific area. It also describes human desires and explains a little more about human behavior as one matures and grows.

Similarly, I design a 'hierarchy of needs' for a child or school-aged Kindergarten student, by starting with the basic needs (food, shelter, and water) at the bottom, and then moving to developing love, security, and friends, finally to self-regulation, independence, and identity. As the child learns and becomes comfortable in the school environment, he / she develops creativity, imagination, and ideas. Thereafter, through maturation, the child becomes a problem-solver and critical thinker and engages in higher-level thinking.

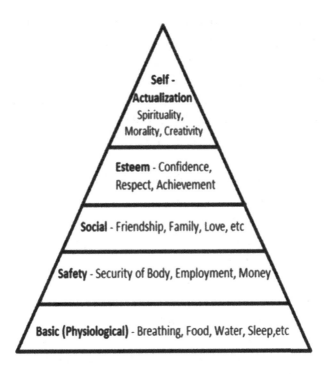

Looking closer at Maslow's Hierarchy of Needs and adapting it from a child's needs / perspective illustrates the movement from the basic needs to the safety needs, to social needs, and the importance of self-esteem and eventually self-actualization during the process of completing Kindergarten. This image was created to visualize the place of schooling and the importance of understanding the levels and steps that even a child needs to move through to reach important milestones before the age of six. Specific details pertaining to a child's hierarchy of needs clarify a child's different needs and levels of needs. Therefore, once these basic needs are met, children should also move to higher-level needs for their own self-development. The teacher can help meet the child's basic needs and support his / her higher level needs as and when the child is ready. The physiological, socio-emotional, cognitive, and self-actualization needs can be linked to the domains of child development, such as the physical, social, emotional, cognitive, communicative, and spiritual needs of a child.

Teachers can also prepare the learning environment for the child with spaces for meeting his / her levels of development. A space to meet basic needs such as a snack table, a quiet space for sleep, a water fountain or bin for water bottles accessible for use both inside and outside meet some of the basic needs of children for a full day away from parents. Teachers often communicate to parents about the importance of warm clothing for outdoor play in the winter, and proper attire for the different seasons. Teachers establish rules and routines to set limits, provide order, consistency, safety and security. There is also consideration for work groups, ways to connect with family and building a sense of belonging in the school community or within the classroom environment. The respect to teachers and peers and even the sense of responsibility to tidy-up and take care of personal belongings are all part of the needs of a child. As children develop throughout the school year, teachers can track student achievement and personal growth, display work and share success with the children, colleagues, and parents.

Higher level thinking in a child includes self-expression through voice, dance, song and visual arts where creativity, individuality, and the use of imagination can engage the learner. The self-actualization stage is also linked to the spiritual domain in the developmental stages of a child where morality, critical thinking, and problem-solving skills develop. Children are capable and creative. Individual teachers can enhance and build stronger relationships and connections as the school year progresses, children move from learning basic routines in the classroom, feeling secure and safe, to building voice and self-esteem. By the end of the school year teachers can shape children's thinking schema to reach their higher potentials, foster creativity, individuality and imagination.

Higher level thinking in a child
includes self-expression, voice,
creativity, individuality and use of
imagination, morality, critical thinking
and problem-solving skills which are
part of spirituality

Children's Hierarchy of Needs

Developing the Spiritual Domain in the early
years of learning is a priority to build
intelligence, character and confidence

Figure 3. Adaptation of Maslow's Hierarchy
of Needs to Kindergarten Children

Figure 3 is an adaptation of Maslow's hierarchy of needs and the pictures are symbols or visuals to remind educators to look specifically at children's hierarchy of needs to make sure they are being met. When we look at each individual child in the classroom, teachers are looking at all types of needs. The levels are represented from the bottom with home life considerations such as an environment at home where food, shelter, and sleep needs are being met. If a child is hungry, this will affect their learning as will the habit of going to bed at 11pm each night and being in school. A child in a room without heat may also not have proper shelter and this will affect learning.

As we move to social, we can see how the element of play, friendship, community, and school bridges the child to the world around him / her and deepens connections and experiences outside of his / her home life. Furthermore, self-esteem is what builds confidence, mastery of skills and a sense of achievement. With all the basic landscapes built up, a child then has the potential to reach higher-level needs. Building imagination, creativity, critical thinking, and problem-solving skills are part of the self-actualization tier where identity and self-motivation drive a child to greater and bigger spaces and places as they move out of the Kindergarten years. It is the creativity that is also connected to the spirituality domain which is added to the domains of child development. The idea of a strong and solid foundation in the Kindergarten years will nurture future success in school life and learning.

The work of Maslow (1954, 1970) inspired focusing more on the specific needs of the child and also led to the design of new models, keeping the whole child in mind. The Integrated Child Development Model was designed as a tool and developed as a theoretical framework. It highlights how Hierarchy of Needs can be applied to considering a 'Child's Hierarchy of Needs' that would be specifically useful for the Kindergarten years of child development. This tool can be used by educators to bring awareness to children's needs and to encourage more integrated approaches in learning. The visual representation of the domains of development and the child-centered focus can also be useful and insightful, in that it allows educators to see the big picture as well as details of the parts. The components in this case are developed based on child development theories and recognizing developmental domains related to children as we look at schooling and education. Specifically higher levels of thinking go beyond intelligence and include nurturing creativity and imagination, building self-expression, voice, critical thinking and problem-solving skills. Furthermore, a term coined by Maslow (1971), 'metaneeds' or 'metamotivation' describe the motivation of people who are self-actualized and strive for higher level thinking as they navigate a path for growth. It reaches towards excellence, truth, knowledge, beauty and creativity. Maslow's (1971) list of 'metaneeds' includes: wholeness (unity), perfection (balance and harmony), completion (ending), justice (fairness), richness (complexity), simplicity (essence), liveliness (spontaneity), beauty (rightness of form), goodness (benevolence), uniqueness (individuality), playfulness (ease), truth (reality), autonomy (self-sufficiency) and meaningfulness (values). Furthermore, curiosity, oneness with nature, humanity and increased identification with human species, global awareness, a loving and kind nature, and being generally more altruistic are all part of 'metaneeds' which Maslow identifies at the peak of his Maslow's Hierarchy of Needs and are a part of higher perceptions and higher thinking.

The Theoretical Framework

The theoretical framework defines the core components that will be used to look closer at key research findings. Developing an integrated and comprehensive way to look at child development and early years practices led me to consider designing a model for better understanding. The PIE Model in *Figure 4* was developed as a way to examine classroom practices. Each time I analyzed teaching practices, I would consider several factors / questions: Was it student-centered? Was the teacher taking on the role of a facilitator? Was the teacher central to scaffolding in the learning experience? Are students reaching and engaging in their zone of proximal development? Is there evidence of identity and consideration of background knowledge and experience in the learning? Are there connections with play, inquiry, and experience? Sparking curiosity and investigation, and considering the pathways for discovery make a significant difference in the learning process.

The outer circle represents the teacher who is overlooking the student and observing. The inner circle is represents the child who resides in the center. The sections of the circle each represent a domain in child development. All areas may develop at the same time, when students are engaged in play, inquiry, or experience. The integration is evident for the child's development. This model emphasizes the support of the teacher as a guide and the focus of learning as child-centered. The strong relationships build support and create a secure environment for children. The child at the core is of central importance. The outer influences and the role of the teacher are on the peripheral. Teaching and learning are related to the various domains to consider in child development.

The physical domain in children is the development from head to toe and large to fine muscle control (in that order), understanding senses, perceptual motor, fine motor and gross motor development of the child. The social domain requires students' ability to cooperate with others, listen to others, follow directions, make connections to prior experience, conflict resolution, self-discipline, and understand the world around them by interacting with peers and people in their environment. The emotional domain is the ability to develop trust, autonomy, express feelings, self-regulate and build self-esteem. The cognitive domain depicts the intelligence, logic, intense curiosities, matching, classifying, sorting, grouping, ordering, relationship of cause and effect, knowledge, and skills. The communicative domain is the language, understanding verbal interaction, problem-solving aspect, and imagination. The spiritual is the moral development and understanding, development of creativity, imagination, visualization, and inner voice along with the acknowledgment that each child has its own identity and uniqueness.

The different domains can be integrated with the child's development during play-based, inquiry-based and / or experiential learning experiences. Child development has long been based on developmental domains, and the fundamental premise that children are continually an unfolding process as they pass through stages. Children's interests and learning are directly related to this developmental process. During play, for example, children often express emotion and feelings (emotional domain), and they may also be engaged in conversations (social) and thinking (cognitive); as they engage in activities of interest, they use their imagination and their creative minds (spiritual domain). By encouraging children to pursue and deepen their self-awareness and interests, curiosities and wonder, children are developing a new way of thinking and approaching learning that invites more critical, creative, original, and unique thinking at a young age.

Critical thinking is a part of educational practice in the twenty-first century and educators can develop individual voice, self-expression, and confidence by allowing more dialogue on topics of interest for students. This may mean asking more open-ended questions, and presenting information in a way that invites thinking and sharing of ideas.

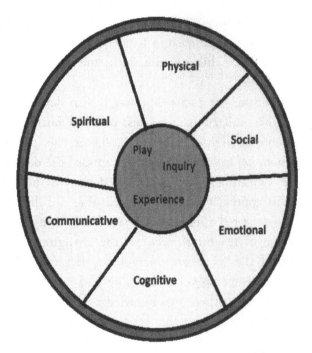

Figure 4. **Integrated Child Development Model—PIE**

It is important for educators to understand typical growth and development of children by understanding early years educational theories that investigate the series of developmental stages. As we have seen from the work of Piaget, more than a half-century of research went into developmental stages. Piaget's characteristics of children's cognitive processes and the later Vygotsky's importance of dynamic interaction between children and the environment are important for enriching knowledge, questioning, cultural and social influences, and interacting assisted performance. The Integrated Child Development Model in *Figure 4* also provides a lens through which to look at Ontario curriculum and FDK in the classrooms. Understanding the domains of child development and acknowledging the role of spiritual development as a path to higher level thinking, creativity, and imagination is highlighted in this research. There has been a shift from the instructivist approach to a more constructivist approach in Kindergarten learning. Both in theory and practice, a child's nature, spirit, interests, and ways need to be acknowledged.

Understanding the focus on what is also developmentally appropriate has shifted to a process-oriented outlook from a product-oriented goal. McQuail et al. (2003) list this in their *Early Years International Evidence Project* that guided the development of FDK in Ontario. *Figure 5* identified the instructivist and constructivist approach to early years learning and the emphasis on the child-centered approach. The comparison highlights the new direction of teaching practices, the changing role of the educators and the focus on emergent curriculum. The play-based environment emphasizes learning and not just teaching, as children construct their own knowledge, discovery questions, answers and solutions, and the 'High Scope' focus is on more hands-on learning experiences.

Instructivist Approach	Constructivist Approach
Teacher-initiated-directed	Child-initiated
Teacher-centred	Child-centred
Didactic/traditional	Play-based, progressive
Basic academic skills	Personal/social development
Developmentally inappropriate	Developmentally appropriate
Product oriented	Process oriented
Formal/structured	Informal/emergent
Core knowledge	Children construct their own knowledge

With the constructivist approach, the role of the teacher is re-positioned and the focus of the learning shifts as does the style of teaching. The classroom management strategies, the types of activities the students are engaged in and the assessment tools being used in the classroom may look different in the constructivist learning approach. Building in the freedom of choice, freedom of expression, and consideration for child interests is an open-ended way of looking at early years education, as it is more informal and authentic.

Role of the Teacher in Kindergarten

Classroom management and ability to sustain and deepen thinking require the teacher to facilitate with a close eye on end goals. With no clear direction and awareness of the journey, the student may not get the full enriching experience. Furthermore, shifting the learner's thinking to use vocabulary and processes that are leading to exploration, discovery and inquiry allows the learning to be driven by the student at his / her own pace. This is in keeping with what Vygotsky (1978) calls 'scaffolding'; that the teacher can guide the inquiry and integration of cross-curricular approaches in education.

An example of such scaffolding is simply having students build boats in class, which can be a very different experience from having students build a boat, taking it on their nature walk, letting it sail down the stream and letting children discover why it moves and why it gets stuck in the water pathway. This inquiry can lead to different discoveries directed by the children themselves. Lastly, the teacher draws attention to what the children are curious about in nature and how the boat works and why it gets stuck in the river. The teacher's role is to observe and then guide the inquiry, but let it be built on the child's own wonder and curiosity. Furthermore, as Bruner (1961, 1967) suggested, the teacher can ask open-ended questions that require investigation and allow children to further test ideas to find their own answers and solutions.

As the research has shown, play, environmental education, and inquiry-based learning are essential components of a well-rounded Kindergarten program. Children also learn through interacting with their environment. There is evidence of alternative schools adapting various concepts and philosophies of education. There are also elements of these three components, play, environmental education, and inquiry-based learning, in the Ministry's FDK curriculum, and in the FDK classroom practices. In the curriculum document, it is stated that using 'initial engagement' to raise questions by using language such as 'I wonder why this happens,' or 'Let's do an exploration,' invites inquiry-based learning. Furthermore, encouraging children to plant and explore living things in an outdoor garden space enriches their learning. Setting up areas in the classroom that invite learning and ignite curiosity is part of enhancing the physical classroom space. Activities should enhance cognitive development and they should reflect children's interests. Teaching children the language of exploration and modeling it is important in both small group and individual settings. The deeper thinking and use of all senses in these approaches during the early years set a platform and invite critical thinking and problem-solving skills.

Fundamental Principles outlined by the government (Ministry of Education, 2010) for FDK include partnerships with families and communities, knowledgeable and responsive educators. FDK curriculum also encourages using play as a means to capitalize on children's natural curiosity and exuberance, and using a planned curriculum supporting early learning with respect for diversity, equity, and inclusion to honor children's rights. With the optimal development and understanding that early child development sets the foundation for lifelong learning, behavior and health high (Cleveland et al., 2006; National Research Council, 2001; Sylva et al., 2004) early years programs are an important priority with FDK in Ontario. These principles, developed after examining current research, reflect important beliefs and guide the Full-Day Early Learning Kindergarten Program in Ontario schools.

The role of educators is outlined in *Figure 6* as it is defined by the government in the *FDELK (Ministry of Education, 2010)* document. The EL-K team is comprised of the kindergarten teacher and the early childhood educators. The team determines the quality of the learning program that young children will experience and they recognize that learning is continuous and reciprocal. In this visual, it is evident that educators are involved in 'scaffolding' and 'facilitating' in the learning. The role of educators in FDK involves more reflective practice, providing both differentiated instruction and a balance between educator-initiated and child-initiated activities.

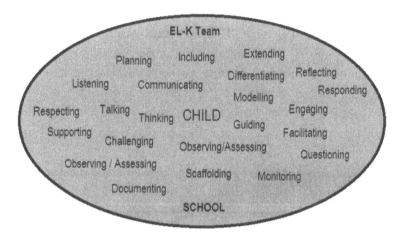

***Figure 6. EL-K Team—Role of Teachers
and Early Childhood Educators***
(Full-Day Early Learning Kindergarten Program, 2010, p. 8)

Tool for Teachers: The Five Key Elements of the FDK Program

As Froebel argued, children, like plants, need to be cared for, and the full benefit of play-to learn requires adult guidance and direction. The teachers are the designers of activities and experiences, and they facilitate learning and plan the environment. *Figure 7* below summarizes the five Key Elements of the FDK Program that teachers can consider as they create conditions conducive to learning. The **PIECE** model identifies five key elements in a quality Kindergarten program: 1) **P**lay-based Learning—using play as a process of learning, 2) **I**nquiry-based Learning—building natural curiosities, 3) **E**xperiential Learning—providing various experiences and hands-on opportunities, 4) **C**hild-centered Learning—acknowledge personal background, interest and self-identity, 5) **E**nvironmental Learning—using the indoor and outdoor environment as a third teacher. The landscape of Kindergarten is grounded within these essential components as they develop an integrated approach to early years education. The teacher must develop and facilitate learning with these in mind, in order to optimize learning experiences and build a quality FDK program. The steps are of equal size and stacked to represent equal importance to each of the five key elements in the FDK program.

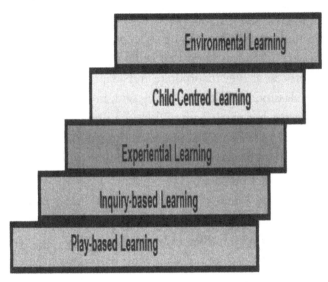

Figure 7. **Five Key Elements in the Kindergarten Program—PIECE Model**

Conclusion

The Five Key Elements of the FDK program summarize areas to develop teaching approaches and practices. The practices integrate various educational philosophies in a comprehensive pedagogical approach to meet the needs of individual learners. The learning approaches are designed to consider the whole child and build curiosities and wonder among children and the elements are not just connected to one educational philosophy.

With international acclaims, global perspectives and awareness can deepen our own understanding of the underlying philosophies of education. Each alternative school may have different beliefs about what education should include; Waldorf schools, Alternative Holistic Schools, Montessori schools, Reggio Emilia-inspired Schools, considers specific beliefs and values in their philosophies of education. While these schools have some elements incorporated in their values, it is the individual teachers and their experience, training, understanding, teaching style, personal values and beliefs about how children learn best that bring different dynamics to the learning process as they incorporate and adapt teaching approaches into their classrooms. With that being said, in this current research study, each teacher participant will have a unique style, focus and philosophy; his / her personal understanding of FDK teaching and learning practices based on Ontario curriculum will be reflected in his / her classroom practices.

My research interest and focus is on understanding the application of teaching methodologies in the public school system and, secondly, understanding and articulating FDK approaches in the Kindergarten classroom. For the most part, the implementation of whole child education has been primarily instituted in the private sector or in alternative schools, but more recently, there is evidence, as shown in this study, that holistic and integrated approaches to teaching are visible in the public school system classroom practices.

A review of the literature leads one to conclude that holistic education cannot be readily reduced to a set of principles and practices. This review also reveals that there is little research on the empirical aspects of holistic education and that there is a need for further research on how teachers actually implement holistic education ideas into practice. The goal of this book is precisely that: to examine holistic approaches in Kindergarten in the public schools sector. I believe that teachers, by telling their stories, sharing their experiences, and discussing their specific classroom practices build upon education theory, which in turn empowers them to have authority in research.

In addition, my personal reflections as a researcher will be a voice that contributes to the understanding the life in a Kindergarten classroom. Creating a theoretical framework and a lens to provide a better understanding of the theoretical concepts was insightful. This journey has transformed my understanding of best teaching approaches and reconnected my spirit with more meaningful engagement with students. As Ron Miller has repeatedly asserted, there is no one correct method of holistic education. In this research study, key elements identified in the Kindergarten classroom include play, inquiry-based learning, environmental education, child-centered, and experiential learning. In the classroom, we learn that engaged learners are empowered, involved and focused.

Chapter 3

QUALITATIVE RESEARCH DESIGN - A FRAMEWORK TO STUDY THE CLASSROOM

Introduction

Pedagogical documentation can serve to make teacher's pedagogy more transparent and thus communicate what teachers' value and honor. The world of educating children is ever changing and pedagogical documentation serves as professional development and as an integral part of Kindergarten. Teachers are valued as producers of research not only consumers of research.

This chapter offers a detailed description of the qualitative research design which was used for this research study. Two qualitative methodological approaches guided this study: i) case study, ii) narrative inquiry. The main methodology was the case study approach and it was weaved with a narrative-style in this qualitative research. A general description of the various data collection procedures identifies the different types of data that built the depth of this research. This also links to the use of the triangulation process where multiple sources of data collection allowed for a deeper look at the eight teacher participants.

In this research study the three areas of data collection included: 1) semi-structured interviews, 2) classroom observations, and 3) review of artifacts and photographs. Therefore, while a small sample group of participants was used in this study there was consideration for a detailed and in-depth research approach to draw on individual and unique teachers' experiences and perspectives. This would provide data that was reflective and meaningful to highlight effective teaching practices useful to educators. Lastly, this chapter discusses the ethical considerations and guidelines, the recruitment and selection process for key participants and background information on the research sites, eight teacher participants, and demographics of the eight classrooms. At the end of the chapter, an overview of the data analysis tools and the limitations of this study are summarized.

In the academic world, there is an increasing interest in qualitative research as narrative voice gives us insight on our participants' practices in a more descriptive way. The subjective stories collected through qualitative methods capture the richness and complexity of our understanding of the phenomena. Through the triangulation process, which involved conducting individual interviews with participants, classroom observations, and collecting artifacts, I was able to explore participants' voices and gain a deeper understanding of their personal experiences and knowledge. This deep exploration of individuals' practices and beliefs also led to identifying patterns and underlying themes which all contribute to enriching the data findings for this research. It is important to discuss and understand the value and multidimensional perspective of qualitative data.

Qualitative Research Design

This section discusses the qualitative research design employed in this research study. Qualitative research scholars, such as Creswell, Stake, and Freebody provide some insight, as do Bogdan and Biklen. The use of qualitative research design for an educational research study allows the researcher to capture rich experiences, provides meaningful information and deeper insight for understanding various teaching practices and perspectives.(Bogdan & Biklen, 2006; Creswell, 2007, 2013; Freebody, 2004; Stake, 1995).

Bogdan and Biklen (2006) use qualitative research as an umbrella term to refer to research strategies that share a set of characteristics. According to Bogdan and Biklen (2006), qualitative research is naturalistic, descriptive, inductive, and concerned with process and meaning. I use these characteristics as a framework for understanding qualitative research, paying particular attention to the implications for my study. Similar to Bogdan and Biklen, Creswell (2007) validates qualitative research and research design. Creswell (2007) recommends using the interview protocol to help organize thoughts such as ideas for starting the interview, guiding the discussion, and leading to concluding ideas. This proved useful in this research study, as I found it helpful to guide the focus of the discussion and organize the data.

Stake (1995) argues that qualitative researchers seek understanding of the complex interrelationships among all that exists and affirms that, "the function of research is not necessarily to map and conquer the world but to sophisticate the beholding of it" (p. 43). According to Stake (1995), this requires that the researcher pay close attention and strive to continuously interpret what is observed. Stake (1995) also specifies that the qualitative case study research can also take the 'collective case study' approach whereby multiple case studies can be compared and it is possible to explore similarities and differences.

In qualitative research inquiry, the setting is also important. The term 'naturalistic' implies that qualitative research takes place in the natural setting of the subjects or case under study including the classroom, the home, or the community (Bogdan & Biklen, 2006). In contrast to quantitative research, "qualitative research involves a particular concern with context, with the notion that action can best be understood when it is observed in the setting in which it naturally occurs" (Bogdan & Biklen, 2006, p. 4). Cohen et al. (2000, 2007) also discuss research methods in education and the importance of understanding the educational environment.

Freebody (2004) noted that the conditions under which teachers teach, the children they teach, and the subject matter they teach, play a significant role in shaping the lived experiences of teachers and learners; these are lived dimensions that are indigenous to each teaching–learning event. I conducted interviews in the teachers' own classroom setting and followed up with a few visits to deepen my understanding of their teaching approaches. Observing their classrooms was insightful. It also enriched the data collection because not only did teachers talk about what they did, they could show the materials used, and the way it was set-up, as they described a particular teaching practice. Lastly, seeing teaching practice in action in the classroom setting brought things to life, as teachers were able to speak to their practice with the organic flow of the day. In addition, connecting teaching practice directly with the learners and seeing how it worked in the classroom setting validated some details from the interview data. Yin (2003) also supports this approach by affirming that "observations are often useful in providing additional information about the topic being studied" (pp. 92-93). Thus observations are an effective way of collecting data in qualitative research.

Bogdan and Biklen (2006) note that classroom settings have to be understood in the context of the historical life of the institutions in which they are a part. Thus, in the case of this study, the relationship between the classroom, teacher, school, and the policy positions on Kindergarten education taken by the Ontario Ministry of Education will all be relevant to putting the data collected into context. Bogdan and Biklen (2006) emphasize the need to examine data with the assumption that nothing is trivial, in that "everything has the potential to be a clue that might unlock a more comprehensive understanding of what is being studied" (p. 5). Furthermore, Bogdan and Biklen (2006) are concerned with process in qualitative research in contrast to the concern with outcomes or products inherent in more quantitative approaches.

According to Robert Stake (1995), qualitative research tries to establish an empathic understanding for the reader, 'thick descriptions,' intended to convey what experience itself would convey. According to Bogdan and Biklen (2003), the concept of thick description in Clifford Geetz's work on ethnography defined descriptions that consisted of layering the multiple meanings created by the research participants and the researcher. The fieldwork in a classroom is unique in that there are many layers and levels of data collection. While this research study aims to capture teachers' perspectives, it is not only the teacher's voice and opinion that is under study; equally important are what they do as well as how they do it. A researcher needs to continue to interpret what is being presented with an understanding that there is a multiple-layered approach to qualitative research.

Bogdan and Biklen further state that qualitative research is "inductive in that researchers do not search out data or evidence to prove or disprove hypotheses; rather, theories are built as the particulars that have been gathered are analyzed" (2006, p. 6). Meaning is essential to qualitative research. Researchers who use this approach (Bailey, Hutter, & Hennink, 2008) are interested in how different people make sense of their lives. In my research, I am interested in both the children's experience of play-based pedagogy and the teachers' experiences, while incorporating teaching approaches and FDK learning strategies into their existing practice. Hence, interviews, classroom observations, artifacts, photographs, and sample student work were gathered, and enhanced the data collection process.

Researcher's Role

These characteristics of the qualitative approach are grounded in the constructivist epistemology of the qualitative tradition. According to Stake (1995), most contemporary qualitative researchers are of the belief that knowledge is constructed rather than discovered. As Stake reinforces, "the world we know is a particularly human construction" (1995, p. 99). As a result, the researcher presents to the reader with different perspectives. In my role as the researcher, I aim to provide readers with a balance of interpretations and also relevant raw material for their own generalizations. The emphasis is on providing various details to readers such as information on the people, places, and practices. Therefore, the focus is on using teaching practices and classroom details, given that "description in this context is not only commonplace description but thick description" (Stake, 1995, p. 102).

Case Study

According to Creswell (2007), a case study is a holistic inquiry that investigates a contemporary phenomenon within its natural setting. It also considers multiple sources of information, and this provides an in-depth picture of the subject being studied. Case study methodology involves qualitative research, which focuses on the uniqueness of individual situations.

Creswell (2007) offers that case study research "involves the study of an issue explored through one or more cases within a bounded system" (p.10). By describing the classroom setting or context in which the research is to be conducted, more insight is given about the data. Yin (2003) further elaborates upon this observation, affirming that case studies allow investigators "to retain the holistic and meaningful characteristics of real life events" (p. 2). Furthermore, examining participants' everyday experiences within their specific contexts, allows for a method that is both exploratory and explanatory in nature.

Case studies are designed to bring out the details from the viewpoint of the participants, by using multiple sources of data. In his book, *The Art of Case Study Research,* Stake (1995) offers many tips on conducting in-depth interviews and the use of case study methodology in research. For example, he discusses data gathering, including document review, coding, sorting, and pattern analysis, the roles of the researcher, triangulation, and reports a case study. According to Stake (1995), the data generated by case studies often resonate experientially with a broad cross section of readers, thereby facilitating a greater understanding of the phenomenon. Stake (1995) defines triangulation as the protocols that are used to provide further explanations in research data. The need for triangulation arises from the ethical need to confirm the validity of the processes.

In case studies, this could be done by using multiple sources of data. The goal in case studies is to establish meaning rather than location. Furthermore, Yin (1994) identified six primary sources of evidence for case study research. The use of each of these might require different skills from the researcher. The six sources identified by Yin (1994) are: documentation, archival records, interviews, direct observation, participant observation, and physical artifacts. Adapting to Yin's recommendations, all six of these sources were used to develop the eight case studies, which are each representative of individual teacher perspectives. Not all sources are essential in every case study, but the importance of multiple sources of data to the reliability of the study is well established (Stake, 1995; Yin, 1994).

Interviews are an essential source of both narrative (Clandinin & Connelly, 1998) and case study information (Creswell, 2007, 2013; Stake, 2005; Yin, 2003). In this research, interviewing was chosen as a primary way of collecting data. During the data collection phase of my study (from May 2011 to May 2013), semi-structured interviews were conducted with a total of eight Kindergarten teachers. According to Banfield (2004), interviewing is valuable for the following reasons: i) It provides the opportunity to generate rich data; ii) language used by participants was considered essential in gaining insight into their perceptions and values; iii) contextual and relational aspects were seen as significant to understanding others' perceptions; and iv) data generated can be analyzed in different ways. Furthermore, in social science research, discussion, conversation, and questioning are effective ways of providing insight. According to Ritchie and Lewis (2003), semi-structured interviews, although guided by questions, are more open and allow for new ideas to be brought up for deeper exploration through "pausing, probing and prompting effectively and appropriately during the interviews" (p. 141). Through interviews, Ritchie and Lewis (2003) show that the researcher values personal language as data and one may even argue that choosing to interview face-to-face recognizes the potential significance of context.

Narrative Inquiry Style

Teachers' narratives provided many specific and descriptive examples of classroom practices, centers, and activities. Each participant had the opportunity to provide more detail and share the various teaching practices they used and what this really looked like in their classrooms. Further, this allowed them to elaborate, as needed, on various areas and share artifacts and visuals.

The narrative inquiry, in general, is an emerging discipline within the broader field of qualitative research and is becoming increasingly accepted among academics. According to Clandinin (1998), narrative inquiry is a research methodology that is growing in acceptance and practice in such disciplines as nursing, medicine, law, especially organizational studies, therapy in health fields, social work, counseling, psychotherapy and teaching. In addition, Creswell (2003, 2008) affirms that narrative inquiry often focuses on the experiences of one or a few participants rather than on those of a larger group. One of its goals is to give voice to those whose stories have been previously unheard in educational research. It may also be a process of inquiry where as a researcher digs deeper and rethink / reformulate the research questions and purpose of the inquiry. In my experience with this research, it was the focus and purpose that narrowly identified the key findings. This process of rethinking provided the impetus to probe further and focus the work as one makes sense of participants' stories. Through interpretation and drawing conclusions, the case study of each participant profile was taking shape. Although this study adapted a narrative inquiry style in order to build on, and shared some personal experiences, it is mainly a case study approach.

Triangulation

Triangulation is often used in qualitative research to indicate that two (or more) methods are used in a study in order to check the results. The idea is that one can be more confident with a result if different methods lead to the same conclusion. In particular, Bogdan and Biklen (2006) affirm that the application and combination of several research methodologies in the study of the same phenomenon allows the researcher to overcome the weaknesses or intrinsic biases that may be a problem from single methods. Therefore, the purpose of triangulation in qualitative research is to increase the credibility and validity of the results. Several scholars have aimed to define triangulation throughout the years. Cohen and Manion (2000) define triangulation as an "attempt to map out, or explain more fully, the richness and complexity of human behavior by studying it from more than one standpoint" (p. 254). Furthermore, Denzin (2006) identified four basic types of triangulation: i) data triangulation (time, space and persons); ii) investigator triangulation (multiple researchers); iii) theory triangulation (using more than one theoretical scheme in the interpretation of the phenomenon); and iv) methodological triangulation (more than one method to gather data such as interviews, observations, questionnaires, and documents).

In this book, a variety of data collection methods and tools such as interviews, observations, photographs, artifacts, class lesson plans, newsletters, video, and lived-experiences, were combined to enrich the data collection process. Evidence from these different sources allowed for opportunities to cross-reference the data. This broader variety of data also led to more detailed analysis and deeper understanding of the research findings. During the data collection process for this research study, the focus was on 'methodological triangulation,' which involved gathering data through three main sources: orally through semi-structured interviews with teachers (giving consideration for open-ended questions to gather rich data), field observations with students present in the classroom, and the collection of various artifacts such as photographs of classroom materials.

In addition, there was also some personal narrative as connections were made where appropriate, from my own teaching experiences in Kindergarten. Creswell also confirms that: "Narrative researchers may interweave their own personal experiences along with the stories that they tell of their participants' experiences" (2007, p. 57). Creswell (2007) further claims that this blending can take different forms, including: i) starting the research report with a personal story to "hook" the readers and / or to help them understand the researcher's particular perspective or connection to the research topic; and ii) showing how they studied their own lived experiences along with those of their other participants, and why.

In conclusion, qualitative research methodology is in fact a more comprehensive approach to research, in that it is multi-dimensional. As Creswell (2007) further points out, qualitative researchers try to develop a more "holistic account"—i.e., a complex picture of the problem or issue under study. This calls for reporting multiple perspectives, identifying the many factors involved in a situation, and generally sketching the larger picture that emerges. In this chapter, more discussion will follow on the in-depth interview process of the eight teacher participants that allowed detailed transcription of each of the eight individuals' narratives. This provided rich data for further analysis. In addition, the details of the recruitment process will provide some more insight on who was chosen and why.

Creswell & Miller (2000) suggest that the validity is affected by the researcher's perception of validity in the study and his / her choice of paradigm assumption. As a result, many researchers have developed their own concepts of validity and have often generated or adopted what they consider to be rigorous or trustworthy terms.I established a process to test the validity and reliability of the study instruments. Follow-up interviews also provided opportunities to clarify or elaborate on information and data collected. Furthermore, consistency, stability, and dependability was considered and also developed by use of the triangulation process, which strengthened the study. Triangulation was a strategy to improve the reliability and validity of the research and the evaluation of the findings.

Recruitment Process

At the beginning, it was important to narrow down the area and start thinking about finding schools that could be considered for the research study. Once the school principal was in agreement, it was possible to approach individual teachers that could be considered for the study. Nine teachers were approached, but eight were recruited and selected for this research study. The selection criteria for participants included having a minimum of two years of Kindergarten teaching experience, as well as individual teacher's general interest and knowledge about the Full-Day Kindergarten model. It was also important that participants were teaching in an existing FDK classroom at the time of the study, as this provided a valid and recent FDK perspective. The aim of the study was to find individual teacher experiences from diverse backgrounds that would provide rich data, opinions, and examples of specific teaching practices and approaches in the FDK classroom. Candidates had teaching experience in implementing the FDK program in Ontario and had some professional development support for running a Kindergarten program. As a researcher, I looked for individuals who would provide insight and varying perspectives. Overall, the teachers were eager, willing and open to participating in a research study where they could share their ideas and opinions and have their voices heard.

In the reporting of the study findings, specific quotes from the interviews are used to illustrate the teachers' voices. Given that the interviews were held in the teachers' classrooms, I had the chance to see some examples of Kindergarten practices as we talked. The teachers shared some student work and assessment tools they used in class, and the actual activity centers they were describing helped deepen my understanding of their answers to the questions. Through observations of different classrooms it was also possible to see ways that creativity was emerging in the learning process. Specific efforts to foster creativity was documented.

The data collection process was most insightful and enlightening. Teacher participants' experience, enthusiasm, knowledge, and dedication were often evident in their detailed answers and the visuals that they shared. There was consideration for preserving the teachers' voices throughout the data collection process. Transcripts were created to scribe detailed answers to the interview questions. Over months, I worked on documenting, organizing, and categorizing the data. Listening to the recordings of each participant's voice in their own words and writing detailed responses, notes, and connecting it with other data sources such as observation notes, photographs, and artifacts, enriched the data collection and analysis process.

Research Sites

In 2011, only some schools were moving toward the FDK model. Schools that were implementing the FDK were considered for the study. The school selection criteria also considered locations with diverse communities, as well as similar size and student population. Other criteria included: same board, same city, same average income category, and similar demographics in the schools. Principals who were approached were those who showed support and interest in this study. Teachers within those schools who gave consent and seemed most open to share their perspective were chosen as teacher participants. Finally, two schools and a total of eight teacher participants were selected for this research study. The following section provides a thick description of the research sites.

The first school, Springfree Elementary School, was founded in 1969 and has a population of over 596 students, with over 97 Kindergarten students. The second school, Summerville Elementary School, has 957 students and over 201 Kindergarten children. Both have a large population of students represented by visible minority groups. The school communities were very similar, and had a high population of ESL (English as a Second Language) students, and mid-to-low income households.

Springfree Elementary School was located in an older two-storey building that had been around for over 45 years. The Kindergarten classrooms were on one side of the school near the back and there was a separate entrance. The walls were painted with murals of children, and featured artwork along the Kindergarten hallway. The classrooms were filled with some round tables, an easel, a large rug, a rocking chair, and low counters with a sink and some storage cupboards. There were older curtains hanging on the large big window of one of the classrooms, from which trees and the soccer field could be seen at the back of the school. This teacher put a lot of time into building up dramatic play areas and had a pretend doctor's office, which consisted of clipboards, an open craft area with lots of different art material, puzzles, and a game shelf. There was also a play dough area with lots of cutters and tools that were put out everyday. The classroom setup and structure informed the understanding of the type of play that would happen in the classroom. In certain classrooms, the layout, physical space, and organization of materials may be more conducive to play.

Springfree Elementary School has a mission to foster an inclusive learning community that promotes respect for all. This school also seeks to promote a love for learning and for building global and responsible citizens. The teacher participants each had their own classroom layout and ran their own Kindergarten program, although they mentioned that they did sometimes collaborate and plan special events with the other Kindergarten teachers in the school.

Summerville Elementary School had been around for eight years at the time of this research study. The design and plan of the schools are more modern, with new furniture and integrated technology; each classroom was equipped with a projector and white screen. The walls were freshly painted with a soft orange color, and there was a modern feel to this school, as furniture was new in the classroom. The teachers were introduced to FDK, but had shown interest right from the beginning in learning and making the transition as early as the first year of implementation. Summerville Elementary School advocated a passion for learning, the arts, and the environment.

The Summerville Elementary School philosophy promoted school performances, monthly assemblies, community building initiatives, parent volunteers, and outreach services that supported new families to Canada. The passion for the arts was evident with the interest from teachers on art-based curriculum development and projects through visual arts, music, drama, and dance. Furthermore, the promotion of environmental performance and sustainable living was unique about this school. There was also an outdoor classroom project and school-wide promotion for saving paper, recycling, planting projects; the school was certified as an 'Ecoschool' because it met criteria that was recognized by the Ontario Ecoschool program.

While each teacher had his / her own style and unique classroom setup, there were some similarities. Each classroom had been setup with many center-based activities. For example, common centers included writing, drawing, art areas which were open and easily accessible, a carpet area to gather, a prominent paint area, a variety of toys, house center, play doughcenter, and a reading area. Although there were some common types of centers, the Kindergarten materials varied widely in the classrooms and each day what I a teacher may focus on was unique. Block play was a prominent and engaging type of play but the types of building materials varied widely.

Teacher Participant Profile

Background information on the gender, age, and number of years of teaching provides some facts about each teacher participant. They all completed a Bachelor of Education degree. Alison completed her Additional Qualification (AQ)—Special Education. Francis and Diya also completed a Master's in Education. Francis, Gillian, Hana, and Cassandra had taken the Additional Qualification (AQ) course—Kindergarten Part One. Francis had also completed AQ course Kindergarten Part Two and Three. Gillian completed Kindergarten AQ Part One and Part Two. Elissa had completed her Early Childhood Education diploma at a college before going to university to complete her Bachelor of Education. An overview of the participant profile is detailed in Table 4 to summarize background information on the teacher participants.

Table 4 *Teacher Participant Profiles*

Pseudonyms	Gender	Age	# Years in Kindergarten	# years teaching in public schools	Education
Alison	F	61	9	17	B.Ed., Sp.Ed.
Bianca	F	46	5	24	B.Ed.
Cassandra	F	35	6	10	B.Ed., K Part I
Diya	F	38	5	8	B.Ed., M. Ed.
Elissa	F	31	3	3	B.Ed., ECE
Francis	M	29	2	3	B.Ed., M.Ed.
Gillian	F	24	4	4	B.Ed., K Part I&II
Hana	F	42	8	2	B.Ed., K Part I

The teacher participants' teaching experience gives information on the total number of years in public school, and subsequently, the number of years teaching in Kindergarten. Alison had been teaching for over 17 years and had taught Kindergarten for 9 years. Bianca had been teaching for over 24 years and had taught Kindergarten for 5 years. Cassandra had been teaching for over 10 years and had taught Kindergarten for 6 years. Diya had been teaching for over 8 years and had taught Kindergarten for 5 years. Elissa had taught for 3 years and all three years were in Kindergarten. There were very few male teachers in the sample pool. Francis, the only male participant, had been teaching for a total of 3 years and had 2 years of Kindergarten teaching experience. Gillian had 4 years of teaching experience, all within Kindergarten. Hana only had 2 years of Kindergarten teaching experience but had 8 years of total teaching experience. The summary of demographics of each of their classrooms is detailed in Table 5.

Table 5 *Demographics of the Eight Classrooms*

Pseudonyms	Number of Students	Number of Boys	Number of Girls	%JK	%ESL
Alison	30	16	14	40%	83%
Bianca	29	15	14	48%	94%
Cassandra	29	14	15	38%	88%
Diya	28	15	13	50%	79%
Elissa	29	13	16	55%	90%
Francis	28	14	14	50%	80%
Gillian	32	17	15	46%	84%
Hana	31	17	14	55%	93%

Data Analysis and Processes

The analysis of the qualitative data began with the gathering of all the interview notes and recordings. Each recording was reviewed and transcribed, and individual statements were subsequently placed into categories or themes. Next, the careful framing of patterns with respect to certain themes allowed for a deeper understanding of the data collected. Bailey described the importance of allowing patterns and themes to emerge from the data by stating that "patterns and themes will be taken out of data rather than being imposed on them before data collection" (1997, p. 159). Taking the time to step back and look at the big picture also allowed me to make connections and understand the themes and their relation to the policy and curriculum documents set out by the Ministry of Education.

Furthermore, the use of methodological triangulation was instrumental in finding specific key themes. The themes that were coded from the research data brought awareness of the attitudes, beliefs, and perspectives of the Kindergarten teachers in different topic areas. Data was gathered from interview questions responses, and classroom observations, as well as field notes. By making comparisons between the eight teacher participants, major findings were gathered and this shed light on key results from this research study.

Data analysis included looking at the interconnectedness of various elements, and the overall relationships between the data were kept in mind as well as the unique data findings that stood out on their own. Finding trends and highlighting responses to specific interview questions, looking for similarities, common themes and new information, as well as evidence from classroom practice led to data interpretation and cross-referencing analysis. This rigorous process led to examining and weaving the data through the theoretical framework, finding a common thread and focus that would allow for making better sense of the data findings, and a move toward the writing stages in my book.

Limitations of the Study

The understanding of FDK among teachers is limited due to the novelty of this educational policy change. The recent implementation also means what is happening now may be different from what FDK may look like ten years from now. The case studies reveal the immediate effect and observations in the early phase of FDK implementation since the introduction of the educational policy change in 2010 and within the first four years.

The understanding of the FDK model could vary among teachers, who each had their own interest, training, and professional development experiences. Some had more of a passion for seeking out information, by attending network meetings, conferences, and by observing other FDK classrooms; others were often using online resources, blogging, reading newsletters, or reading board or union resources. For some of the participants, it was the day-to-day experience and collaboration with other colleagues that provided the primary source of learning about FDK as they were progressing through the school year. Some teacher participants also relied on various resources including books, articles, and websites.

The sample-size considerations were a part of this research study. There were initially four teacher participants interviewed for this study, but with further consideration for building emerging themes and to add more breadth to the perspectives and findings, the sample size was increased to eight teacher participants. Furthermore, these eight case studies provided more insight, as there was a saturation point on teacher perspectives and emerging themes when it came to thoughts on the interview discussion questions.

Moreover, there may be a sense of reflexivity, and the interviewee may be stating what the interviewer wants to hear. It is important to note that traditional criteria such as reliability and validity are often under scrutiny in qualitative methodological approaches; however, with care, the case study approach can prove to be reliable and valid. Both Yin (1994) and Stake (1995) designed protocols for conducting the case study and it was useful to make use of these strategies when considering approaches to improve reliability and validity in this study. Probing questions were used to focus the discussion and get a good sense of the teacher participants' opinions and perspectives.

The school sites were also from a specific demographic area and FDK may vary in a different locations in Ontario. The school sites were also from one specific board, and the FDK program may look different in another board. Teachers within a specific school may work better together and share information and this may mean that FDK classroom practices may follow more of a team plan approach, versus a school where teachers each do their own planning and teaching. Thus, school demographics and teachers' previous experiences, collaboration and teamwork may affect current classroom practice.

Conclusion

In this research study, the lived experiences of FDK teachers provide some rich data and details on the teachers' perspectives.

The qualitative research methodology provided the best way to collect data for the purpose of this study. In addition to being more holistic, rich, and flexible, this approach also connected to real-life contexts. Using the triangulation process also provided more evidence to support research findings from interview questions. This process was most appropriate, and connected to the context of this research study; the findings also provided relevant and meaningful data results. While there are a few limitations with this relatively well-established approach to research, its growing interest and success among social studies educational research experts is evident. Kindergarten pedagogical documentation has provided rich data and while it make more meaning to parents to read about their child with anecdotals than grades, in research it is also the detailed descriptions that really tell the story. It is meaningful to understand why this learning, for this child, in this way, makes sense at this time.

In Chapter 4, I describe the data, highlight key themes, and summarize the key findings. The teacher profiles provide rich descriptive data about the classroom observations. There are some highlights of teachers' understanding of play-based learning, detailed quotes, and classroom examples. The different teaching styles as well as the eight participants' approaches to Kindergarten teaching in the Canadian FDK classroom is unique in its own way. It also sheds light on how we are moving away from planned activities to the study of learning.

Chapter 4

FULL DAY
KINDERGARTEN –
CLASSROOM PRACTICES

Introduction

In this chapter, the major data findings about Kindergarten teaching approaches from the research are highlighted. Further, the teachers' understanding and application of play-based learning in FDK in Ontario are presented. It is interesting to learn about specific activities and classroom approaches to foster creative thinking. Lastly, there are some data findings looking closer at Kindergarten assessment, challenges with implementing FDK, and a comparison of teacher styles. Throughout this chapter, specific teacher quotes and stories are explored.

Looking at Data Findings Process

This qualitative research study focused on gathering rich data that would provide participants' perspectives of, and experiences with FDK classroom teaching practices and approaches. Teacher participants provided perspectives initially through the guided interview questions. Subsequently, through follow-up interviews, classroom observations and examination of documents and artifacts, it was possible to understand more thoroughly each individual teacher's classroom practice, style, and teaching approaches.

Coding the data involved grouping the responses to the interview questions according to specific research questions. This helped to organize the data into subcategories and examine them with specific research questions in mind. The data was coded and summarized using pertinent quotes from the interviews. Tables were used to summarize key findings into various categories, codes and sub-codes, and cross-references in order to track the frequency with which a code was used in the data.

There are several data findings from this research study. Learning more about FDK and how it compared to the Half-Day Kindergarten program from a teacher's perspective begins to give some relevant information about FDK and a deeper understanding of its implementation. Full-Day Kindergarten introduced larger class sizes for teachers. With half day Kindergarten, class size was capped at 20 students; with FDK, the class size requirement was increased. According to the Bill 242, class sizes are to be an average of 26 with a child-adult ratio of 13:1. It is required that the board manage class sizes as close to 26 as possible. All classes in the study were over 26, the largest having 32 students. Class size can affect the quality of the learning that takes place. Classroom management is also more difficult and challenging when there are more children. Research findings provide insight into what is the reality of classroom learning.

In the past, HDK had one teacher and a limit of 20 students for about two and a half hours of the day, either morning class or afternoon class. With FDK, teachers mentioned that there is now an Early Childhood Educator (ECE) in the classroom, and that constituted for another relationship, which they had to manage. Within the FDK program, an ECE was also a co-teaching partner in the classroom, whereas with Half-Day Kindergarten there was only one teacher in the classroom, or maybe the support of a Teaching Assistant, if there were identified special needs children in the class. A comparison between some of the teaching practices in the Half-Day Kindergarten and the FDK program helps to provide some background information. For example, with FDK, teachers are required to plan and teach differently. Having two educators in the classroom can also change the way a Kindergarten program is run. Planning is also changing. It has also become more difficult to do long-term planning because the programming depends largely upon the children's interests. Some teachers also reported that they found it challenging to adjust to the idea of letting the children have so much control over what they are doing.

The FDK model encourages inquiry, play, and a free-flow of learning that is driven by the students themselves. Evidence from classrooms reveals specific teacher practices, which show that teacher philosophies, beliefs, attitudes, and perspectives are shifting to a more constructivist approach. Each teacher had a different classroom that was unique in its own way. Each teacher integrated the FDK model and developed a Kindergarten program that continued to evolve in a very fluid and organic way. Each classroom flowed differently; the children, the teacher, the rules and routines as well as the focus were slightly different. This study aims at capturing a glimpse of classroom practices, while comparing and studying key findings.

Teachers' Understanding of Play-based Learning

The teachers reported that they found play gave children more opportunities to problem-solve and more freedom to explore areas of their own interest. For the most part, the teachers take on the role of the observer of the play. Play also is a holistic approach to learning as it engages mind, body, and spirit. There is an excitement in children at play that deeply connects and engages them. Teacher participants in the study expressed their perspectives on play-based learning in Kindergarten. Alison stated:

> Unstructured play would be just the ability to use your imagination, to show leadership, maybe cooperation, during an activity, see how people get along, how they might resolve a conflict or let them just do whatever they might want to do, and observe their choices in play.

Francis found free play provided no right or wrong ways and fostered more creativity and imagination from the children. When the teacher would demonstrate or give an example, more children tended to just copy the teacher's way, but when they were given more open-ended tasks children were all coming up with their own ideas. Francis shared that "there was a greater variety in the student output during open-ended activities."

Hana found that there were some things children just loved to play with and some things they never touched. Hana paid close attention to what types of play excited and interested the children and developed those areas of the classroom. She stated that "every day the children loved big blocks and Lego and each day they came up with a different structure or way to play with it. The straw connectors were another fascinating toy for the children and they connected them in many different ways." As Hana shared, the paint center in her classroom was also popular; the idea of being artists and creating their own portrait, scene, or masterpiece by mixing colors, applying color on paper and seeing it drip and blend was very interesting and exciting for the children.

According to Elissa, play-based learning does not only mean letting children do what they want, but it means taking the time to observe and facilitate learning while children are engaged in these activities. Elissa indicated that "as the teacher, my role is now as a researcher, observing, documenting, analyzing, scaffolding, and making meaning of what I see." According to Elissa, the follow-up, the sharing, the conversations, the continuation of a process of discovery from the child means becoming more cognizant of what is happening in the classroom and "finding ways through materials, classroom set-up, teaching focus, classroom management and continuous comfort with adaptive and changing ways to hone the learning for the individual students at the right place and at the right time."

According to Gillian, "instead of just listening to the teacher talk, [she] found that through play, children could do more testing and experimenting." Play gave children a chance to think and dialogue about their experience as they were engaged in it. As Diya indicated, "they had a lot more time for play during the day with FDK and therefore more materials to use, more time to use their imagination." Children also had to make more decisions about what to do instead of being told, "This is what we are doing today." All the teachers were of the view that children made choices based on their interests, could move freely from one center to another, and were able to socialize and interact with peers more often. The friendships and sense of community among the classroom were also stronger. The children learned to become respectful of each other very quickly. With a longer time in a classroom setting, they had to learn to deal with various with social issues and communicated with the teacher in order to solve problems, when needed. Children figured out the cause and effect relationship as they navigated the school environment. Overall, by the end of the school year, they had acquired a greater variety of experiences.

Finding opportunities in play to build inquiry and guide learning is also part of FDK. Bianca talked about how children were first experimenting with the ice and the snow and watching it turn into water. The teacher observed and then asked the children to describe what happened to the snow. This gave them a chance to think and dialogue about their experience. The teacher listened and the children talked. Therefore, the teacher was once again observing and using guided questions to get a sense of what the students are thinking, thus gaining a better sense of their understanding and imagination. Letting the children experiment and then finding ways to introduce discussions focuses the learning to be more child-centered.

Teachers also found that role-play allowed children to explore. Students have opportunities for self-discovery when they direct their own learning. They want to learn about things that interest them or are relevant to their lives, and when they are given the opportunity to do so, they learn much better. Self-awareness and self-identity build self-confidence. As children get more comfortable through the year, they open up in a natural way. Hana observed that taking on the role of 'superheroes' or characters they have seen on television was of interest to the children and they could create costumes, use the cut-and-paste center to make a shield, or create masks and props for imaginary role-playing. Hana shared her experience in her class: "I let them share their interest in superheroes, but we may begin to apply math skills to figure out what shapes to cut for the costume, and use a ruler to measure and markers to design details on the costumes and props." Extending the learning and integrating curriculum expectations in creative and unique ways, could also present challenges the educators, but as revealed by the data findings, it can be done.

Francis acknowledged that the one thing children love to do is "dress up." There is always interest in putting on hats or costumes and playing a role. The dramatic play area is an important part of FDK. Francis describes dramatic play activities as follows:

> In my classroom they have been firefighters, police officers, athletes, and pizza makers. I even brought in dinosaur hats once and they loved it. Sometimes we make a vest or hat. They use their imagination in different ways. They take on different roles. They love to pretend to be something.

FDK involves building, constructing, and playing with blocks. Furthermore, the construction center is often equipped with various materials from wooden blocks, to colored cups, recyclable boxes, to lids and straws. Children love to build. Alison communicated:

> The kids like painting, and making buildings. They would cut out the windows, the doors, putting numbers on the buildings, so this whole area had recyclable boxes. It lasted about 2 months until they were bored of it. So you have paint and do everything out there at the table. Then whatever they made they would bring it to the construction site. At construction site there were many blocks, like the foam blocks, wooden blocks, cardboard blocks, and Lego blocks. They continued building.

The teachers reported that they were moving away from organizing lessons geared toward all children learning all the same things in a formal theme such as farm animals, dinosaurs, bears being visible at all centers. For example, one teacher said they do not use theme-based learning at all anymore, except on special occasions such as Mother's Day or Father's Day. Instead, children are encouraged to bring in interesting things from home, and that becomes the focus of learning. For example, as Alison asserted:

> I have two boys. They are very bright, they are very much into computers, but we had to make their own comic club, storytelling center, and then they really got into talking about Pokémon and brought Pokémon bookmarks, drew Pokémon pictures, and did retells on Pokémon.

Teacher participants try to bring topics and ideas that are of interest to, and are generated from the children. Teaching practices in Kindergarten also involve focusing more on the children and letting them lead the topics of learning. Another teacher, Hana, really enjoyed the shift to student-centered learning and talked about how it led to more engaged learning:

> Some students were very curious about space so we started to look at planets online. We even drew different planets. I found books on planets from the school library and brought them into the classroom. They were interested in looking at Mars and they wanted to build a rocket-ship so we did.

The teachers also expressed interest in integrating more natural objects and processes into the classroom, such as planting, touching trees, and looking at flowers. Teacher participants in this research study often make observations about environmental changes and what is happening in nature; letting that guide the learning makes sense. The use of inquiry-based learning, especially connecting it with the science curriculum expectations, is a growing practice in the Kindergarten classroom. Hana indicated that she often takes her class outside—even twice a day.

> I take them out in the morning and the afternoon. We go for outdoor play, walk, and sit under a tree. We love to collect things, and I want them to get their energy out so outside is a good place to run around. Being outside also gives me time to observe the kids and see what they are curious about. I can see what they do, what they talk about with friends, how they use their imagination. I will bring out different bins of things at different times: bubbles sometimes, magnifying glasses sometimes, books, and even shovels at other times.

Language is the foundation of every program. Finding ways to connect children with literacy expectations and covering the language curriculum expectations takes some planning. There are some children who often participate whereas others really need encouragement. The goal is to get children to participate and to be engaged in their learning. Oral language development is a big part of Kindergarten. Bianca stated:

> Through the centers and games, they talk while building Lego structures together. They share ideas. Children are talking about books and discussing what they are seeing in the pictures. Talking is important to their learning.

Furthermore, increasing participation is a focus. It may mean providing opportunities for children to come up and talk in front of the class, or share their thinking through a think/pair/share activity. Having the ability to come up to the teacher and share their ideas and thoughts as they do their work builds confidence. They are learning how to interact while gaining an understanding and this is an important element of the learning process. By asking questions, the teacher also gets the kids to dialogue. Participation also means more access. For example, Diya shared as follows:

> At the water table, we had a rock-washing station. I put out books at that center about rocks. Also, letting the kids create whatever they want is important. I just put out the resources and make materials accessible. At the art center, I have colored paper, glue, scissors, pompoms, markers, pipe cleaners, buttons, cotton balls, pencil crayons, paint, and stickers. Kids come over freely and use the materials.

Diya often uses games and creates problems or scenarios to integrate learning and make connections. Play can integrate games and cooperative tasks or simple problems that generate thinking from the students. Teachers can frame the learning to foster critical thinking by asking more open-ended questions. A vivid example of this is presented in the following quote from Diya, who explained her morning routine:

> We figure out things together, we look for the missing words in the morning message, we play games, solve math calculations together based on real-life situations—[for example], how many chairs to put out for theatre for the play based on how many students are in the class today.

Kindergarten teaching practices should be considering the different levels of learning. There is a need for free flow of activities and open centers that are spaces for children to explore. While intentional teaching occurs in a Kindergarten classroom, there also needs to be room for free exploration based on the individual child's interest and level of development. For example, as Cassandra explained:

> At the same center a 3-year-old can start speaking English, and scribble with markers, and the 6-year-old can write a sentence and draw a detailed picture. The same center can be used by all different students and at any time. We keep tables empty and open floor spaces so children can come over and spread out materials and get right to it. The activities and the centers can be used at all times. It doesn't matter what level the children are. They are open all the time. We always have a paint area,

snack area, drama area, writing area, reading area
open all the time.

Small-group instruction is becoming an increasingly important
teaching practice in the FDK classroom. Working with small groups,
of children can constitute for more effective teaching at this age.
Small group instruction is more effective than using the whole-class
teaching approach in the Kindergarten years. As revealed in this
study, this also helps to target individual learning goals and develop
differentiated instruction. For example, Cassandra divides the class
for small-group instruction. Francis also finds developing reading
skills requires more direct teaching and this is more effective in small
group instruction. Diya reinforced this and stated:

> Creating a corner for more guided instruction is
> also effective. I have someone who needs a little bit
> extra help with letter recognition come over with
> magnetic letters and the cookie sheet and we will
> play the magnetic letter activities. We have block
> area which is the center of the whole classroom.
> We can always see what they are doing. We have
> a water area, a sand area, a math area, reading
> area. We notice the kids are not using the math
> manipulatives in the math area [so] we put them in
> the block area and have them start measuring their
> structures. Kids can use manipulatives for math
> skills actually in their play.

Examining how literacy and numeracy education looks like
in a play-based learning classroom was fascinating based on what
teachers said. The teachers are conscious of school-wide goals, and
curriculum expectations and they focus on meeting them throughout
the year. They are aware of specific learning goals. The teachers

shared some examples of learning in their classrooms. Cassandra shared as follows:

> For math, I have objects in one basket and some in another and then we figure out how many altogether. We sort the objects, lay them out on the table, graph them on the table and talk about the most and the least number. We see if we can sort them another way, too. I see them try to use the math language. They are getting the math concepts.There is a time for reflection on what they do throughout the day. They realize different strengths and different skills as they explore. We talk about their success with learning and what they did in the day. We share our ideas and discuss as a group.

Learning letters with movement, song, and meaningful contexts works with young children and builds environmental print awareness. There is a shift from the letter-of-the-week approach to a more open-ended literacy approach. Alison elaborated that 'word walls' are more personalized and child-created in a FDK classroom. Children add their names to an alphabet line and there is a concerted effort to carefully choose the word, which goes up on the walls. The words that are familiar to the students are added to the word wall. Furthermore, as Cassandra noted:

> Today, I have children taking pictures of themselves, attaching it to a piece of paper, and printing their name underneath.Then we attached it to our alphabet line. Well, it's a play-based curriculum. It is all about the child as a whole and trying to understand their interests, where they are coming from, and their experiences up to now. Some only know the letters in their name and that is what

they have been learning. Adding notepads and clipboards at centers is great because it encourages experimenting with writing.

The activities and the topics prescribed by the child are all part of the learning. The child chooses according to his or her interests and the teacher's job is to assist in the learning. They determine what the children's interests are and then work in that context to meet the learners' needs. For example, Diya talked with a lot of enthusiasm about her hairdressing center:

> I brought in a hairdressing table, and my kids sitting in hairdressing table have been talking a lot about putting it on a fashion show, so I am going to be designing my drama centers around the fashion show area. So it would mean a lot of the art things are to do with designing clothes. I encourage math patterns on the clothes. Their drama would show acting out the fashion show. I noticed that the boys are more into some other aspects. Maybe I would put cameras and other types or pieces of technology that they could be using to incorporate themselves into that area. Maybe they don't want to do clothes-decorating, maybe some girls don't want to do that. Maybe they too want be a photographer or write a script for the show. I am sort of guiding the talk, guiding, you know, by making some suggestions on their outfits. But they are playing, they're playing the fashion show, but [with] the guidance of a teacher who has an idea: I don't need to do this pattern sitting at a desk and on a paper with a pencil. Children develop their understanding of patterns or shapes in drama centers. As far as they're concerned they're playing fashion show, but I am

assisting their knowledge of patterns and shape, colors, and all of that.

In the following excerpt, Bianca clearly articulated her views on the effectiveness of play-based learning, when she stated that:

> Play-based learning approaches can go beyond Kindergarten. I think it is hard to do it well, but when it is done right it is amazing. If it's done well, there is much better learning in the classroom as demonstrated by teachers in this research project. Through play, they are getting so much more. They are much more engaged. Learning this way is more likely to capture their excitement and interest. We can reach more children with play-based curriculum. Think about how boys who do not like sitting at a desk writing on a paper and how they would enjoy play-based learning.

In addition, Cassandra mentioned:

> Well anything tactile also works well. For example, like play dough, this week one of my activities is the big dice that you can individualize, and put different shapes on them, and roll them. You pair them and whatever shape comes up you will also make it with the sticks and play dough. We also do play dough numbers and letters. They love play dough.

Understanding each participant's understanding of play-based learning sheds light on the teachers' perspectives onthe use of play in the classroom. With specific examples, the teachers explained how play looks in their own classroom. Alison sees play as more unstructured activities, more choice in activities, role-playing, problem-solving, socializing, singing, constructing, and games. Bianca is focused on how to make learning more fun, and therefore, integrating more science into the play-based centers became her focus. Cassandra elaborated upon the idea of integrating more mathematics into play-based learning. Diya talked about a variety of centers, touching upon building on subject-specific areas in the class and building oral language development with the use of guided questions.

Cassandra talked about the reading and writing area, and the use of magnetic letters on a cookie sheet. But it seems that none of the teachers had a comprehensive and detailed plan for literacy development. As some of them indicated, a structured time for letter sound recognition was not as popular anymore.

Key findings from the data collected highlight what the teachers were thinking and talking about. This section gives a summary of the major perspectives and areas of focus that emerged from the interviews with the teachers. Many key elements of the Kindergarten program were identified. It is clear that a lot of consideration goes into the design of a play-based program. Below is a summary of key themes identified in the data.

When integrating play into the classroom, key factors for consideration included: integrating learning with activities, redefining the role of the teacher and role of the student, focusing on intrapersonal child development, movement and learning, inquiry in learning, problem-solving, and the physical space in the classroom.

The process of reviewing the transcripts and examining specific quotes led to getting a sense of key perspectives of the eight teacher participants. A close examination of the topics, and how often they were discussed by the teacher participant in the interviews helped to identify frequency trends as I began to code the data. This process was facilitated by creating data summary tables; this also helped to summarize key findings and make sense of the major themes that were emerging. Fifteen components were identified in these findings and these were becoming clearer as I sifted through the data and examined it more closely. Some of the topics, which were mentioned by the majority of participants, also helped in identifying significant trends.

It is important to examine in more detail, the key themes that emerged from analysis of the teachers' remarks about play-based learning; these have been summarized below:

1. Teaching Approaches: integrating learning with activities, the role of the teacher, intrapersonal child development, role of the student, movement, and learning;
2. Physical Space: room layout and setup, access to materials, floor space for play;
3. Integrated Curriculum: focus on problem-solving and inquiry-based learning; and
4. Holistic Practices: focus on natural science in classroom, use of inquiry, exploration, discovery and experiential learning approaches.

Trying to keep learning fun and interactive, managing boredom, and some of the other challenges of Kindergarten teaching were also common themes in the participants' narratives. I will be presenting the teacher's perspectives. The use of the play-based approach reported, shows evidence of hands-on and experiential learning opportunities for the child in Ontario Kindergartens. The shift from a teacher-directed approach to a child-directed learning style also entails a change in the role of the teacher. Examining the teacher's view and evaluating them was insightful. Describing each teacher style defines the individual teacher case study.

Classroom Connections: A Closer look into the Kindergarten Teachers' Classrooms

After transcribing the data, I had a good sense of each teacher's style of teaching. Some of the teachers definitely had a deeper understanding of and greater confidence in experimenting with the different Kindergarten teaching approaches. Others established routines and various areas in their classroom, which they often managed in much the same way throughout the year. A couple of teachers often moved around the furniture in the classroom and tried to make changes monthly. There was a spectrum of methods for classroom management techniques as well. The entry and end of day routines could look very different in different classrooms. A couple of the participants always started off their day by first taking the children outside of the classroom. Others only went outside just before lunch, while some went outside twice a day. The majority went outside in the afternoon or at the end of the day.

The journey of change is individual and each teacher is on his or her own journey. When a new approach is introduced, it takes time to implement the changes in the classroom. There's a great deal of change in teaching practices with FDK—one's own mindset, one's ability to think of ways to inject new ideas, and one's comfort in trying out new ideas. The examples and ideas shared by the teachers gave a glimpse into the classroom. The dialogue with the participants enriched my understanding of the range of teachers' perspectives. Each teacher's level of comfort with the language of FDK varied. Each teacher's understanding of the general and specific curriculum expectations, their confidence with managing children in the early years of education, their own classroom space, routines, rules, choice of topics, and types of activities, were unique in each case study.

It was through classroom observation that I was able to get a better sense of the individual participants' teaching practices within their own classroom. Classroom observation protocol included looking at the classroom setting, routines, layout, interactions, relationships, movement, teaching practices, teacher's role, types of activities, sense of independence, and freedom among the learners. Details of the day in the life of the teacher participants' classroom routines are described below.

Alison's classroom. Alison had a strongly child-centered focus in her teaching practices. For example, it was clear that there was a movement away from paper-and-pencil activities toward more hands-on activities. There was more of a focus on letting the children lead, based on their interests, by minimizing carpet time, and by co-constructing centers of interest with the children. Alison discussed the changing role of the teacher from teacher-directed lessons and moving toward more guided questions in a small-group setting, while children are engaged in play. There was a shift toward a lot more play, less sitting, more movement, and intentional interaction by the teacher to dialogue one-to-one by asking questions about what they were doing and thinking.In general, there were more individual, center-based, and small group learning opportunities rather than whole-class lessons and activities. Children were doing many different things at different times.

In Alison's classroom, there was a welcome sign at the door and a poster with hello in different languages. After hanging up their jackets and backpacks, children came and sat at the carpet which had a globe and faces of children with different ethnic backgrounds. Alison would then take attendance and sing a morning song with the children. Alison often sang songs for routines such as lining up, snack, lunch, tidy-up and she had a 'good morning' and 'good bye' song, which she sang with the children each day. She often chose songs that related to the topic that they were focusing on. Children all engaged and participated in songs with actions activities. After the morning circle, Alison introduced centers that were open, and within about 20 minutes, she would invite the children to go to specific centers. Once they made their choice, they would then proceed to the center. A couple of children headed toward the art counter where several materials were left out each day. In the play dough area, there were placements and seats for four. At some of the other centers, there was a crafts table or an activity related to the song she introduced. Bin toys were shelved on a wooden rack and contained building materials, cars, train tracks, matching game cards, puzzles, plastic colored bears, and snap cubes. The house center was open and had a table with placemats and settings with cups, plates, and bowls. Children had created menus for a restaurant with pictures of food items such as sushi, pizza, samosa and rice. The environment had visible signs of multiculturalism with the books on the shelves, the things on the wall and the materials at centers.

The ECE sometimes sat with the small group of children at the table with the activity related to the song or topic for that day. She would prepare this activity and set it up in the morning that day. The morning center time lasted about one hour and then the children were asked to tidy-up and get ready for their snack, which they ate as a whole class, and individual mats were placed out after two helpers sprayed and wiped down the tables. The ECE helped to redirect children during tidy-up and transitions; she also helped to supervise during snack.

After snack, the children went outside and played in small groups among friends; some children played hopscotch, others would draw with chalk on the ground, and some blew bubbles. Outdoor play time lasted about thirty-five minutes, then the children came in, washed their hands, got their lunch bags, and sat down to eat lunch. A lunchroom supervisor and an ECE remained with the children while the teacher had a lunch break. The ECE would sometimes put on a video after lunch and there was also a comfort corner in the classroom where children could rest as they finished eating; some would read a book, others sat and watched the video; some were just slow eaters; and others talked most of the time with friends. The afternoon routine was very much the same. The centers would be re-opened but this time board games and book bins with different types of books, some non-fiction, some fiction, and with a variety of topics were brought out. The children went outside again before they went home, and a mailbag was handed out to children, which they tucked away in their backpacks. They sang a 'goodbye song' in the hallway as they kept jackets on ready to return home. The ECE helped with the dismissal routine and the teacher also communicated with a few parents.

Creativity in the classroom was evident in different ways. There was a 'creative center' in the classroom filled with clear containers with buttons, yarn, Q-tips, beans, foil paper, recycled paper, markers, pencil crayons, and crayons. It allowed for the child to use scissors and glue with different materials to make what their imagination allowed. Art supplies such as brushes of different sizes, paint and rollers were set up on the counter in the classroom.

Bianca's classroom. Bianca found the changes more demanding and challenging. The noise and chaos with working with Kindergarten children all day and the larger class-size seemed overwhelming. The dynamics of the classroom is different with an ECE worker working with the teacher, and Bianca admitted that she initially did not like that at all. Bianca had some basic understanding of the new FDK curriculum expectations, but it was not clear because there were so many resources, and she did not know which one to use. She admitted to feeling nervous and uncomfortable with the change, as it was not an easy transition for her. Her strategy was to first focus on one thing, try it out, and then start something else; otherwise, it was difficult to introduce too many things all at the same time. Evidence of changes in practice included: awareness of greater opportunities to socialize; encouraging use of home language between friends who could not speak English, buddying up children and using a visual schedule and pictures on bins to encourage children to put things back where they belong, building confidence by encouraging participation in activities; building leadership skills a letting SK children model routines for JK children; and the active use of a morning message with built-in questions. Sometimes students were asked to answer a question by putting a tally mark to indicate their response as they came to the carpet. Other thoughts from Bianca included the need for appropriately-levelled reading materials and a clear writing area with a writing book. Having some control and structure to manage the classroom is as important as teaching them to sit and listen. Bianca discussed how having some control manages the noise level and creates quiet space to concentrate. Bianca found it difficult and challenging to get all children to sit on the carpet. She set up a quiet activity for those who found it hard to sit still. The ECE would work with them on a small group activity.

Bianca started the day by having the children come in and answer a question on the white board as part of the morning message and then they would pick a book and read as they waited for others. Once everyone gathered, they would wait for attendance and then put their book back on the shelf. The morning message also stated what was going on for the day. It was used for identifying words and teaching letter sounds. It was read by the whole class with the lead of the special helper who used the pointer and came up in front of the class to lead the reading. After circle time, students were introduced to centers for the day, and students put up their hands to indicate which one they wanted to go to first as the teacher asked one by one. There was a limit of four students at each center and once at centers the teacher circulated the classroom and then sat a small table and asked specific students to join her for levelled reading, as did the ECE at another table. These books were also sent home as part of a snuggle-up and read program. Children used the listening center to listen to a book tape, some were also building with blocks, some using chalk on a chalkboard, and some playing with dolls of different ethnic skin. After forty minutes inside, the children went out for a walk and to the park to play for about forty minutes each day. In the afternoon after lunch, there were sight words up on the wall in big font, and many writing tools out on the counters in the classroom and specific poem cards in a basket that students could read with a magic pointer they selected from a tall container located beside the book bin. Some used the computer center, and some did puzzles, and some went back to house center and used the dress up clothes which had some capes, tutus, scarves, and community helper hats.

Bianca used many classroom management strategies and she used her firm tone, pauses, and moments of waiting as students made transitions giving them time to settle before she would talk. There were some discrepancies on how she presented her style and how it actually appeared in the classroom. Although Bianca commented in the interview that she found FDK very demanding, she seemed to have a good hold of strategies to manage the class. She also had children listen attentively and engage in discussion as she modelled interactive lessons and teaching approaches. The walls in Bianca's classroom had some student paintings with their name card and picture below and other artwork hung near a bulletin board.

The ECE had specific tasks and the teacher had others, so they talked to each other, but not all the time, as they interacted frequently with the children on a one-to-one basis. Bianca mentioned that the afternoon circle was run by the ECE and she often read a story and maybe set up a craft connected to it. There were community helper toys out and a police station set up that engaged some of the students during free play in the afternoon. She still mentioned the use of journal books and making mini-books an important part of her program. There was a sense of routine and structure that students were familiar with, and she used a rattle as a noise control method, to signal if it was too loud and mentioned to students to quiet down. Some activities included labelling the pictures they drew or making cards. Bianca built classroom practice on repetition, routine and visual gesturing both in classroom management approaches and teaching style. She also used eye contact and proximity to students as a way to get attention of students.

Creativity was captured with the use of puppets, props and dolls. There was often dramatic play opportunities and children could use their imagination to play a role or character. Music with instruments was also encouraged during circle time and children even made some of the instruments. Children loved to use instruments as they sang songs. Art and craft materials such as construction paper, cardboard, straws, pipe cleaners, glitter and beads were available for the children. Different art techniques were explored and mixing and making colours was welcomed. Even what they used to paint may change and this created different textures.

Cassandra's classroom. Children in Cassandra's classroom sat against the wall after hanging up belongings and waited for morning announcements then once announcements were over children were ready they could enter and choose an activity at the carpet. Four bins were placed out with games. Children knew what to do. The teacher quietly strolled around took attendance. Some children also went to look at the fish and discovery area where plants were growing. A couple of children looked at a board that had the agenda for the day. Cassandra made choice, decision-making, and problem-solving a bigger part of the day. For example, students decided when they wanted to eat and there was no formal snack time. Learning to make independent choices early on was part of children's self-regulation skills. According to Cassandra, this was part of her teaching style and was a big part of the new FDK curriculum.

Self-regulation and self-directed learning nurtured listening to one's body and mind. A child who reached for a jacket because it was cold, and sat to eat a snack when he / she was hungry also was aware of the need to use the washroom or the time to tidy-up. Building awareness of one's environment at an early age also builds independence. This also made learning self-initiated and relevant, and built connections at a deeper level. The role of the teacher was to take the time to dialogue with individual students. The teacher maintained authority in the classroom and established that early in the year because at the end of the day, they were still liable. Cassandra's understanding of whole child learning focused more on the integration of specific subjects and making the child experiment with materials.

Cassandra commented that the ECE in her room plans activities and brings in different types of materials, books, and enjoys baking, making play dough, papier-mâché, and melting crayons. She often introduced new ideas; she communicated suggestions and was highly interactive and involved in the classroom management techniques, as well as classroom setup. She also introduced new songs and poems to the children on a regular basis and had them posted on the walls, class website and printed on a paper that was laminated and placed in a basket. Some children would sing songs andfollow along with the pointer. Pointers were also used at the listening center where books on tape were placed and accessible for children. She organized things in the classroom, cleared off and sprayed down counters to disinfect them, and sanitized and washed toys daily. The ECE was also actively involved during dismissal time, talked to parents and provided updates and reminders.

Both the teacher and ECE spoke different languages and at times they would interact with students in their home language. Children also were encouraged to wear their national clothing and make storybooks about their family life. Pictures on the wall included a family picture and places they had been. A map of the world hung and a string with flag under the picture showed the diversity of representation from around the world of children in the class.

Creativity corner was open for students to use water colours, coloured glue, sponges to sponge paint, and there was also a focus on collaborative art. For example, all children coloured popsicle sticks with sharpie makers in different patterns then each stick was used to make several squares as they were lined up in a row. It became an abstract piece of art. There was also the idea of each child coming up to splat paint on the mural paper on the floor and then the large painting was used to decorate a wall. Using guided questions, children used their voice to express creative ideas, solutions, and designs before, during and after they would create art pieces.

Diya's classroom. Students entered, picked a book, and sat on the carpet during entry. The teacher did a good morning song, and then took attendance once everyone was at the carpet. She also had each child answer the question of the day when their name was called. On my observation day, the question was 'what is your favorite fruit?' Children would give an answer when their name was called. After 10 minutes at the carpet the children would choose tabletop activities and math bags. The morning play was limited for 20 min to these activities and then once complete children could make a choice of any center in the classroom. The teacher also read a story, *The Very Hungry Caterpillar*, and children had to remember the words as the teacher pointed to the food pictures. They enjoyed interacting with the teacher as she read the storybook. For transitions the teacher used song as a way of giving instructions. She sang, "It's time to read a story, so gather here today. It's time to read a story, so join us everyone."Most children put down their materials and came to the carpet to sit and listen to the story. A few were distracted and busy at the center. The teacher continued anyway with the story and let the two boys at Lego continue to play.

Diya said that having children take initiative and self-regulate in the classroom was a priority; therefore, the children had more time to play, discover, and be creative. The teacher became the observer. Sharing during circle time was what may have happened during an afternoon circle time. There continued to be challenges in delivering an excellent program because of the class size. Problem-solving, and critical thinking strategies were posted on the wall with step-by-step directions integrated into daily classroom activities. Curriculum expectations about connecting children with the world around them were also posted visibly. There was a sense of structure with the established routines, the placement of materials in specific areas, and the organization of supplies. The assessment and documentation binder was full, with many observation notes connected to specific curriculum expectations. A systematic tracking of students' skills, abilities, and knowledge was documented and filed.

Diya encouraged self-regulation with many tasks in the classroom such as entry and end of day routines, circle time expectations, and tidy-up. Her teaching practice focused on co-construction and involving the children in different designing centers. They created a hair salon and beauty parlour, and children who were interested in it helped to paint a sign, draw hair style posters, and set up an area.

They also discussed ideas in small groups as the teacher facilitated the time of sharing thoughts and opinions. Lighting was set up with lamps and distributed around the classroom, and often the main room lights were off and the lamps were on.

In Diya's classroom, the ECE had specific tasks and this is written out. The teacher often had meetings with the ECE to make plans. Subject areas were also divided up and the ECE taught some subjects areas and the ECE taught others in a small group setting. The ECE was also responsible for creating a document panel to share student work or put up artwork. The teacher divided classroom newsletter making and had the ECE write up comments for the report card. There were low-level cubby areas for each student to put artwork or things to take home. It was also a place where the teacher could leave notes and had the children put art, work of the day, and notes in into their own backpack on a daily basis. The ECE spoke the home language of many children and would tell the teacher the meaning of a word if the teacher was not sure what the child was saying. During parent teacher conferencing, the teacher arranged for a translator she said to assist with communication. She said she also tried to connect with parents early in the year about home language and would find out if the children had siblings so she could note this.

Elissa's classroom. Elissa had a lively classroom environment equipped with many different types of materials: tissue paper, cotton balls, cloth fabrics, silk material, wallpaper paper pieces, yarn, buttons, rocks, tiles, foil paper, brown bags,newspapers, and flyers. The walls were filled with instructions for drawing such as: add detail, use five colors, and use shapes. There was a buddy system in place and names were listed on the board. Elissa described her FDK as being inspired by transformational practices. She had taken the time to see other classrooms and also used the internet to research ideas. Elissa often tried to look at other teachers' practices, connecting with others, reading about FDK and using different teacher resources to figure things out. She was familiar with the board's diversity resources and had them on a shelf. She know about the board policy on social justice education and inclusive practices. She also had a daybook with festivals to recognize and shared that.

When children entered the classroom, they walked down the hallway and their hook was labelled with their name and a piece of artwork hanging above. Children changed to indoor shoes, took their lunch and water bottles out, and stored them in a bin laid out in the hallway. They turned in their mailbags at the start of the day and sat by the wall next to their name cards. After listening to "OCanada," the national anthem, they stood up and walked into the classroom pick up their name cards, which were laid out around the circle, and put them in the basket. They then sat, and the teacher took attendance, read the morning message, and had a book at the easel. She started her morning with a story and children sat quietly and listened. She asked the occasional question and children put up their hands to answer. If someone shouted out, she reminded them that she was looking for a quiet hand. The story she read that day was entitled *I Love Rain*. She finished the story and asked the children what they thought of rain. Some children said they were scared of rain. Some said they were sad and did not like to get wet. The teacher then talked about how rain could be fun and how it helped plants grow. She introduced a journal entry and had students on a daily basis do one writing or drawing piece, which they hung up on the clothesline by their pictures.

Elissa's teaching practices focused on using natural materials, books about water, wind, rain, sun, and rainbows. She also made class books that were based on children's interests. There was one entitled *Heros* and another entitled *Making our Garden*. There was also a place to put artwork or display structures built that day, and children were encouraged to share their work during a show-and-share time in the afternoon. Children were used to moving to center choices and they were familiar with the rules at the centers and how to use them. They moved freely around the room illuminated by natural light. There was also a singing bowl that was used purposefully to calm the children, if the noise got too loud. There was an emphasis on setting up the classroom with 'invitations' and 'provocations' for learning. For example, rocks with lines were put out in a wicker basket, with frames and children could align the rocks to make shapes, letters or numbers. There was also an area of 'loose parts' that included clear containers of materials such as beans of different color, beads, pennies, different shaped pasta and cut string and yarn and each day different 'loose parts' were put out on a tray at a table where children could make 'loose parts' art. One day they made faces from 'loose parts'.

The ECE in Elissa's room worked to create student portfolios and arranged small groups to get children to use letter sounds as they scribbled down their thoughts on a question or drawing. The ECE is also very actively involved in choosing books and teaches during the circle time; further, she brings in classroom materials, organizes crafts, and redirects students as needed. The teacher and ECE sat and planned together, often discussing weekly lessons while setting up areas in the classroom. The ECE was very actively involved with sharing her opinion and ideas, and coming in to set up activities. A good working partnership between the teacher and ECE made for more effective teaching practices in FDK. Quite often, the ECE would also work with half of the class, and the teacher would take the other half outside. They divided up the class and worked in small groups for science inquiry, based on student interest or in different groups by skills and abilities for guided reading tasks. Classroom management strategies were visible on the walls and effective grouping and buddying system was laid out on a bristol board. As observed, the teacher had visible strategies to manage the classroom effectively while allowing some choice but managing chaos and building on experiential learning, literacy, and numeracy skills. There is a good balance of structure and free choice that guided the children in a calm way.

Creative ways were brought in based on ideas from storybooks. The details the illustrator used in pictures became a topic of discussion and led to inspirations for creative art ideas for the children. There was a drawing book children could pull off the shelf if they wanted to add a picture to their own personal portfolio. Little tables with markers in cups and sharp pencil crayons of various colours were accessible all the time.

Francis' classroom. When children came to school, they were required to line up for entry and go directly to a hook with their name to put their things, then come sit on a bench outside the classroom by their name card on the wall. Once they entered they found their name card and answered a question of the day by placing their name card in a pocket chart. There were clear established routines that the children were well aware of and they followed. Francis' classroom had a lot of artwork on the walls. Francis pursued his passion for the arts, which he integrated in many ways with cross-curricular approaches. He believed that creativity and imagination are core components of early years and strived to develop these elements in many different ways. He also encouraged sharing cultural art and dance. He had a table with cultural artifacts and children wrote in their home language and things were posted on the wall above it.

There were many unique arts-based activities that allowed the children to explore the integration of subject areas. The teacher combined math with art and had students build a rocket ship then measure it and sort materials. The use of different shapes and objects to paint and the blend of art with science were also visible with the rock art; the children also engaged in ordering the rocks from biggest to smallest. Classroom materials were sorted in small baskets and kept in labelled bins at a low level for easy access. Children did less open-ended art as many structured art activities and lessons build on curriculum connections. Children had a choice to make paper maché masks, paint them, and add feathers and shapes for details. The ECE in Francis' classroom took half the class at times and conducted her lesson with this group, while the teacher worked with a separate group on writing activities and word lists. The ECE supervised children and often redirected them during activity and clean up time. The teacher was responsible for building up long range plans, and then ECE occasionally added in a craft activity connected to the big ideas. Francis was particular about putting things back exactly where they come from and reinforces this in his classroom. There were two distinct carpet areas and foam padding over the tiled flooring. During the 'quiet time' after lunch, the lights were dimmed and children could lie down, read a book, or play a quiet game; they silently engaged in these activities for about ten minutes. Francis mentioned that sometimes children enjoyed doing yoga and watched a video called 'cosmic kids yoga' and followed along. Yoga was an effective way gathering the children and introducing them to exercises within the classroom. It was well-liked by the children and they remembered the different poses and refocused during this time.

Student portfolios were detailed with student drawings, a writing sample, many photographs of a variety of activities, and thinking captions that highlight the exact words the child said to answer a question. Student portfolios gave a good idea about the variety of activities they children were engaged in. The construction area was a large section in a corner of the classroom and many sample photos of structures were posted on the wall near that center. Samples of buildings and structure such as a skyscraper, a house, a hut, an igloo, and a bridge were labelled and hung near the construction center. Portfolios also had many pictures of the different group and individual structures created by the student.

Creativity through construction was a focus in this classroom. Three-dimensional models and block play were areas of interest and inspiration for many children. They used small Lego, big Lego, shaped blocks and wooden building blocks during center time. Children also built structures from rolls, boxes, tubes, and egg cartons and used them to build community buildings. Doing science experiments was a way to rekindle enthusiasm and curiosities, and using technology to research and design models and interests was encouraged.

Gillian's classroom. Gillian loved to pursue classroom transformation practices on a regular basis as she discovered new books, ideas, and good examples of effective teaching practices; she is eager to experiment and test out how to integrate diversity practices in her classroom. She infused her teaching with the use of technology; she took pictures of students engaged in play and then talked to the students while she recorded their thoughts and answers to questions during the play. She often talked to the children about world events. She added her own notes and electronically filed her anecdotal notes through the 'Evernotes Application' on her iPad.

Gillian had an interest in bringing in a variety of materials such as buttons, wallpaper books, egg cartons, popsicle sticks, lids, yarn, threads, fabrics from different cultures and colored and textured papers for the children to use at the art center. Gillian herself dressed with bright colors. She sang often and had children dance and engage in movement throughout the day. She enjoyed 'spirit days,' which got the children excited and moving. Not only did the children dress-up, but Gillian also enjoyed dressing up for lessons and spirit days and had a drawer full of spirit day props. The children responded to her enthusiastic, energetic and creative teaching style.

Children entered the classroom and went straight to specific bin / center activities. The children had a ring of pictures in the bin that showed examples for the activity. Children often got ready at different times so those who were quick to get ready could get busy instead of sitting at the carpet. The morning activity time was about 15 minutes. Gillian had many ideas, which she was quick to implement. She enjoyed talking about her teaching practice, had many experiences, and shared various student work samples. Gillian is highly driven by the challenges in FDK, which she finds very exciting. Her joy for teaching young children was clearly evident, and she had a passion for making learning fun and engaging. She loved science experiments and inquiry and made this an integral and central part of her teaching practice in her classroom. She mentioned the importance of inquiry and building teaching around the student curiosity and interest. She advocated for equity, diversity, and inclusive teaching practices and tried to understand ways to be mindful of teaching practices that met the needs of the learners. She took interest in different cultures and recognized the celebrations from diverse cultural traditions by often reading to the children stories about festivals and setting up a center on each festival. Creating opportunities for learning about other cultures builds cultural connections and children learn about interacting with peers from different backgrounds. Quality and diverse relationships are important parts of equity initiatives. Supportive and sensitive values and beliefs foster building compassionate, responsible and respectful citizens.

The ECE in Gillian's classroom worked with individual students and supported ESL and special-needs children. She was comfortable supporting the activities the teacher introduced but did not take an active role in planning, designing, or creating centers or activities. She interacted and played with the children. She often sat and did a puzzle with one child while the teacher worked with a small group or read to the other children. The ECE was comfortable working with the children and brought many ideas forward, interacted with teacher and was an enthusiastic educator.

Hana's classroom. When children come to class, they put down backpack in the line and then go to play outside for about half an hour each morning, whether warm or cold. Parents were told from the beginning of the year to ensure children are dressed well for the day as they spend a good portion of the day outside. Children climb, run, jump, and skip. Some children are engaged in conversation, others are busy with play, and a few draw with chalk on the ground, but all are busy doing something. Children sign-in by writing their name with chalk on the ground and they put their mailbag in a bin that is kept near the door once they line up and get ready to come in. Once inside the chart stand has a morning message that children eagerly look at to find clues of what they are doing today. The morning message has words, pictures, and some blank lines for missing letters in a word. The children are busy trying to figure things out as soon as they come in. There is also a book held closed with an elastic band and a picture which is partially covered. There is a clue box beside them and children have the choice to put in their guesses on what the picture or book is about. The picture had seemed to be an animal that resembled stripes from a zebra. The picture was a photograph that looked like a real-life photo.

Hana has a deep sense of connection to nature in her teaching practice. She enjoyed creating learning opportunities using natural materials and allowed children to explore in different ways. Building on the awareness of the environment, she took children on a walk and made a slide show of the walk; she then shared it with students and encouraged them to dialogue about their experience. She recorded these dialogues and used them as a way of guiding discussion and asking questions. She also visited the local pizza store and recorded it and then brought it to the classroom to show students, thus creating a real life context to a pizza shop. She may do a similar activity involving a walk around the lakefront and share that experience with the children through video in the classroom. Her personal interest in nature, insects, animals, and her appreciation for natural beauty is part of her teaching philosophy. Boys loved bugs she said.

In Hana's classroom, the walls are filled with questions and scribbled answers from the children. She ensured that student voices were represented visually by having the children share their thoughts and by writing down what they said, often in play or during class discussion. Hana liked to guide learning but let the children lead the interests and focus in her classroom within a landscape of strong environmental education, science inquiry, art activities, and fine motor skill development centers. Hana found that she needed to balance student interests with curriculum expectations; the idea of creating an environment where both can be done effectively is a real art. She studied the Ontario curriculum and photocopied important expectations. She created a binder of the expectations that she shared and how and when she planned to integrate them. She asserted that the play is important, but enriching the play and deepening the learning is also equally important. She found that separating JK and

SK students allowed for meeting needs in a more effective way at times. Overall, lots of documentation was a big part of building the program and was something she could share with students, parents, the principal and colleagues.

The ECE in Hana's class will often take half the children outside, usually the JK, so the teacher can work with the SK on a guided lesson. Hana also has SK students work on a sign-in question in more depth, whereas the JK students may have to answer with a check mark under 'yes' or 'no'; the SK may have to print a word or draw a picture to answer the question. This classroom management strategy also helps manage the numbers and noise, and provided the opportunity to share ideas and participate in the lesson especially during carpet time. The ECE would bring in the JK students and work with them on the carpet or outside, by sitting in a circle on the ground and using visuals to discuss a topic in a lesson. This was usually a shorter version of the lesson that the SK may have had. It is clear that the relationship between the ECE and the teacher is established and managed differently in the various classrooms.

Creativity was evident with the brainstorming that preceded an activity. The teacher encouraged ideas to flow by having deep and interesting discussions with the children with a topic of interest to them. Allowing them to list ideas on the class chart paper for a ship they were going to build as a class. They would describe the materials they would need and the things they could bring from home. They did a lot of planning and sourced out many materials that the children felt they needed to complete their creative project.

Kindergarten Teaching Approaches

There are different ways that learning can happen. Students can engage in a variety of learning methods in the Kindergarten classroom. There were some key teaching and learning practices within the FDK classrooms that were evident and in this section data findings highlight the types of practices and significant areas of interest amongst the eight teachers in this study. Some areas of interest were amongst all teachers and others were among only some.

Integrating Learning with Activities

All of the teachers described integrating learning with activities as the basis for their teaching approach in Kindergarten. In their view, the interactive and hands-on experience is very important. Through unstructured play, children can also use their imaginations. Teacher participants described tactile approaches, such as learning letters by making them in play dough, as a better approach than just having the students write them down using a pencil on paper. Using multiple senses and actually feeling the letters helps the children to remember letters better. Teacher participants have used sandpaper letters in the classroom. Children have even drawn letters in the sandbox, painted them, and made them out of pasta or fruit loops.

All teachers reported that doing and playing are significant parts of the Kindergarten program. Diya, in particular, often talked about play-based learning in her interviews. Diya described the various literacy activities that she had tried in her class using the alphabet line, playacting, and play dough, among other materials and activities. Diya builds learning opportunities into the play by asking questions and guiding the dialogue. Diya also talked of her attempt to do this by building a shape-awareness activity into the 'fashion show' game in her classroom. Teachers can also add books and a clipboard to a center to build in literacy. Diya spoke of adding books about rocks to the rock-washing station in her classroom. For math, Diya described her use of real-life situations in which calculations are required to determine, for example, how many chairs are needed for a particular activity. Alison talked about how much the children enjoyed building things and what they could learn through this activity. Gillian found that mathematical concepts were evident in that as the children played 'restaurant,' some of them were engaged in sorting, counting, writing numbers, and creating patterns.

In addition, during role-play children focus on their interests and use their imagination. The teacher can listen and observe children in dramatic play centers and see what roles they take on. Alison talked about focusing on their interests:

> In role-playing children are able to discover what interests them. They see what interests them, and it is much more relevant to them. They want to learn certain things and use their imagination, so they learn much better that way. Children are allowed to just explore. Students discover their own directing [direction] and learning. During role-play you can also ask questions. By role-playing, they are able to access more information.

Bianca incorporated more natural science into her teaching approaches. Using rocks, sticks, leaves, and flowers to spark a love for nature and the natural materials in centers by placing books about rocks, flowers beside them and inviting inquiry. Bianca further explained her thoughts on integrating play into the Kindergarten program as follows:

> I've been trying to incorporate more kinds of natural science, so more planting, more touching trees, more looking at flowers, especially in the spring. We are making observations about environmental changes all the time and seeing what is naturally happening and letting that guide our learning.

The emphasis continues to be hands-on and play-based learning, which is appropriate when teaching young children, especially in the early years, in a way that is geared toward deeper engagement in learning. Building laughter and fun into the Kindergarten program helps make children more enthusiastic and allows them to grow up with a greater level of love for school and learning. The children make choices, and explore at their own pace, but the teacher can get students to engage, reflect and think more about what they are doing, why things are a certain way, and how things work.

Furthermore, as Cassandra affirmed, "unstructured play is the ability to use your imagination." As she described in the following citation, she also finds calendar to be an important part of the day, but it is shortened and an interest driven by children.

> We begin in the morning with our calendar. I am talking slowly, we sing and we all participate. Some people are being told not to have calendar. In fact, I've heard it's actually taken off their wall. I still do it. I really believe in it and it forces us to work with numbers, do counting, learn days of the week, months of the year, and whether [or not] the children understand all of that, at least they learned something about the progression of numbers. And they love it. They look forward to it every day, and they ask why we did not do it if we miss doing it.

Role of the Teacher

Alison talked about the role of the teacher and the need to observe children's choices in play. It is important to see what learners like and then do things to meet their needs. Sometimes a teacher will explicitly tell the students what to explore and then observe to see how they engage with the material. It is helpful to videotape the child in play to see how they experiment, engage, and dialogue as they play. The children lead and the teacher follows. Hana vividly captured the essence of this experience as follows:

> Teachers' role is also to understand the child, who they are and what they like and then build on their prior knowledge and frame what they are learning. Instead of talking to the kids and having them listen to us, we always have them experiment and show us. They talk and we listen.
>
> In science, Gillian said "we were experimenting with the ice and the snow and seeing it turn to water, and then I would ask them what happened to the snow." This was one way to express ideas. Elissa also found building the Kindergarten garden encouraged children to play in nature. Some children were interested in the insects, others just wanted to touch and dig in the dirt.

Diya also talked about observing with the purpose of finding out a child's interests:

> It is all about the child as a whole and trying to understand their interests, and where they are coming from their experiences up to now. Then we build on their learning and try to design the frame and what they are learning. Well, it's a play-based curriculum. It is all about the child as a whole and trying to understand their interests, and where they are coming from their experiences up to now....We are also aware of our school success goals. For math, I have objects in one basket and some in another and then we figure out how many altogether. We sort the objects, lay them out on the table, graph them on the table and talk about the most and the

least number. We see if we can sort them another way, too. I see them try to use the math language; they are getting the math concept.

Diya also elaborated on the idea that it is the teacher's role to scaffold the learning:

> Instead of being prescribed by the adult, the environment, the activities and the topics are all part of the learning that is prescribed by the child in their interest and the teacher's job is to assist the learning.

There is a need to understand child-centered play. By using play, inquiry, and / or experience, children will become better engaged in the learning. Combining and integrating play with inquiry or experience with play provides a more enriching and integrated approach to learning in the Kindergarten years. In the following citation, Bianca shared her views on the importance of looking at each child as an individual and understanding the child's perspectives.

> Looking at the child as an individual and bringing their ideas a lot more in the classroom, expanding on the child's natural abilities, natural desires to learn about things in a child[like] way. The full philosophy of the holistic education is basically looking at the whole child and then looking their perspective, putting more nature in learning and more inquiry basis learning this is all [that] whole model building on is based on that philosophy.

The teacher can nurture diverse and inclusive teaching approaches by paying attention to equitable and quality teaching practices that consider accessibility and varying intellectual abilities, varying child interests, gender differences in learning, and consider assessing and engaging students with song and dance and not always language-based assessments. There are also varying socio-economic status of students and providing resources, materials and support as needed is part of equitable practices as is consideration for religious accommodations, disability, race, ethnicity, ancestry, and special needs children's modifications. Strengthening class values and beliefs for a safe, inclusive and nurturing learning environment.

Interpersonal Child Development

In Kindergarten, children socialize at different levels and begin to build a voice in the classroom. They become more comfortable sharing ideas and talking in front of the class. Bianca stated that oral language is the foundation of every program; children talk with each other about games and books, and these interactions are important for their learning. Interaction in both informal and formal ways provides great opportunities for language development. In addition, many children enjoy 'special helper' roles and take more interest in leadership opportunities, which are also great for building communication and interpersonal skills.

Alison contributed to this discussion as follows:

> You can see leadership skills in play. You see how children resolve conflict and how they get along and their ability to cooperate during an activity. [The] calendar is an opportunity to come up in front of the class to foster social, self-esteem, and leadership skills.

Diya shared her thoughts on the value of having time for reflection during the day. At this time, children explore and talk about their successes and share them as a group. Learning from others provides good examples and opportunities for presenting and sharing one's own creativity and thinking.

> There is a time for the reflection on what they do throughout the day. They realize a different strength and different skills as they explore. We talk about their success with learning and what they did in the day. We share our ideas and discuss as a group.

Skill development can be embedded in interpersonal play experiences in different ways, and this is particularly evident through children's daily use and development of mathematical concepts and skills; for example, Cassandra's experience with numeracy and integrating math skills during calendar routines:

> We begin in the morning with our calendar. I am talking slowly, we sing, and we all participate. Some people are being told not to have a calendar. In fact, I've heard it's actually taken off their wall. I still do; it you know I really believe in it and it forces us to work with numbers, do counting, learn days of the week, months of the year. And whether [or not] the children understand all of that at least they learned something about the progression of numbers, and they love it. They look forward to it every day and they ask why we did not do it if we miss doing it.

Observing children in play and seeing how they use math resources or materials also allows them to share their thinking. Alison had this to say about integrating the use of the number line and counting into play:

> Play that involves games that use a number line, one-one correspondence, and counting [i.e., simplified

variations of Snakes and Ladders] helps children master [math] and integrates understanding about numbers.

Diya integrates math at a block center by encouraging children to measure and record the height of the structures that they build. She stated, "Instead of a math area, we put the math learning into the block area and by putting math into their play, it is a better way to excite the students about the numbers she describes."

Movement and Learning

Cassandra described movement and learning as essential parts of the day in Kindergarten:

> We begin our adventure with an active morning and the majority of the time they are at centers. Children are always moving, playing, and doing.

Diya commented on the success of play-based curriculum, especially for boys. She found it to be so successful that she thought it should be used in grades beyond Kindergarten because when it is done well, the students, especially the boys are so excited and more engaged.

Learning through singing and dancing is another kind of learning through movement. Diya shared her classroom experience with learning the alphabet through movement by using alphabet songs accompanied by movement. Combining kinesthetic, visual and oral language learning with auditory learning deeply engages the learner and uses different senses. Bianca also agreed that boys often have less attention and finding ways to engage and connect boys to learning experiences may mean teachers have to think and plan alternative learning centers to meet the differentiated needs of learners.

> I do a lot of movement when we do learning letters of alphabet. We do a lot of singing and dancing. There are specific movements. I do a lot of Dr. Jean songs, and Dr. Jean had tons of alphabet songs. There is an activity where the kids say the letter and they push their arms to one side over the mid-line when they say a letter they push the body to the other side, so they say a letter and punch on the one way. So today, I had the children add their names to an alphabet song. They did an action for each letter of their name.

Bianca said that less structure means less sitting and more doing. In the less-structured classroom, the role of the student is to initiate his or her own activities. The teacher then supports the learning by asking guided questions and providing resources such as materials, books, pictures, and children's websites on the topic, to extend the learning.

Alison stated that letting the children do whatever they want to do in play is part of the unstructured learning. They use their imaginations. The children guide the direction of their learning as part of their own personal inquiry. Bianca agreed, but remarked that sometimes children only want to participate in one particular activity:

> We try [to encourage them to do] other things, but they also say let the kids focus on their own interests so that is what I do. I have one little boy, he constantly wants to be on the computer all the time, and he hardly ever seems to be at other centers. So I let him be on the computer every day. Then there

is only one computer and then I have to schedule time for other kids too, but he just sits behind and wants to watch the other kids on the computer. I want him to self-regulate and take initiative for other centers, but he always ends up back at the computer. That is his interest. He just does not want to do anything else.

Diya is of the view that learning is child-centered, and that the interest and the voice of the child guide the focus of the learning:

Instead of being prescribed by the adult, the environment, the activities, and the topics are all part of the learning that is prescribed by the child in their interest and the teacher's job is to assist the learning.

Physical Space

The access children have to materials and centers, and the amount of floor space available, constitute the physical space factors in the FDK program. The layout of Full-Day Kindergarten is different from Half-Day Kindergarten in that there is less focus on starting the day by having students simply come in and sit on the carpet for calendar and formal lessons. FDK involves movement and more interactive ways of involving the children. In a few classrooms, 'sign-in' activities are the focus for the start of the day, by using a chart stand for students to come in and sign their name. At the start of the day, a morning message routine can be established whereby students are expected to find their name cards. Using the message to identify numbers, letters, and set the agenda for the day focuses the children.

Some ideas from participants for centers included: art center, paint center, creative center, block center, drama center, play doughcenter, literacy center, math bins, and sensory center. Furthermore, as mentioned by teacher participants, a recyclable materials center, or a water, sand, or discovery table may invite learning and inquiry. The drama center is often co-constructed and can change every month. Inquiry is guided through a discovery center and the use of an "I wonder" wall. There might be a word wall made up of words suggested by the children and some common sight words also called 'popcorn words' (I, see, went, etc.) that they could use in their journal writing. Document panels, which display the process of learning, are process-oriented rather than product-oriented. Showing pictures of the children doing the work and captions that share their thinking by stating things in their own words at the time of play helps deepen the understanding for teachers of what the child is thinking while doing an activity. Audit trails such as a writer's wall can show work from the beginning of the year through to the end. These are examples of ways to show progress and child development that are also informative when it comes to understanding the individual child.

Diya reported that in her classroom, there is a corner for guided instruction. She said, for example, she might use this corner to work with a student who needs a little more help in letter recognition. Diya also talked about having the block center in the middle of the classroom so she could always see what the children were building. The block centercould be used most of the time and by all children at all levels. In addition, the art center in her classroom is a hub of activity, a space for interaction and creative freedom that could be used by all the students in the class, regardless of their level. Diya reported that in her classroom, there are several different areas for various activities such as block, paint, drama, writing, reading, water, and sand center.

Elissa mentioned that the classroom layout was developed by giving due consideration to 'quiet spaces' and 'loud spaces.' The blocks and house centers were located near each other, given the high volume of interaction and movement around these spaces. The paint area, along with the reading and writing spaces, were situated in a quieter corner to allow students to focus and to work more independently. Hana thought that keeping materials at low, accessible levels and allowing children to move freely were very important. Francis liked more floor space and fewer tables and chairs. Children could sit more naturally on the floor while doing puzzles, playing games, and building with blocks. Gillian thought that classroom management could be improved with improved spaces. This teacher often considered avoiding crowded areas and trying to spread out children and movement in the classroom. She often modelled setting up easels, clipboards, and white boards in accessible ways so as to encourage children to draw, paint, and write during the day when centers were introduced.

Integrated Curriculum

Play-based learning lends itself to opportunities for integrating subject areas. In Kindergarten the informal teaching also provides flexibility in what needs to be covered at a particular time. Not all children are doing the same thing at the same time. In fact, many children are all doing different things at the same time. There is movement and interaction most of the day. Inquiry is an important focus in the classroom.

Inquiry

Inquiry-based learning is a key component of the Kindergarten program as many science- related inquiries can happen all the time. Making notes and writing down the children's thoughts on a topic of inquiry allows them to go back to it and revisit it. It could be posted on the wall, and the inquiry could grow over time depending on the child's interest and the teacher's guiding questions.

Bianca indicated that there is a need to put more inquiry into learning by having kids experiment and then giving them a chance to think and dialogue about their experiences. Gillian loved to build inquiry into science investigations all the time, and in order to encourage this activity, she would strategically place such items as magnifying glasses, clipboards, and books in a particular area situated near a window that overlooks a tree. Hana observed children, and when she saw they were looking closely at—or were deeply involved with—something, she would go over and ask questions about what they were thinking. For example, there were new ideas and opportunities for inquiry at the block center, where new structures were continuously being built. It was important that this inquiry was coming from the children and that they could investigate and explore things based on their own curiosity.

Problem-Solving

The shift toward engaging children and making them think was evident. Part of the self-regulation in the early years is giving children choices, having them engaged in decision-making, having them take risks, and encouraging them to figure out what to do next. This process of thinking develops critical thinking and problem-solving skills. When children are encouraged from an early age to share opinions and are given a voice, they are participating and developing in a more meaningful and connected way, and at a higher level.

Gillian talked about the many opportunities in the classroom for developing higher thinking skills and how her program encourages this in many ways. Gillian stated:

> I often extend the learning by asking questions and getting students to explain their thinking. Also,

through inquiry-time or sharing-time children are figuring out what to say and how to present it to others. The thinking in social interaction is also an important skill—knowing how to share your ideas and how to get others to hear you.

Similarly, Diya reported integrating problem-solving into classroom activities. She tried to have the class figure things out together, such as helping to determine how many chairs to put out based on the attendance for the day or what words were missing from the morning message. Francis also reported using play-based learning as opportunities for developing problem-solving skills. For example, one of the ways of introducing this idea is through the use story-telling and literature to get children to think. As Francis explained:

> I often ask them to predict what the story will be about by just looking at the cover. They can use clues from pictures to figure out text. I like to sometimes read half the story and then get them to share what they think the ending will be. I like to change the character or a trait and ask questions about what they think.

Natural Sciences

Teacher participants found the inquiry-focus in the classroom allowed for integrating nature, natural materials, and nature art as part of building environmental awareness. Bianca was of the opinion that there needs to be a greater emphasis on nature in the classroom. She described letting the children's observation of changes in the environment guide learning in the classroom. By incorporating more natural science into the classroom, we can build on an inquiry-based learning model. Hana discussed strategies for classroom transformation using nature as the basis. She started with the physical appearance of materials. Hana described her approach as follows:

> I learned that natural materials in the classroom are better. I try to use more wood, mirrors, glass, and less plastic. I also bring in many found materials and unique things. It can be[anything]from lentils, to beads, to metal coin-like materials, to clear transparent materials, buttons. We collect many things from nature and use it in different ways in our learning. Materials do not always have to be ordered from an educational catalogue.

Elissa acknowledged that the use of inquiry-based learning is an important part of FDK. To her, it is "the bigger part of learning." It is also about connecting the inquiry to things around the children every day. Elissa shared an example of how spider inquiry developed in her class:

> It is all about inquiry-based learning now. We were in the classroom and the students found a spider. So many students were excited about the spider. They ran over with a magnifying glass to look at it closer. They figured out it had 8 legs. We put it in the bug box. A few wanted to figure out what to give it to eat. We had to get books from the library and googled it and we learned more about spiders. The kids loved our classroom spider.

Fun and Learning

FDK was more about making learning fun and exciting in order to engage the student. This leads to the development of a love of learning that will be the foundation they will carry forward in the schooling years. The lasting memory of relationships and connections to their learning experience provided more stimulation and lead to better cognitive development. Hana found that change was an important part of her strategy to keep learning moving. Hana discussed her way to keep learning fun as follows:

> I bring out new materials, new games, new toys, and new ideas all the time. The variety of experiences including what they touch, feel, and see is important. Each week we make something different. We make playdough, flubber, bubbles, slime, moon sand, play dough, or even bake or make juice.

Bianca also talked about the value of making learning fun for older children such as in Grade One:

> It is about making learning more fun. I think [it's important] to have fun, and to learn [while] you're having fun, and no matter what age. Over the last year, there are some thinking about how many "baby-boomers" [there] are, and all the things they are used to doing. Nowadays, they are even thinking of building playgrounds for seniors. It's true because when we're having fun, it's much better and a more natural way to learn about things. So I do agree with making learning more fun.

Alison clarified: "We don't do themes anymore—only special occasions like Mother's Day or Father's Day. We try to avoid themes

such as farm, apples, pumpkins, and focus more on centers of interest to the children." Children are having more fun when they are coming up with ideas and working with them at their own pace, and at the time that they want to. This attention to the child is part of holistic philosophy as each child is developed according to his / her needs.

Understanding Holistic Education

The teachers shared some thoughts on holistic education. Generally speaking, they were aware that it is child-centered and requires a full understanding of children. Alison described it as expanding on the child's natural abilities and looking at the child as a whole. Bianca stated that she did not know exactly what holistic learning means; however, she shared some of her thoughts about it. She suggested that it is related to bringing a child's ideas into the classroom and expanding on the child's natural abilities and natural desire to learn about something. Furthermore, it involves looking at each child as an individual and including more about the natural world in the classroom. Bianca further elaborated that it is important to be "looking at the child as an individual and bringing their ideas a lot more in the classroom, expanding on the child's natural abilities, natural desires to learn about things in a child way." Bianca further discussed her understanding of holistic education in the following way:

> The full philosophy of the holistic education is basically looking at the whole child and then looking their perspective, putting more nature in learning and more inquiry based learning; this is all [that] whole model building on is based on—that philosophy—and I think they may not presented to the teacher as the holistic model but it's just a practice and showing the classroom and the

direction with that even the documents showing it's based on that philosophy, so I may think it referred to that and talked about it. I think it's evolved over the year—the whole philosophy, different people, different interests have contributed too. It means letting the child guide. Less structure means less sitting and more doing.

When Cassandra was asked to share her thoughts on the meaning of holistic education, she enthusiastically offered the following:

I would say yes, we use holistic education in the classroom! Especially in Kindergarten, it is sort of the main thing. Educating the child as the whole. The curriculum is integrated the way it is to make the child whole. It's like we don't have science time, math time, art time because we are looking at the whole child and also looking at the whole learning process, so we don't see anything that they do in isolation.

Researchers (Piaget, 1969; Vygotsky, 1986) have discussed the importance of attachment in early childhood and it is accepted that relationships play a part in healthy developmental processes. Relationships are essential to learning, and developmental achievements also come from the interactions with other people and objects. A student that has a good relationship with his / her teacher will feel safer and more motivated to learn (Zull, 2002). Cassandra also shared the following perspective on learning, relationships, interactions, and her understanding of how the social aspect contributes to this:

The more laughter and fun you can build into the Kindergarten program, the more enthusiastic they are and the more growing up every day they are doing, and when you build that love of school and the love of learning, then you can capture them on such a greater level. That is what I want to do and that is holistic learning. The social aspect of learning is important.

Cassandra further discussed her philosophy on inquiry-based learning and how her understanding of it has evolved:

It has more inquiry-based learning and the model shows the classroom differently and the direction has changed to letting the child guide. Different people, different interests have contributed too. There is less structure and this means less sitting and more doing. You capture them on a greater level and that is holistic.

Diya said that she wants children to self-regulate and take more initiative, and that building on the child's interests, voice, and connections becomes very important. Diya also expressed that "...holistic education is about addressing the needs of each child and understanding the whole child. It is about becoming more of an observer and then building a program around the needs and interests of the children in the classroom." This connects with the understanding that there is more attention to many areas of development: social, emotional, physical, cognitive, and intellectual developmental needs; they are all equally important. Therefore, Diya argues that: "Authentic learning is based on deeper and deeper connections with the child in a balanced program."

Understanding the Full-Day Kindergarten Model

The eight teacher-participants saw the benefits of the Full-Day Kindergarten learning program. They all said that they believed that more time for students meant more time for learning and also more time for self-regulation, self-discovery, and extending learning. A child-centered and student-interest focus was a great part of the new FDK program as it engaged those who wanted to be doing something; it did not mean that everyone had to do everything all the time. Moving toward encouraging choice, decision-making, and risk-taking was a bigger shift in the delivery of the program. The new full-day learning model would also allow students to get deeper into topics and explore learning in different ways. Students could research, build, and engage in what they wanted to do.

Alison described the following benefits of the FDK learning model:

> The full-day lets them relax and get into things. They also have more time to problem-solve and get into play-based learning. I think that it is fantastic. I just saw that children are able to socialize, which is the most important thing about Kindergarten. For them to learn to get along with other children is huge…Without play, they don't have to challenge themselves and problem-solve—not as much time to do this in [the] half day.

Bianca felt that the full-day program really benefited the Senior Kindergarten (SK) students and stated that: "As far as kids progressing, SK definitely progress, probably further than [they] would [in] the half day. The JK [Junior Kindergarten] is not [progressing] so much. Cassandra conquered and reported that the children, especially the JK students, are exhausted in the afternoon.

Sometimes there are inconsistencies with their attendance as well in FDK. She stated:

> The kids are very tired as the whole day is a lot for them. They are tired and cranky, and they want to sleep when they get home. I have three little boys whose attendance is very poor. They usually come every other day.

On the other hand, Diya felt that: "In the full-day they have more time to play; this is the time all children learn, discover, be creative, and think."

Play and Activities

Teachers commented on the greater use of centers, play, and choice during the full-day learning. Whole-class activities are kept short. Teachers start centers earlier in the year. They also do more open art activities rather than whole-class art activities. Bianca offered the following explanation:

> Before, I would have the whole class doing one activity, but now after a few weeks, we start centers. They have the choice of what they want to play. They do centers depending on what they decide to do.

Bianca further stated that: "The children are more independent. They decide when to eat, they are the ones who determine when and what they will play and who they want to play with." Furthermore, Bianca explained that instead of telling the children how many people should be at the center, she posts a sign on the wall near the center so they can self-regulate. The crowd control for centers provides some class structure. Children learn the rules and then they follow them on their own.

The co-construction of centers is also emphasized in the Full-Day Kindergarten program. The children can, for example, make suggestions about how the drama center should be set up. They can brainstorm a list and then vote. The students have more input into what the focus of the centers will be. Thus, the centers are based on student interests. Bianca mentioned that the integration of various subject areas (such as gym, language, art, math, and science) and the flow of play have become more natural. For example, for outdoor play, the children might sign in by writing their names with chalk on the pavement; they then play ball and count their bounces, or run around and look for bugs. They also engage in cooperative play in order to foster their social development. Engaging in activities such as riding bikes and visiting the park also helps them develop gross motor skills. Ball skills are also good for hand and eye coordination. Bianca explained how she integrated math at the co-constructed shoe store in her classroom:

> Right now, we have a shoe store, we measure feet, and we make a chart of the length of the children's feet.

Diya acknowledged that play is the focus of FDK:

> They all are doing different things. Play is the focus not just centers and rotation around them.

Cassandra commented on the children's interest in show-and-tell. She said that children have a lot more to talk about when they bring something in from home to share with the class. As she explains in the following quote:

> We usually have to repeat the center from the morning because kids get used to being with certain

things and will they get to do it again and finish something if they did not finish it. Then we usually begin in the afternoon with show-and-tell.

Cassandra also shared that singing is an effective way to learn in Kindergarten. Letting children choose the songs to be sung builds on ideas that they themselves have generated. The teachers also mentioned that they address the individual child and his or her needs and interests and bring these to the class for discussion. Diya stated:

> Every child is individual. I don't know if I can answer that as a whole, and thinking of my kids, they are each different in different stages. I have one child who is much into learning [about] things we bring from outside. She is very curious about science things and that is part of full-day learning. We address the child and their needs and we use their interest to bring into the class for discussion.

Alison highlighted the importance of asking guiding questions:

> By asking them guiding questions, [we get them to] think a little deeper and get more information on their background and about what connections we can be discussing.

There are some challenges with Full-Day Kindergarten. Bianca mentioned that finding a quiet place can be quite challenging, especially when the children are less mature. She shared that:

> I find it's very difficult this year. I don't know if the kids are less mature. I had 18 boys and eight girls. Even working with an early childhood educator

(ECE), you know we're both different people and have different expectations.

Socialization

The research findings revealed that children are given opportunities to socialize in FDK. As Alison mentioned, a full day of learning gives children more time to socialize, to be around different people, and experience different stimulations. She elaborated as follows:

> I think that it is fantastic. I just saw that children are able to socialize, which is the most important thing about Kindergarten. For them to learn to get along with other children is huge. After all, socializing and stimulation are important skills; most children have only been in the home environment with no siblings; they come to school to be around others and be stimulated.

Bianca concurred, adding that: "Getting the chance to come up and participate in the class and it's really good for their social skills and leadership skills." Children develop oral language skills and learn to talk to others, express their thoughts and ideas, and also learn how to ask for assistance when needed. Using words, sentences, and asking questions develops their thinking. Francis discussed the importance of free play, outdoor play and gatherings on the carpet as social times for the students as many children are learning for the first time to socialize away from family members. Throughout the year they build confidence to socialize with classmates. Lastly, social media is another way to encourage interaction between parents and teachers. Hana created a class website, and uses 'reminders' app where teachers can send pictures to parents of things children are doing in the daytime. Some teachers also used 'weebly' website to share information. Using technology is also a way to improve communication between colleagues.

Reading and Literacy

FDK literacy skills development was embedded with the play. Letter and word awareness started with discussions during whole class activities and eventually small group activities. Some teachers had a strong literacy component in their FDK program. Cassandra talked about her carpet time, language development in her classroom, and literacy learning among Kindergarten children, and elaborated as follows:

> They see the repetition of the words and it gives them an idea what we're going to do during the day, especially their activities or something special for that particular day. I write it down in the message and they also start to identify letters. I see them try recognition of words [and recognize] the fact that there are spaces between the words. I do every sentence in different colors, to learn about sentences-the fact that there is a period in every sentence. Now, actually, I'm having kids coming up to do what I normally do by pointing to the words with the pointer and [the] class is reading along as the child is pointing and it's not been a controversy. I do [it] a lot and see benefits around that. Is there any controversy about coming up and reading? Well, the whole fact that they are sitting on the carpet.

There is some controversy around reading, as many of the participants thought reading skill development was not a priority while others thought they should do it every day. Bianca elaborated on this as follows:

> I do totally agree some kids are not ready [for sitting on the carpet], but they can learn some other things [from] the fact they have to, you know sit for a while and listen to have self-control. I see a lot of good things and you know it really matures children. I know it's hard to sit them, but you know the fact of life [is that] they have to during the rest of the school. That's the important thing.

The morning message helped the students learn about sentence structure, punctuation, and word repetition as they learned to identify words and use a pointer to point to words in sentences. This was also helpful as it gave children an idea of what activities will be done on that day. Bianca highlighted oral language and encouraged children to talk about the books that they were reading

Furthermore, Elissa tried to incorporate some form of literacy skill development into her teaching every day. There were clipboards in play spaces and children could easily access a pencil and clipboard and make a plan, write a list, draw a picture or just scribble as they played at a center. Elissa described the following scenario in her class:

> I have built in many invitations for learning in my classroom by leaving out clipboards and pencils. At water table or block center you will see clipboards and pencils. I encourage children to complete one literacy work daily. They have a cubby space that is for their completed work so they have somewhere to collect and store their creations. This literacy work can be anything they want it to be—a drawing, journal story, a plan, a list.

Self-regulation

The purpose of the snack center is to develop self-regulation. Children can choose when they want to eat their snacks, and they need to know whether they are hungry or thirsty. They need to open the containers and learn to use scissors to cut open the wrapper. Children can build independence and self-regulation in simple routines, such as during snack time. At lunch time, children all eat together, but concerning snacks, they need to make choices about what to eat and if they even want to eat. As Cassandra commented:

> Snacks are the part of the morning and the afternoon, a lot of the time the kids don't snack in the afternoon. Sometimes kids are so hungry right from the start. They need to nourish themselves and pay attention to their bodies. They learn to take care of their basic needs.

Bianca shared that they do not go outside during lunch hour, and that some structure keeps the day organized:

> They don't go outside during the lunch hour. No, because the other kids are outside. Sometimes they may watch a movie. Sometimes it is more of a quiet time and children can relax and listen to music or read. But all classes keep children in at this time because the rest of the school is out at lunchtime.

Bianca acknowledged that in Full-Day Kindergarten, carpet time is different, and that this activity has become very difficult given the increase in class size, which used to be capped at 20 children in a half day Kindergarten classroom. The fact that the class size has increased to over 30 in FDK does not always make sense and presents many challenges. For example, it has become more difficult to get children to even sit at the same time. To overcome these challenges, Bianca had to change carpet time to include a quiet activity for kids who did not want to sit:

> There are too many kids that you have to focus on. I had less time with my kids— 27 kids, it's so hard. Carpet time is so difficult; that's why this year I had to say if you are not ready to sit on the carpet, do the quiet activity somewhere else, where[as] in the past everybody would sit down and do the story at the beginning of the year. [It is the] same size classroom but just more students in the room and longer time of day.

Alison observed that if children are not allowed to experience different activities and discover new things, their learning becomes stifled. As she observed, play also allows them to challenge themselves, think outside the box, and solve problems:

> I think without play they wouldn't be able to challenge themselves and be able to think outside the box and problem-solve as effectively. Making choices and decisions for themselves is also part of self-regulation. I redirect children to come up with ways to solve problems to get them thinking.

Cassandra also reported that decision-making constitutes a bigger part of the Full-Day Kindergarten program. A lot of learning is happening when children are making choices. Socialization skills development allows children to access more information and ask questions of the teacher and other students. These interactive activities help deepen their understanding and both students and teachers have the opportunity to ask questions. Cassandra explained as follows:

> They spend the time in Kindergarten learning by socializing, learning from each other, and by role-playing. They are able to access more information and ask questions. They are allowed to just to explore with the teacher and students.

The students' learning is self-directed based on their various interests, and because of this, what they are learning becomes more relevant. They are allowed to explore in different ways and discover through their own self-directed learning. The teacher can ask guiding questions to engage the child in dialogue about their learning. Through dialogue, the teacher can deepen the learning for the children by making them reflect on what they are learning.

Looking at Assessment

Assessment is an important part of classroom teaching. The process of understanding where the student is and scaffolding learning in order to develop their interests is based on the teacher gathering information about the student. Assessment is done in different ways. Literacy skills assessment can be done by using magnetic letters in a basket and having a child pull them out and name them; students can also use the white board and write the letter that the teacher shows or says. Memory or Bingo games are fun and allow the teacher to evaluate who really knows their letters and numbers, as they play. Alison shared the following thoughts:

> We still do alphabet recognition, but it is done less formally. We might set up the center and the kids play come over and play games to get to know

letters and then to recognize the alphabet, they're supposed to read a letter on a card. They can also use either white board or magnetic letters, read in the room, and this kind of thing. But some kids do not do all the centers, so again it's a little harder to assess them.

Bianca shared the following strategies for assessing literacy skills:

They are always thinking of the alphabet. I don't call it letter of the week anymore. It is just a letter. For letter W, we did watermelon. We cut out triangles like a watermelon slice, we painted it red and green, and I had white stickers that they colored black for seeds. We had a watermelon to cut up and eat. We also sang "Wheels on the Bus" and lastly we drank water. They loved it. I could tell who was getting the 'w' sound and who could recall 'w' words.

Diya also contributed the following ideas:

Instead of asking them to recognize letters on paper, you might set up a center and have the kids come over to play a game and they may use a white board or magnetic letters at that center and you ask probing questions to see if they are showing literacy skills and letter recognition and sounds....The new assessment approach includes creating an audit trail. An audit trail captures samples of student work to show how the child has developed from September to June. For example, a journal may have drawings where children at first could only scribble or make lines, but after a few months in the journal, you could see that the child was making stick people, and as the year progressed, they were adding more detail in their drawing such as features on the face when they drew a person. This could also be valuable to capture the child's experiential writing. At first, they may only write random letters, but over time they write letters in their name and later they may experiment with using beginning and ending sounds to write.

In addition, teachers are capturing and sharing learning through documentation panels where photos, quotes from students, sample work, and simple explanations of the process of learning are highlighted. This adds more value than simply putting up many finished products that look very similar on a bulletin board. Finding ways for children to individualize their thinking and creativity in the classroom allows them to express themselves in their own unique way. Art centers are open all the time, and children rarely all do the same craft.

Less paper-and-pencil assessment and greater use of technology have helped to reshape assessment in Kindergarten. The use of the video and digital cameras, along with various teacher apps and the iPad, allows teachers to make quick notes with lots of visuals of each child's artwork. Teachers are also using technology to communicate with parents. On a daily basis they are able to send some photos on an app such as Remind that shares learning experiences as they are happening at different times in the day. Furthermore, as Diya elaborated:

> In the full-day learning you are using more photos and videos to understand the children's learning abilities. The video can be played and is more authentic and tells you so much.

Videos of children involved in play activities present a way to observe the children and create an electronic portfolio. Often, the play itself explains the context in which children are meeting specific curriculum expectations, and showing a video during a parent-teacher interview explains more clearly what the child has been doing in the classroom. Alison also talked about her experience with using photographs and videos:

> This year we used a lot of pictures and videos. You can sit back and watch the video to make sure that the child is assessed properly. We don't videotape all the time that is for sure, because we're doing much more than that, but we use it a lot more than we used to. I videotape and watch the kids in the classroom. Photos help capture their work.

Observation is always a great way to assess children. Observing them in play gives a good idea of their approach to learning and understanding. The teacher is always moving around and paying attention to the children. Francis discusses the importance of observation:

> We have to observe and walk around to assess them, not just sit at one place. We assess during co-construction, too, to see who is giving the ideas and participating in the discussion. During co-construction, we can see who is getting into it. We let the kids take ownership of building up a center. You see the excitement and enthusiasm build. You see who is absorbing.

Following instructions and understanding expectations is a part of daily learning. Some children follow instructions well, whereas some need reminders. The teacher guides the children and guides the learning. It can be extended when appropriate or shortened when needed. Cassandra described her approach:

> Sometimes giving them activities and seeing if they can perform the activity within the steps expected, they may be asked to complete it. I am observing as they perform their activity and if they need assistance with it.

Even during outdoor play, children get opportunities to make choices. For example, bike time, ball play, skipping, jumping, running, balancing or playing games such as octopus, tag, duck duck goose. Children play and interact differently inside versus outside the classroom. Both are important types of play in Kindergarten, as they help children develop different skill sets. Sometimes there are organized Diya described observing the choices made for outdoor play:

> I write notes during outdoor play noting the choices and interests children show, their gross-motor skills such as running, climbing stairs and ball skills such as bouncing a ball, playing catch and tossing bean bags back and forth.

Cassandra commented on the importance of taking the time for one-to-one interactions with the children as a form of assessment. Children behave differently in a whole group, small group and one-to-one setting. As she explained, the teacher needs to make the time to sit and dialogue with each child:

> One-to-one question-and-answer period with the child gives you a good perspective of the child's understanding of the topic. Oral communication as an assessment tool is great. Say within science

when they telling me about the life cycle of the chicken. I try to sit down the child one-on-one and have them explain what they are learning and what they know about the cycle. Finally, participation in small group and whole-class discussions tells you more about the child.

In addition, portfolios of sample work are of great value, using checklists is an easy and quick way to make an assessment, and taking anecdotal notes on the spot are also helpful. There are many ways to assess, and more time to assess in a full day of learning. The teacher can really get to know the child, and more records on progress are available to really understand the child. Connecting with parents and developing a rapport to build trust and a sense of community or family, helps build security.

Each teacher adapts to change in different ways, and it is interesting to hear their individual perspectives and specific examples of teaching practices. Through the process of creating tables for coding, the data became more coherent and organized, and this led to the emergence of key themes. The specific quotes within each table give rich data and present the bigger picture, as well as various perspectives on a specific question asked. Drawing out details from the transcripts and capturing data in tables constituted a significant part of the process of data analysis. The process of separating teaching practices from teacher's challenges with FDK was also informative.

Challenges with Implementing FDK

Implementing policy change such as FDK does not really mean changing practices but contributes to a shift of mindsets. The shift may be gradual for some and quick for others, but for teachers, the journey itself is always ongoing as they are challenged in many different ways. The community of learners, the school administration, the professional training they are given, the leadership and experience of staff, the support, and expectations from colleagues, the materials, budget, and resources are all factors that may be thought about as part of the move toward Full-Day Kindergarten learning. It can often mean taking pieces of the puzzle and figuring out how it will all be put together. No classroom will look exactly alike, but some key elements and challenges may be faced. Highlighting challenges presented by teachers will also identify gaps and areas for making improvements. Below are some challenges identified by the teacher participants with the move toward Full-Day Kindergarten.

Teachers discussed several challenges. The most frequently discussed is the class size. Teachers feel that the class sizes in Full-Day Kindergarten are too big. They feel that class size should not be increased because the physical space has remained the same. There are more people in the same space, moving around more often. It is a busy room. The teachers reported that they need more space and fewer students. The following comments from Alison aptly shed light on these challenges:

> To be very honest, the class size that they are suggesting scares the pants off of me. There are 26 or 27 children, but it could go up to 32. I fully support full-day learning, but I think we have to stop and look at the square footage of the classroom. I have a hard time with 27 chairs in the classroom and still building in play centers, floor-based centers to get on the floor to play their train, trucks and plane, and sort things on the rug. And then when 27 are here all day they are here for lunch which means you need table space for everyone, you need chairs for everyone.

Diya agreed, stating that:

> My biggest thing is to reconsider the numbers.
> There are too many kids in the classroom. An ECE
> working with me helps me a lot and I spend more
> time with the children, but over 30 kids is still too
> many. It's not because it's too busy, there are just too
> many kids that you have to focus on. It is so hard to
> do your best and deliver an excellent program with
> too many kids.

Alison suggested that the program should be structured differently, in that Junior Kindergarten (JK) should be for half a day, whereas Senior Kindergarten (SK) should be a full day:

> I would say and suggest that they begin with the
> Junior Kindergarten at half a day see how it goes,
> you know, they are adjusting. And SK will be a full
> day. That's how I see it.

Furthermore, there are more messes to clean up, and deciding who should clean them up becomes an issue at times. Both the ECE and the teacher often talk with each other and with children during a carpet time about things they can work on and what kinds of behaviours are expected in a classroom. Alison commented as follows:

> I think they had probably problems with custodial
> things. In the beginning of the year there are a
> lots of accidents when the kids [here] are all day.
> Sometimes they are not the nicest washroom stalls
> at the end of the day. One day, we had to evacuate
> the classroom [because the blocks were soiled] and
> [it] got to be a question—who will clean the blocks?

I called the Union but the Union said certainly it's not my job; even the ECEs said it's not their job either and what ended up happening is one of the custodians got paid an extra half an hour to come and clean the blocks, but I was told it's not common practice and would not be happening all the time. I don't know what is going to happen in the future if it happens again because it seems custodians are not happy because of the extra clean up. With so many little boys you can imagine [how it is] in the bathroom at the end up of the day. It needs to be cleaned more than just once a day or just at the end of the day for sanitary reasons.

The constant moving around in the Full-Day Kindergarten classroom requires teachers to be more alert and active. They have to make sure no one is getting hurt. There are more children to watch in a smaller space, so there are more likely to be accidents, especially when they are there the whole day. Cassandra commented on the challenges of managing the larger number of children:

You cannot just sit down and focus on one group if you are in charge of the whole class and you have to watch and are making sure they're doing okay. You have to make sure no one is getting hurt.

Cassandra also commented as follows:

It's too busy in the full day; there are just too many kids that you have to focus on. There is also so much happening and the children need lots of attention. Teachers get tired, and the kids get tired too. One more thing to worry about in the full day is kids falling asleep. The kids are very tired, as the whole

day is a lot for them, they are tired and cranky, and
they want to sleep when they get home. I have a
very young poor little guy. He is young. He will
be sitting on the carpet and his little hand goes up
and right back down and he is fast asleep. We have
children fast asleep on the carpet.

Teachers find that they need a bigger budget to provide more
experiential learning opportunities. They need more materials to
build centers, especially as they are trying to move away from paper-
and-pencil activities. There is definitely a need for different types
of materials. Cassandra talked about how she ordered a light table,
transparent shapes, mini chalk boards, and chalks to add to her
classroom.

Communication among the ECE and other teachers, and also
with parents becomes more important in a FDK. Communicating
with parents is challenging because when there is an ECE in the
class, sometimes parents are not sure who is in charge. There needs
to be a effective communication system that works between the
partnership. Alison shared her thoughts and experiences:

I find it's hard for [me to] communicate because,
and I know it's happened throughout, but you know
the parents tell [one of us]something important and
I feel it's very important to make [sure] the other
one knows. Again, it is not that easy. I don't know
what the parents say to the early childhood educator
sometimes. For example, even in this week one of
my parents is in the hospital, I taught the child last
year too, and I taught them again this year, and
she's been in the hospital very ill and nobody told
me about it until she was out of the hospital, and
I feel very bad because I could have called. I could
have talked to the child and kept a closer eye on

them in the class with emotional and mood swings. I am often wondering what is going on. With two people, parents even get confused with who is in charge.

Kindergarten is very different from the rest of the grades in the school, in terms of both classroom configuration and the way in which the classroom is run. Its uniqueness can present more challenges. The maturity of the children varies a great deal, too. Self-regulation, which can include taking turns talking, putting things in the right place, zipping up a jacket if one feels cold, eating one's own snack when hungry, has to be taught and this takes time to develop because many children come into the class unable to do many things for themselves. Diya commented on the challenges further:

> There is a huge gap between your immature JK and your mature SK [in terms of] their learning needs, their self-regulation habits, their interests, and abilities. There is a lot going on and it is challenging meeting all their needs. I don't feel I am meeting all their needs.

When the classroom gets loud there classroom management strategies are essential. Having ways to manage when children make transitions, clarifying expectation during carpet time, using a song for times when they line up or move from one part of the day to the next provides signals and communication in an effective way with so many children. It is not an easy task when you are many so many children for the full day. Cassandra described the challenges of all-day play-based learning:

> Play all day is chaotic. There is very little structure. Sometimes I find it extremely hectic. There's a lot

of movement. There's a lot noise. That is my feeling on it.

Understanding the role and dynamics of ECE in the Kindergarten classroom has been evolving with each teaching partnership. Bianca commented that the ECE's role is not very clear, and that often presents a challenge. It is nice to have two adults in the room, but Cassandra remarked that the teacher is the main authority in the classroom, and she needs to establish that early in the year:

> I think it still comes down to who is liable, you know the teacher's role, and it's not like an ECE. We are essentially liable; it comes right down to the teacher's responsibility at the end of the day.

Bianca described the relationship between the ECE and the teacher as being difficult because they have different perspectives, different educational backgrounds, and thus, they do not always agree:

> We are working as a team, but the relationship dynamic is challenging. We are two different people because I am a teacher and she is an early childhood educator. We've got different backgrounds and you know different amounts of education and yet teachers keep referring to the documents. We almost have to be doing exactly the same thing. That's the relationship challenge.

Cassandra commented that planning ahead becomes more difficult when learning is based on child-initiated play; although she can think about units ahead of time, what actually goes on depends a lot on the children and where they want to go with ideas.

There are also challenges associated with not having formal circle times. As she explained:

> The other thing is you can't really plan ahead. Before we might spend some time thinking about units ahead, but now it is all child-initiated play and we can't really plan ahead. We are not supposed to have circle time, but I don't agree. There are always hurdles every day.

Given the movement and noise, a quiet space in which to learn is not always available for those who want it as the room is often loud and busy. Cassandra found that there is more chaos, and children are not as able to sit and listen. There are different levels of maturity and different learning styles, but children still need to learn to sit and listen. A lot of time goes in teaching this skill even for a short time:

> Sitting is hard for children, but they need to learn to listen to important things. I try to get them to sit for a story, but they are more restless. The kids are not well-trained and it is hard for control. Often when I look at the room there is complete chaos. The behaviors get worse if nothing is done.

Alison commented that the teacher needs to be aware of things the children are not using or getting bored with, and change things often in the classroom in order to keep them engaged and excited. Alison talked about her focus on bringing more interesting things to them, such as bringing in new material and developing centers for specific interests. For example, if children get bored of the construction center, the educators can think of ways to excite children about learning and change the centers.

Finding ways to effectively manage the movement in the room with more people and less space, finding ways to share resources and gather more materials, along with thinking of effective methods to manage children for the full day away from parents can be challenging. The first month of school, Kindergarten teachers are dealing with so much from both parents and children; it can be a challenging and busy time of the year.

Hearing from each of the teachers and trying to understand the reality of the classroom was a wonderful experience. Having visited each classroom and seen their style of teaching was informative and valuable; this helped me to gain a deeper understanding of each participant's perspectives and a better sense of a 'day in the life' of their classroom.

FDK has brought more access to classroom resources (books, online resources, conferences, workshops, etc.), an increased budget for classroom materials, and more attention to the Kindergarten program from the administrative staff in a school. Some may even say teachers are getting more information and training, but teachers are feeling they are not equipped with the right type of training, and the board is not giving them the expertise they need to manage this new FDK program. Teacher participants feel that they are thrown into a classroom setting that is very different from what they were once used to. They are expected to adapt and learn and make it all happen. The pressure is high and the job of a Kindergarten teacher has become more difficult.

There has been some awareness of the FDK program and direction it is taking—shifting to more child-centered approaches, more movement, choice, and stimulation. However, classroom management issues, difficulty for partnership planning time, difficulty meeting student needs/ levels with differentiated instruction, lack of support for behavioural and special needs children, and dealing with transitions smoothly with larger numbers are some of the challenges that teachers are facing with the FDK program.

Summary and Conclusion

Integrating new expectations and implementing them in the classroom means changing the way one thinks. Through the process of taking interest and the initiative to learn, one can broaden perspectives and knowledge. Sometimes looking from above or from the outside gives a different perspective than looking from the center or from within. It was wonderful to have both to rely on in the self-discovery process in my work. In this case, research informed practice and practice informed research. Likewise, teachers continue to reflect on practice in their classrooms.

It was interesting to gain insight into the different teaching experiences and styles. Often times we don't always see the challenges with working partnerships and how a classroom is managed. This research gives insight into how teachers teach and what they have to consider and also introduces many relevant educational and brain research studies that continue to show the importance of this work. The quality of teaching between the ages of 4 and 6 years of age can make a difference in life-long learning.

It is important to see ways that teachers weave creativity in the classroom. The variety of activities, understanding the creative process and ways to explore in the FDK program, but *Fostering Creativity* is also about facing the realities of the job of teachers. Figuring out ways to make things better is part of quality management. It was important to look at this research with an openness to all that could be found and it was enriching to see the true picture of life as a teacher.

Next, I will discuss more about the findings from the eight teachers and how they relate to the early years education literature.

Weaving teacher's perspectives, literature and research data highlights key areas, essential components and the array of experiences and learning environments. My personal voice and conclusions from findings identify teaching practices which will also be part of the discussion and analysis chapter that follows. Implications of the research findings and suggestions for future research are also included.

Chapter 5

DISCUSSION AND ANALYSIS—CONNECTING PRACTICE WITH THEORY

"Space has to be a sort of aquarium that mirrors ideas, values, attitudes and cultures of the people who live with it."

- Loris Malaguzzi (Gandini, 1998, p. 177)

Introduction

Education is an integral part of childhood, and a strong foundation (Canadian Council on Learning, 1996, 2007; Pascal, 2009a, 2009b) can allow children to reach their highest potential later in their schooling years. The focus of this study was Kindergarten teaching and learning.An examination of different FDK classroom practices as well as a historical overview of Kindergarten learning. Looking at the past, present, and future provided some rich perspectives on the direction in which Kindergarten teaching and learning is going.

Revising the history of Kindergarten education, during the second half of the 19th century, Froebel provided a major direction in the Kindergarten curriculum (1887, 1889). With the 20th century came the development of influential educational philosophers such as Montessori, Waldorf, and Reggio Emilia. Seminal theorists such as Piaget (1950, 1962, 1969), Vygotsky (1978), and Gardner (1983, 1987) studied and contributed developmental milestones for children while in the process of exploring teaching and learning practices. At the turn of the twenty-first century, holistic education scholars such as R. Miller (2000, 2002, 2006), J. P. Miller (2006, 2010, 2011), and P. Palmer (1993, 1998, 2004) brought insight into deepening and broadening teaching and learning practices, bringing awareness to the complexity of transformational teaching and learning practices that enrich the educational experiences of children.

It appears that no one theory proved adequate to describe and explain learning and development but each contributed to better understanding specific aspects of it. The Integrated Child Development Model—as presented in this book (see *Figure 4*), creates a landscape to view early years developmental domains and was inspired by the need to connect concepts and ideas from different educational philosophies and theorists in order to meet the needs of Kindergarten students. The model provides the lens which guides the discussion on teachers' perspectives on the FDK program in Ontario. Through their lived experiences in the FDK classroom and their openness to share, the teachers provided valuable insight on FDK teaching practices. This research study gives a voice to teachers concerning how children are taught in Kindergarten classrooms in Ontario and also informs educators, policy-makers, and administrators on the FDK program and how it is being implemented in schools.

Connecting with the teachers and letting them provide an understanding of what the FDK curriculum looks like in the classroom as well as share their success stories related to teaching practices broadens one's knowledge of twenty-first century

Kindergarten teaching approaches. Moreover, hearing teachers' opinions and getting a sense of their thinking about FDK can be meaningful and insightful. The complexity of this province-wide educational initiative can be further examined by considering the effectiveness of delivering the FDK vision, along with possible concerns, issues, and challenges, which can eventually inform the future direction of the program.

This chapter focuses on the discussion and analysis of research findings and making connections to concepts and theories introduced in the literature review. Connecting practice with theory and weaving the two will clarify some key elements such as play, environmental education, inquiry-based learning, experiential learning, and teacher presence. Teachers' understanding of play-based learning is influenced by their training, knowledge, skill, experience, values, beliefs, interests, and motivation.

The questions that will guide the discussion in this chapter. The research questions included:

1. What kinds of teaching practices are evident in the Full Day Kindergarten (FDK) 'play-based' learning classroom?
2. What are the key elements for consideration in setting up of the FDK classroom?
3. What are teachers' perspectives of and challenges with the implementation of the FDK program?

To address these questions, I first connect the ideas and experiences of the Kindergarten teachers who were interviewed in this study with key elements that are considered in play-based learning. Second, I address the question by looking at how teachers are implementing the Full-Day Kindergarten (FDK) program. I share the opinions and examples given from teacher participants relating to their implementation of FDK teaching and learning strategies. Third, I consider what challenges teachers face with

FDK and then discuss what changes teachers want to see with the Kindergarten program.

In these qualitative case studies, triangulation was used to overcome weaknesses or intrinsic biases that might be a problem if using single methods. The purpose of triangulation in qualitative research is to help increase the richness of the data and strengthen the data results. The methodological triangulation involved the use of more than one method to gather data (such as interviews, observations, artifacts, photographs, and notes), and this provided insight into each teacher participant's style, philosophy, and practices. Teacher profiles were each represented in individual case studies.

Through this triangulation process, specific key themes that were coded from the research data brought awareness to the attitudes, beliefs, and perspectives of the Kindergarten teachers in different topic areas. By gathering data from interview questions/responses, classroom observations, notes, and making comparisons between the eight teacher participants, major findings were revealed. The key themes are summarized below in Table 6.

Table 6
Major Findings from this Research Study in Ontario

Key Themes	What affected quality of FDK?
Teaching Approaches	Integrating learning with activities – all eight participants adapted to a centre-based learning approach
Physical Space	Room layout, setup, access to materials, variety of play
Integrated Curriculum	Inquiry-based learning, encourage problem-solving and critical thinking and finding ways to extend learning and use different senses
Holistic Practices	Whole-child focus – look closer at natural sciences, nature as a classroom for learning, different perspectives, children's ideas

Ella Karia, Ed.D.

An analysis that includes looking at the interconnectedness of various elements and the overall relationships as well as the unique data findings that stand on their own will be presented. The process of data interpretation and cross-referencing analysis involved the following: finding trends and highlighting responses to specific interview questions; looking for similarities and common themes as well as new information; evidence from classroom practice, artifacts, and different teacher perspectives on a topic.

Teaching Approaches in the FDK Classroom: Play-based Learning

Looking back at theory and connecting it to practice, we can see how classroom teaching practice is developing with play-based learning approaches. As discussed in the literature review in Chapter 2, educator Froebel, the 'Father of Kindergarten,' introduced play way back in 1887. Since then, there had been evolving perspectives on what type of play experiences are of most value to children's development. Froebel's (1887, 1889) philosophy of education rested play on four basic components: i) free self-activity, ii) creativity, iii) social participation, and iv) motor expression. Scholars such as Dewey (1938) also believed play to be a primary vehicle for mental growth; however, Dewey believed more strongly in the importance of scientific inquiry in play. Therefore, keeping children interested and engaged in play activities that are meaningful means teachers have to think more about the type of play they want to develop, and thought must be given to materials, set-up, and extension of learning during play-based activities.

Gardner (1987) also acknowledged that play experiences bridge and adapt to different learning styles and make sense as a teaching approach in the early years. Furthermore, Piaget (1962), Vygotsky (1986), Bruner (1967), and Sutton-Smith (1997), reinforced play as an important activity for the development of various skills in a child, including cognitive, social and problem-solving, critical thinking, and imagination. In this research study, all eight teacher participants agreed that play-based learning is an integral part of their Kindergarten program.

Some types of play were common in all classrooms. For example, all eight classrooms had engaged in block play, sand and / or water play, house center play, and dramatic play. Outdoor play was also integrated in the daily routines twice a day. Some examples of outdoor play activities could include: bringing centers outside for the day, a tent/camping area, gardening, blowing bubbles, art with chalk or soapy bubble paint on the walls, a nature walk, playing at the park, bike and scooter riding, using a wagon, doing hopscotch, playing ball, hula hoops, skipping ropes, as well as engaging in organized sports or cooperative games.

Less teacher-directed learning and more child-centered learning seemed evident in all eight classrooms. Dewey (1938) continued to impress that change brings about new opportunities; by embracing these changes, educators can continue to assist children in making sense of the world. Rather than directly instructing children, educators need to allow children to work collaboratively with others in order to engage their body, mind, and spirit more fully in the learning process, especially during the Kindergarten years. Children are capable of using all of their senses and connecting to the world around them in different ways.

Miller E. and J. Almon (2009) discussed the different faces of play and the different ways in which it can be accessed and integrated into the daily routines in the classrooms. Six classrooms had open access to playdough as well as cut-and-paste with construction paper and crayons. What made each classroom unique were the different types of activity-based centers. Four classrooms had a puzzle center. Two classrooms had open access to paint and to a puppet center. The physical learning environment, classroom layout, accessibility for children, and the variety of materials were different in each case study. Some examples of other play centers included car-and-ramp, construction, art, planting, animal figures and farm-house, and dress-up or dramatic play areas. During this research, there was evidence of the great variety that existed in the type of play as well as the range of materials teacher used in FDK.

The focus and style of each teacher and the flow of the day became more evident during the observation visit, which provided a good opportunity to see, not only how the teachers established rules and routines, but also how they extended learning. Some teachers asked questions to deepen inquiry, shared learning experiences on a daily basis with children, and also focused on the variety and type of materials they were introducing to the children. Other teachers were less involved in interacting with the children and let the children make their own choices throughout the day

The data findings revealed evidence of Reggio Emilia (Malaguzzi, 1993), Montessori (Montessori, 1967, 1972a, 1972b), and Waldorf (Steiner, 1994) approaches and inspired practices, which transformed classrooms. For example, by using logs for stools, building an outdoor garden or bird houses, and using various play type materials that were open-ended and made with natural materials in the classroom, teachers were able to transform the learning environment. Furthermore, rocks and crystals in baskets, sectional trays for sorting branches, and mirrors for placing materials were at one center, and books and papers at centers also provided for more open-ended writing experiences. There was also much evidence of the use of various items from nature. For example, some teacher participants encouraged students to use nature in rock art, leaf art, and branch art. In one classroom, a teacher participant often communicated that there is not just one way to do something with the materials. Through this approach, the children are really encouraged to come up with ways to engage with the materials in different ways. It was also evident that the teacher participants added literacy tools and materials at centers in order to build interest in reading and writing. Very often, the choice of topics was also inspired by the children's interests in the subject matter.

Regardless of the simplicity in the materials, the children were required to build creativity skills based on what they can do. This means and approach for presenting play in the classroom is unique and meaningful. There is careful consideration of the type and variety of materials to introduce to students and what to avoid in the classroom. The idea of a child (Barr, 2002) as a creative, compassionate, caring, expressive independent thinker was a common value in Reggio-Emilia, Waldorf, and Montessori's educational approaches, and these similar values are shared among these pedagogical practitioners.

Evidence of deepening thinking through creativity (Bruner, 1976; Schirrmacher, 1998) was visible in arts and crafts activities in several classrooms in this research study. At times, children would use a sponge or a stick to paint; they would also use the bottom of bottles or lids to make circles for different textures. Children experimented with, and mixed, colors; they also introduced various shades, by sometimes using water colors to create art with different tones and colors. A couple of teacher participants used techniques inspired by specific artists or stories they had read. Art was integrated as a follow-up to a nature walk or another experience the children may have been involved with. A couple of teacher participants tried connecting learning to real-life experiences and building awareness of their environment. A few teachers were creating cards, a class mural/ quilt/collage, and many simply always had drawing materials such as pastels, pencil crayons, chalk, pencils, and markers available to students daily as their attempt to inspire new creations. One teacher even created colored paper samples when children dipped white paper in a tray of boiled blueberries to create blue paper, and onion peel water to create yellow paper.

In one classroom, recyclables were used to create critters and a rainbow made out of colored wrappers hung on the wall. The awareness of environmental print, and the use of recyclables on the one hand established an increased awareness of reusing items in our environment and on the other hand, encouraged creativity. In another classroom, materials such as buttons, lids, caps, material, cardboard, or sticks inspired creativity and the use of imagination. Many classrooms were making three dimensional art. Artistic expression was visible with the complex block play, Lego models, and use of connectors and / or a combination of the above. In some classrooms, students also worked on projects or self-created mini-books over the week. This allowed them to develop and broaden their thinking and their ideas over the week. The concept of ongoing project work added to the quality of children's creations and also expanded ideas and thinking.

Play may look very different depending on the various educational philosophies. For example, in a Waldorf classroom, instead of the toy-like materials, home life materials such as knitting materials, table settings, logs, blocks and baking products, are used. Steiner (1994) reiterates that there is also an aspect of Waldorf philosophy that reinforces that children learn best with movement. In the Montessori classroom, the idea of individual learning experiences is prominent and children are working independently on different things, and at their own level, as was evident in many of the classrooms observed. Montessori (1967, 1995) encouraged the use of less plastic and more natural wood materials, including beads, wooden geometric blocks or sorting sticks, and posited that other materials such as puzzles may be more directly connected to the curriculum. Reggio Emilia (Malaguzzi, 1993; Edwards, Gandini, & Forman, 1993) inspired classrooms to sort colors by the rainbow, use light tables, investigate, and explore with nature materials such as rocks, trees, flowers, and leaves.

Nurturing Individual Identity

When we consider Gardner's (Gardner, 1983, 1999) multiple intelligences, it is clear that one size does not fit all and children have different ways of learning. Teachers in this research study felt that it is important to minimize the time at the carpet and at sitting activities, as this gets children moving, and in turn, helps them learn. More tips and information on the importance of physical activity to improve learning is available on a website for Healthy Families BC at https://www.healthyfamiliesbc.ca/home/articles/importance-physical-activity-children. There was a conscious effort to plan the day with time for movement, choice, and both indoor and outdoor play. Teachers were aware that children learn well with movement and interaction. Vygotsky (1934; 1978) and Banchi and Bell (2008) showed that more group exploration, less table-and-desk work, less paper-and-pencil activities, and more inquiry-based activities were embedded in FDK. Furthermore, the data findings revealed that there is a broad spectrum of play-based pedagogy/teaching practices in the Kindergarten classroom and a shift away from only a paper-and-pencil activity approach in FDK to a more play-based, creative and activity-based learning approach.

Each of the teacher participants reported that their experiences with play-based learning approaches had been enjoyable for the children. One teacher mentioned that she felt the kids were getting more through play and were more engaged, excited, and interested. All teachers also indicated that the shift toward child-centered learning, individual inquiry and exploration, and finding opportunities to extend student interests was working well in the FDK classroom. All the teacher participants found that there was an improvement in children's level of interest, as well as their level of excitement and engagement. Thus, the shift from instructivist to constructivist seems to bring about positive change that fosters creativity. McQuail et al. (2003) emphasize the shift toward process-oriented outlooks and child-centered learning approaches build on the freedom of choice, expression, and interests.

Ella Karia, Ed.D.

Play with Multi-layered Facets and Making Connections for the Child

Teacher participants indicated that from their classroom experiences, play develops a child's imagination, creativity, literacy, numeracy, social, and problem-solving skills. Play theorist Sutton-Smith (1976, 1996, 1997) advocated for the value of play and its deep connection with children. For example, in role-playing, children are able to discover and pursue what interests them. They learn to cooperate and decide who plays what role, and what should be said. Children take the lead in their learning in many ways. This allows them to build their confidence in talking and performing in a play-based setting, where they can make mistakes, have fun, learn from others, and try new things. Vygotsky (1978) demonstrated that pretend play allowed children to explore everyday situations and social roles. W. Haiget and P. Miller (1993), in their research, proved that by the age of four children are 'prolific pretenders,' spending over twelve minutes per hour engaging in pretend play and spending more time in pretend play episodes with peers than in solo play episodes. The data findings from teacher participants in this study confirm the value of pretend play in the classroom. Teachers reported that the dramatic arts center was a good area for pretend play, but also as students constructed and created things they would engage in pretend play using materials and art created as props.

Interviewees identified several other factors as contributing to effective, comprehensive and quality play experiences. One teacher mentioned the need to integrate more natural science into the program. Another teacher stated that introducing new materials in the classroom is often important and exciting for the children. Other themes identified included the role of the teacher, the role of the student, integrating activities into play, physical space in the classroom, movement and learning, language, numeracy, boredom in play, intrapersonal child development, and inquiry. It is important to integrate and balance the key elements such play-based learning, inquiry-focus, experiential opportunities, child-centered interests and environmental education in the FDK program.

Furthermore, the play itself is seen as a starting point, and finding ways to develop and extend the learning is something teachers are thinking more about. Integrating subject areas from the curriculum (Ontario Ministry of Education, 2006a, 2010) into play is another goal teachers are working toward as they rethink and reflect on best practices in the Kindergarten classroom. For example, in this study, instead of the paper-and-pencil approach to teaching numbers, and the representation of quantities or patterns, children were encouraged to look for numbers in the environment around them. Some teachers developed more questioning techniques and practices whereby children were asked a couple of questions in a careful way to allow them to continue the natural flow of play. During block play, children were asked about their structure and a connection was often made to a mathematical concept. Sometimes, simply letting children talk freely about their personal creations allowed dialogue and insight about their play experience. In addition, encouraging the children to become more observant and see what was naturally occurring was a new focus in teaching and learning for many FDK teachers.

A peak period for creative self-expression occurs between the ages of 4 and 6 (Schirrmacher, 1998). The arts curriculum is also an important part of the Waldorf (Steiner, 1994) philosophy of learning. Teacher participants also found that it was important to foster creativity in their classrooms by providing free-flow and plenty of time to access diverse materials such as paint, clay, cut and paste, and drawing tools. Rather than always providing a model for children to copy, teachers tried to foster originality. Furthermore, all teachers in this study discovered that creativity could be expressed in block play. For example, blocks are timeless and classic play materials that all the teachers found extolled benefits for young children. As they concentrated with devotion on block play, they were provided with opportunities for building whatever they wanted, using their imagination. The children were also developing visual-spatial awareness, and perceptual-motor skills as they fosteredcreativity.

To reiterate, all the teacher participants identified play as an effective and integral teaching practice in the Kindergarten years. Teachers confidently acknowledged the importance of play. All the teachers shared specific examples of play activities and experiences in their classes, and during the classroom observation, there was clear evidence of play-based materials and play-based teaching practices. The study's findings clearly showed that play-based learning was an integral and important focus in different ways in the various FDK classrooms. In addition, teachers actively experimented with child-centered and inquiry-based learning during their implementation of FDK.

Teachers' Perspectives on Implementing FDK Curriculum in the Classroom

When examining the teacher's perspectives on the FDK program, the findings revealed that all teachers felt moving to a full day from a half day benefited the students, especially the SK students. They also stated that with more time, teachers could get deeper into learning, giving children more opportunities for both structured and unstructured play. While teachers felt that students were learning more, they also felt it became more challenging to manage a less structured Kindergarten program. Three teachers reported that it became difficult to integrate subjects with play. It was not so easy to get on board with the FDK expectations. Many teachers experienced a learning curve at the beginning and a lot of experimentation before eventually developing a good quality Kindergarten program that they could implement and run smoothly. For example, teachers found that they were trying to find effective and creative ways to meet the needs of the curriculum, as well as reach all the different learning needs while trying to honour the natural flow of play.

There are some advantages of FDK as revealed in this research. The majority of the teachers agreed that spending a longer day seems to make a big difference in children's learning. In a full day, there tends to be more time for creativity, conversation, and context learning, as revealed by the teachers. There is more small-group learning time and less whole-class instruction. Children are moving more freely and in a less structured way, thus can work at their own pace and depth. It was reported by many teachers that in the Full-Day Kindergarten, students spend little time on calendar routines and whole group lessons, and more time on individualized activities. Children sit on the carpet for only 10 minutes at a time to get instruction or participate in a discussion, then spend longer periods on the carpet for story time or for sharing their work. There is awareness among teachers about the importance of choice and movement and building those elements into their FDK program.

In addition, when compared with children in Half-Day Kindergarten (HDK) classrooms, children in FDK classrooms spend more time (in absolute and relative terms) engaged in child-initiated activities (especially learning centers), more time in teacher-directed individual work, and relatively less time in teacher-directed large group setting(Lee et al., 2005). Teachers of FDK expressed higher levels of satisfaction with the program schedule and curriculum, citing benefits such as: more flexibility, more time for child-initiated discovery learning, and more opportunity for in-depth inquiry and creative activities. Teachers were aware of the need to foster gross, fine, and perceptual-motor skills development in young children. Teachers identified social competence, emotional regulation, and self-expression as emerging priorities in FDK. Correspondingly, Bruner (1967, 1976) reinforced the notion of learning as an active and social process in which students construct ideas and express themselves.

Teachers' Perspectives on the Challenges with FDK

Overall, FDK has its benefits but also its challenges in implementation; many teachers expressed their opinion on this. The majority agreed that class sizes are too big, and the student-teacher ratio ends up being too high. Teacher participants did find it harder to run a quality FDK program with large class sizes, especially because there is such diversity in the student population, considering the many special needs issues and the overall trend toward a higher ESL population in many Ontario schools. Controlling class size is also part of holistic learning in that it reduces noise and chaos and creates a space for quieter learning. All teacher participants agreed that a smaller class size would make a big difference in the quality of education that is delivered. Data findings from this research correlated with other research findings on the impact and importance of class size. For instance, Bascia (2009) also confirmed in her research in Ontario schools that a smaller class size does provide an environment for increased quality of education for students, especially in the early years. Research (Bascia, 2009, UNESCO, 2004) shows evidence of the importance of managing class size effectively to improve the quality of education.

Furthermore, there was concern about the lack of understanding and training around the FDK model. There was a definite shift in the way teachers were expected to go about teaching in the FDK. However, the way they embraced the change and dealt with challenges was unique to each individual teacher. Each teacher had his / her own training, knowledge, and understanding of FDK expectations. In fact, even parents and the administrative team at the school are continuing to learn about FDK. UNESCO (2004) identified teacher training as a key indicator of quality education programs. Therefore, to manage quality of FDK programs in Ontario, teachers should be given more teacher training specifically around the FDK model.

Each had his / her own interpretation of FDK, routines, teaching style, and personal identity as a Kindergarten teacher. At times, the need to shift practice was met with resistance. There was evidence of different teaching approaches from each teacher participant. Nonetheless, the teachers also had different reactions to what they had to deal with in FDK within their own classroom. In general, there was definitely some interest, excitement, and enthusiasm to implement FDK among teachers, but there was also a sense of frustration and even confusion.

The ECE and teacher partnership was a continuous challenge for teachers who were used to planning, teaching, and running their own classrooms. There is a lack of role clarity and there are often tensions among educators; regardless, they are forced to make it work, which makes it awkward and stressful. ECE training is also very different from teachers' college training. Many teachers were unhappy with the way the FDK model was rolled out and indicated that they needed more continued professional development opportunities and guidance on the best way to build a quality early years program, as well as nurture and manage relationships with the ECE.

Another challenge for teachers is understanding the new FDK curriculum document—*FDELKP* (Ontario Ministry of Education, 2010). Some teachers expressed that the FDK is not only about play; there is still a curriculum to cover, and this becomes an issue for teachers who are trying to make sure they are meeting all curriculum expectations throughout the year. Interpreting curriculum documents, planning, and developing learning experiences improves with experience and knowledge.

Ella Karia, Ed.D.

Building Learning Partnerships and Quality in a Supportive Environment

Parents are becoming more aware of play-based learning approaches. Instead of having children watch television, they can encourage children to play more at home, to self-regulate and to communicate. Informing and working with parents to let them know about early years centers, community parks and recreation programs, and the value of outdoor experiences for children mean that parents—and not just educators—have a role to play in child development. Quality family life and teaching important values such as respect, kindness, and compassion are equally important in child development. It could mean simply letting children talk after hearing a story and letting them share their ideas and opinions; parents can ask questions at home instead of providing all the answers.

Learning partnerships and community support for early years education have improved with the opening of Ontario Early Years Centers, as well as the seamless and manageable before-and-after-school care programs for children. Along with Kindergarten, many Ontario schools provide before- and after-school care in the school. This has made it easier for parents, and the seamless transitions also help children. There is the need to continue strengthening community relationships and connecting families as well as providing support for parents and children. Communication and awareness are especially important as many new immigrant families are adjusting to the educational system in Ontario, and as the population of ESL students continues to grow. Encouraging children to write their own stories, make books about their life experience, and letting them make dual language books or share their learning in different ways through audio, video, and drawing. Newcomers to Canada are also connected to community resources and teachers can continue to develop classroom strategies for English Language Learners (ELL). Literacy development in multilingual school environment adds to the complexity of teaching and learning, and also means teachers need to celebrate the linguistic diversity and capitalize on it in this move to becoming global citizens.

The awareness of community support services, building of quality relationships and accessing quality resources make a difference in the quality of learning. The special needs support, ESL small group instruction, and speech therapy in addition to the various psychological services that help identify issues and assist children earlier can also address children's learning needs in a more effective and timely manner. Improving the quality of education also means addressing the needs of children in today's society and providing the necessary services to students when needed.

The diverse community of learners also means that educators and teachers need to adapt and be aware of teaching practices that are inclusive and address the needs of learners in today's society. With increased awareness by teachers of the backgrounds and different learning styles of students, differentiated practices become more important as teachers are at the front line of addressing children's needs. Teachers can be empowered and equipped to refer services and gain more support from administrators and the board by sharing their insight on children in an effective and timely manner so each child can get the support needed sooner than later. This means managing the allocation of both time and money in an efficient manner so children get the support they need. Everyone's experience is enriched when children are from diverse backgrounds. A good Kindergarten program honours diversity in its many forms. Some teachers encouraged students to bring in and share pictures of their families and even posted them up on a classroom family wall, other made a family tree by adding the photo with a clothespin to a plastic potted tree plant on a table. The classroom space reflected the learners and promoted interactions about understanding different cultures and personal backgrounds

Equity needs to be an active part of teaching practices and an intrinsic aspect of the school culture. Equity needs to be embedded in the values and beliefs of individuals and groups. Twenty-first century learning is not only about technological integration and building a green team for environmental education, but also emphasis on social justice, culturally responsive pedagogy and inclusive education. Ontario is multicultural, a great asset, and Canada's most diverse province and there needs to be a greater evolution of practices to meet the changing societal needs. Schools and teachers can ensure more accountability for achieving equity goals, being actively involved in removing bias, eliminating discrimination, and eliminating barriers. An equitable and inclusive educational system is fundamental to achieving high levels of student achievement. It is recognized internationally as critical to delivering a high-quality education for all learners (UNESCO, 2008).

In 2009, the Ontario government established *Ontario's Equity and Inclusive Education Strategy* that reports, "Equity is a condition or state of fair, inclusive and respectful treatment of all people. One must remember that equity does not mean treating people the same without regard for individual differences." (Ontario Ministry of Education, 2009, p.4).In the past, voices of marginalized groups may have been silenced, but in future generations starting from the Kindergarten years children are learning that their voice counts and their presence is does matter. Diversity in knowledge production, varied opinions, innovative and creative ideas are valued. Diversity is represented in many ways. Furthermore, the Ontario government's (2009) inclusive education vision considers the diversity of the population:

> Diversity is the presence of a wide range of human qualities and attributes within a group organization or society. The dimensions of diversity include, but are not limited to ancestry, culture, ethnicity, gender, gender identity, language, physical and intellectual ability, race, religion, sex, sexual orientation, and socioeconomic status (p.4).

In essence, diversity in Ontario communities is an asset and educators and society at large should understand how it can enrich one's life and how it truly can give an advantage.

Enriched and Modified Curriculum Guides Learning Goals

Research also showed that the FDK curriculum document is guiding teachers and the new version of the *Full-Day Early Learning— Kindergarten Program (FDELKP)* would be helpful. Boards can also consider revising report card systems and updating the format of the report card to reflect the new FDK curriculum. Teacher participants in this study commented that the report card is still the same and that the structure and reporting on student achievement is reflective of the 'old' learning expectations. Resources on FDK are also available for teacher support and continue to be helpful. The Ontario government can continue to inform and guide teachers on the FDK curriculum, including studies, reports, website information, and tips for teachers. Continued updates on the Ministry of Education website build more awareness and inform all stakeholders. More communication fosters better relationships to help manage change.

Oral communication, particularly social skills development, constitutes an important part of FDK. Vygotsky (1978) encouraged and emphasized conversation between children to facilitate the acquisition of knowledge and language development. Reggio Emilia (Cadwell, 2003, New, 1993) consistently demonstrated that talking together can help children put ideas into words, increase their ability to use language to explain their thinking, and help them make cheerful social contact with others (Edwards, Gandini & Forman, 1993, 1998). Teachers can be aware of the need to increase the amount of talk in the classroom among children whenever possible. Teachers also talked about the importance of building children's vocabulary.

Teachers are developing language and print-rich environments to provide pressure-free opportunities for experimenting with reading and writing. Storytelling, inferring, predicting, role-play, and finger-play are all enriching literacy learning opportunities in the Kindergarten classroom. Teachers also all agree on the value of books and having them available and connected to learning in the classroom. Children continue to love to hear the teacher read a story during story-time. Elissa read a story about rain in her classroom and it led to various interesting dialogues among the students that extended learning in multiple pathways.

Many Kindergarten teachers want to develop emerging reading skills and experiential writing opportunities. There is a need for balance between an unstructured program and a rich literacy experience for each child in the Kindergarten years. There was some evidence of literacy opportunities in FDK classrooms; various texts were available at different spaces in the classroom (whether at centers, or on the bookshelf), and there were charts written out on stands or in pocket charts, paper and pencil at centers, labels in the classrooms and a word wall. Words and text were visible on the morning message. The idea of more balanced literacy in the classroom may be an area of development for teachers. Dale Willows, Professor of Child Studies Education at OISE, University of Toronto, focused her work (2002, 2008) on literacy education in classroom instruction on reading and writing. Willows (2002) is the school administrator of 'The Balanced Literacy Diet' website, which is a useful tool for practical ideas for elementary literacy instruction and describes areas of development and focus,such as building phonemic awareness systematically and sequentially, building print awareness and facilitating letter sound recognition-specifically during the Kindergarten years. Willows (2008) argues that teacher development is another key factor to reducing literacy failure. Teachers can keep a range of books in the classroom and implement a variety of activities.

Some teachers were also using graphic organizers to discuss a topic and share information. Writing down the students' thoughts and scribing for them is also part of literacy development in the Reggio Emilia philosophy. The Reggio Emilia-inspired emergent curriculum (Cadwell, 2003) emphasizes the importance of a child's natural curiosity, independence, and sense of personal wonder. If we want students to produce original thoughts, we need to facilitate learningbyinfusing more questions than answers and helping children document their thinking.

Balanced literacy initiatives (Willows, 2002, 2008) are important and need to reflect the diversity of a school community. There are many English as Second Language (ESL) learners in the student population. This also challenges the literacy component and teaching approaches. Teachers in this research study often developed a repertoire of chants, rhymes, and songs and let children learn to sing and repeat lyrics to build vocabulary. Finger movements and actions with songs improve children's memory and make learning more fun. In many Kindergarten classrooms, teachers use sign language, visuals, gestures, and pictures to differentiate teaching and meet the needs of different learning styles. Movement, song, and repetition are effective strategies for early years learning. An integral part of transformational practices involves understanding the learner and shaping teaching practice and approaches.

In future research, examining the literacy component in FDK may provide evidence of best practices and guide teachers through more explicit instruction on what can be done in the classroom. It is important to find out what knowledge teachers have about the literacy goals in the early years, and then see how teachers can be empowered to broaden their understanding and use of resources to meet the divergent needs of learners in school today. More work can also be done to gain a deeper understanding of the long-term effects of students within the FDK program in basic and advanced literacy development, reading, writing, and oral communication. Therefore, until more research is conducted and reported on the FDK program in Ontario schools and made available, it will be difficult to see the true effects of this policy change. It would be interesting to compare the experiences of children in Ontario schools with those of other provincial schools; it may also be of interest, to consider and examine national and global teaching and learning plans and practices that build global awareness on early years educational developments. The novelty of FDK means there are definitely areas for future research within the classrooms, across the province, and across the nation. Many researchers (Gullo, 2000; Rothenburg, 1995; Da Costa, 2005) have been comparing the benefits of FDK for JK and SK in comparison of HDK programs.

Kindergarten builds on children's desire to make sense of the world. Comparing quantities and encouraging children to touch each object builds one-to-one correspondence awareness. The act of moving, aligning, and sorting objects, as well as organizing materials encourages children to organize their information. Planning experiences where children can compare two quantities encourages more math talk. In participant teachers' classrooms, making the center with moveable andincludinginteresting manipulatives made it more interesting for the child. Froebel (1887), with his 'gifts," used geometric wooden blocks and found that the aligning of blocks was often the basis for the development of simple math and physics concepts. Montessori (1964) found that the counting of beads and grouping of numbers with visual representation helped build a solid foundation for number representation that could assist with mathematical operations later. Some teacher participants did refer to the use of the tens blocks and tens frame, and they integrated dice or card games with building tens activities. Some teachers also created math bags with dot plates; children were also engaged in sorting, patterning, or matching activities using visual representation.

Estimating and determining quantities is always built into early day real-life experiences. For example, teachers can ask the children, "How many large pails are needed to fill the water table to the blue line?" First the children guess, then a child comes up to fill it and the children all count. Another question could be, "How many children are here today?" The special helper uses the special pointer to count and point to each child sitting in a circle on the carpet. This child reports the number for attendance purposes, and all children see that counting is important for everyday life. The teacher can also ask probing questions with calendar routines, such as, "How many days until our field trip?" In this case, a child comes up to count the squares and put the sticker on the date for the trip. As in these cases, real-life math learning is meaningful learning. Francis integrated formal math concepts each morning into classroom centers. There were sorting biggest to smallest, measuring objects in a basket with paper clips, filling in missing numbers on a calendar, and ordering number cards.

Problem-solving and reasoning that involve "big ideas" are foundations of mathematics in Kindergarten programs. They can do this by measuring, comparing, classifying, sorting, and by answering simple questions and solving simple problems. Teachers can identify, extend, reproduce, and create a repeating pattern with many types of play materials. Children can thus learn to describe shapes, size and color and use math language to explain their thinking during a one-to-one conference. All five strands, as described in *The Full-Day Early Learning Kindergarten Program – Draft Version, 2010-11,*—Number Sense and Numeration, Measurement, Geometry and Spatial Sense, Patterning, Data Management and Probability—are introduced and have specific curriculum expectations that teachers are developing in their FDK program.

Physical Space: Building the Indoor and Outdoor Classroom

The teacher needs to establish both a physical and the cultural environment in which children have the opportunity to wonder and be curious. In this research study, the majority of teachers were aware of the importance of both the indoor and outdoor classroom. Many teachers were also experimenting with the environment as a third teacher. It is important that more time is given for outdoor inquiry for children. It is vital to support a program that provides children the opportunities for outdoor activities such as gardening and trips to the farm. Thoreau (1999) argued for the value of field experiences and the importance of acquiring the ability to foster inquiry and observations. Thoreau was a man who grounded his thinking in experience with the natural world. Palmer (1998) argued that the development of care for the environment starts in the early years. Educational philosophies, such as Waldorf and Reggio Emilia, transform classroom practice with nature as the basis for developing young minds.

Waldorf education (Steiner, 1994) also integrates subjects and the relevance of the real and natural world. In the Waldorf education system, children spend a generous amount of time farming and gardening during outdoor play. At one school, children also had an outdoor classroom where they had rocks and logs arranged in a circle; they used this space for seating both for small group discussion and whole class instruction. The school developed garden boxes, vegetable gardens, and integrated a rock garden. Some teachers were also taking children to sit in a circle on the grass. Palmer (1993, 1998) supported environmental educational practices and the value of using outdoor classrooms in the early years of learning.

In planning activities throughout the year, teachers often think about what will excite the children and try to relate it to what is occurring in nature at the time of year. For example, in the fall, teachers may integrate nature walks into a study of the change in season. They may bring leaves into the classroom and integrate them into arts and crafts activities. In winter, students build in the snow and do snow and ice experiments to learn about solids and liquids. In spring, the teacher may bring live caterpillars into the classroom and create an environment where children can watch the chrysalis process and the emergence of the butterflies. Teachers may also arrange the physical environment to promote peer interactions and provide a quiet space, areas for investigation, and allow access to materials, equipment, and books. Introducing learning at appropriate times is part of teacher's planning process. It is important to be aware of integration and making connections in the learning process.

Furthermore, building up centers around the learning is a great way for children to explore and go deeper into learning. When students learned about the life cycle of a butterfly, teachers often brought live caterpillars into the classroom to bring real-life connections to the learning experience. This helped to support the language associated with the investigation, especially for those ESL learners with very little English vocabulary. In Kindergarten classrooms, teachers often try to make a space where children can view live specimens from different angles. A space where children can draw and write about their observations and represent their learning makes learning more engaging as they watch live species. Some teachers find it of value to even add play dough to the science center so children can try to replicate creatures by studying the parts of insects or live specimen. Children start to add more details when they have objects, insects, or flowers in front of them. A science center in the classroom is a place for children to explore and investigate. In this study, teachers would often hang up students' work to share observations and understanding of living things.

Participant teachers often planned activities to extend play experiences. Teachers would ask probing questions as they went close to observe play. By asking questions such as: "How could you build the tower taller?" and ""What did you build?" teachers encouraged children to represent learning and ideas in many different ways. Some examples, such as, drawing about a topic, role-playing it at dramatic centers, and creating things with craft materials to extend learning. Students were also talking about topics with the teacher or peers, sharing their learning with the class, and bringing in materials related to the topic from home. Often, teachers would ask the students, "Wwhat do we need to have at this center?"Teachers would change centers often and add new books or materials to keep them interesting for the children. Vygotsky (1978) believed that social engagement and collaboration with others was a powerful force that transformed thinking. In dialogue, we extend knowledge and learn to think and reflect. Vygotsky (1987, 1986) believed high quality play experiences increased verbalization, language comprehension, problem-solving, questioning, imagination, cooperation, vocabulary, and empathy.

Teacher can respond, challenge, and extend a students' learning experience in many different ways. For example, talking to children about their artwork draws interesting information about their thinking. Using prompts like, "What does it remind you of?" becomes an excellent way to extend learning. Thinking aloud guides children. Teachers noticed students looking at the pictures in a book, and observing what excited them allowed for dialogue about children's interests. Teachers discussed how educators could understand more about what experiences the children had and teach them to link their school learning with home life.

Teachers find that explaining vocabulary with visuals is also important in the early years. For example, one student talked about camping, another student talked about the cottage, but some had no idea what these meant because they were not familiar with this vocabulary or experience. The teacher took the time to look up the word on the computer and project it on the screen. She also brought in a story about camping. The student who is new to the country may not be familiar with a 'camping' conversation; he therefore needs to develop background knowledge. ESL learners and newcomers are a growing portion of the diverse student population in many schools. Teachers are beginning to adapt teaching styles to meet student needs and find ways to build creative thinking into the classroom (See Appendix F).

Teachers also look for understanding by interpreting body language and by taking the time to interact informally with each student at least once in the day. For example, during outdoor play, teachers would go up to quieter students who had not shared ideas or talked during class, and talk to them on a one-to-one basis. All students express and share their understanding in different ways. Some are more orally strong, whereas others are more artistic.

Bringing the outdoors in the classroom and creating exciting and interesting learning spaces open the door of inquiry. The excitement of playing and exploring in nature presents endless possibilities and is connected to whole child learning philosophies. Mother Nature, as a playground of learning, provided real-life connections for the students. The classroom is seen as a place to build curiosities, to wonder, and to share thinking. Gardner (1983, 1999, 2011) also identifies 'naturalistic intelligence,' where learners relate deeply to nature and learn best in a natural environment. Gardner describes the naturalistic learner as one who flourishes by being able to touch, feel, hold, and try practical hands-on experiences, but generally within the outdoor environment, in nature and with animals. Naturalistic is the most recent addition to Gardner's theory. It has been met with more resistance than his original seven intelligences. According to Gardner (1999), in his book *Intelligence Reframed: Multiple Intelligence for the twenty-first Century,* individuals who have naturalistic intelligence are more in-tune with nature and are often interested in nurturing, exploring the environment, and learning about other species. These individuals are said to be highly aware of even subtle changes to their environments. Teacher participants also found that some Kindergarten children had more natural curiosities towards worms, snails, and bugs. Some children really wanted to dig their hands in the dirt and touch insects, worms, and living things while others did not want to get their hands dirty or did not enjoy exploring worms or insects.

This research (Cappon, 2006; Pascal, 2009a; Shonkoff & Phillips, 2000) leaves no doubt that early childhood learning and development is vital for lifelong learning. Many previous research studies (Best Start Expert Panel on Early Learning, 2007) have confirmed the benefits of quality early years education, and it is scientifically proven to help improve brain development (Mustard,

2006; Rushton & Larkin, 2001; Rutledge, 2000; Washington, 2002)in children. Many Canadian children are not yet experiencing optimal early learning experiences. We need to pay attention to research conducted on the impact of the full day early learning goals in order to gain a better understanding of best practices in the Kindergarten years (See Appendix G – Questions for Educators to Think About). Seeing how teachers are implementing FDK practices in the classroom is insightful.

In the Ministry curriculum, key teaching and learning approaches, such as learning through inquiry, learning in real-life contexts, and learning through exploration, are described as holistic approaches. The aim of early years education is to give children the best start possible (Pascal, 2009a, 2009b; Shonkoff & Phillips, 2000).In the Kindergarten curriculum document, the Ministry stated that most children are naturally curious about their surroundings. They have an interest in exploring and investigating, to see how things work and why things happen. Children have an innate sense of wonder and awe and a natural desire for inquiry. We need to be aware of building both indoor and outdoor learning spaces, materials and furnishing that accommodate and ensure in-depth exploration, participation and a high level of engagement from the children.

Integrating Curriculum and Developing FDK

The Ministry also outlined five areas for developmental consideration: physical health, social knowledge and competence, emotional maturity, cognitive knowledge, and communication skills. In the Integrated Child Development Model, developed based on this current research, I have included "spiritual" as an additional domain. According to the guidelines, the key components of the Kindergarten learning environment are: "the use of space in the classroom and outdoor area; the use of time during the day; and the appropriateness and variety of the resources available, including both people and materials" (Ministry of Education, 2006, p.

22). As the findings of this research have revealed this, it is evident that teachers are making use of the learning environment, the indoor and outdoor classroom space, the considerations for building inclusive, safe, and stimulating spaces to learn and explore.

The use of the PIECE model helped provide deeper understanding of the different domains, as well as the types of teaching and learning practices that support each domain. Furthermore, a better understanding and improved clarity on the role of the educators resulted from the study. Teachers are seen as researchers and facilitators. Teaching practices that take a more transformational approach, rather than a transactional approach (J. P. Miller, 2010, 2011) suggest that teachers are engaging, exploring, and interacting with students more with an understanding that the learning should focus on child interests. Parents gain a better understanding of their role and ways to get involved with their children's journey. All educators learn and work together through greater collaboration and professional development. Most importantly, the children learn and explore with deeper understanding as they are learning to be thinkers, problem-solvers, theory makers, leaders, and team members; they are becoming more confident beings along the journey. What is clear is that while on the one hand, it is important to have a better understanding of factors that contribute to children's early learning and development, on the other hand it is difficult for researchers to isolate the impact of any one philosophy (e.g., Reggio Emilia, Montessori, Waldorf). The adaptation of educational philosophies can vary from teacher to teacher, and no one child is the same as another. Therefore, the learning is always fluid and changing. It is clear that in order to be meet the needs of Kindergarten children, learning should to be active and requires meaningful participation, stimulation, and engagement from the teacher and learner.

In addition, the Integrated Child Development Model brings awareness of the domains of child development and the importance of the focus on a child-centered approach in Kindergarten program development. The individual teachers in this study integrated elements of practice from different early years philosophies, and educators are building FDK classroom teaching and learning practice with information and resources that guide FDK program development. The teachers are aware of a 'newer' way to teach Kindergarten than they may have seen or heard in the past. Through this research, it became evident that there is an increasing awareness of the shift in the role of the teacher as facilitator, researcher and observer. Guided questions deepen learning for the children, unraveling children's perspectives and scaffolding the learning.

The research findings have revealed the importance of both teachers and ECEs working together in a harmonious way in order to contribute to the quality of the FDK program. The EYE model, in *Figure 8,* was developed to better reflect and depict the significant role of the teacher and ECE in the FDK classroom and the organic nature of the learning partnership. It also shows the flow and dynamics of the partnership, which plays such a vibrant role in setting the environment, the tone, the connections, and the beginning journey of school life for the child. The role of the teacher and the ECE in the FDK program must be balanced, nurtured, and maintained over time to sustain the child-centered focus and the development of all six domains. The role and importance of both the ECE and the teacher working effectively together need to be recognized and require teamwork. Hence the circle is shared as two partners meet to complete the teaching component in FDK programs. This is a modification from the original design of the PIE Model, which has been renamed to reflect the early years-education context of the research. Furthermore, after joining the two sides of the outer circle the PIE Model looked like an 'eye,' so it made sense to rename the Integrated Child Development Model and call it the EYE Model. The EYE Model integrates and brings together concepts and elements that became important aspects to consider in FDK. The development of the EYE Model was the accumulation of many years of research and design. The EYE Model considers the importance of relationships in the education of the child. The family, educators and child are all important components.

The stronger the partnerships the deeper and more valuable the connections and the greater the benefit. In order to deliver high-quality early years programs there needs to be healthy, supportive and responsive relationships. Only then will we recognize the holistic connection between emotional, social and cognitive development and understand that the child's well-being is inextricably linked.

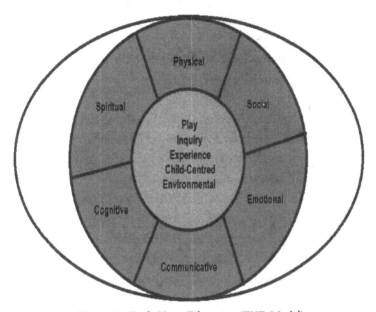

Figure 8. *Early Years Education (EYE-Model)*

Using the PIECE Model also identifies the five key elements in FDK and can guide teachers as they set up their classroom. The PIECE model also assisted in making sense of the data. The data codes established (such as integrating learning with activities, the physical space, and the role of the teacher), represented some relevant aspects of developing good quality FDK teaching practices. Teacher participants were defining their practice in the classroom by using aspects of these elements, and this model resulted from the research findings. It provided a way of looking more closely at FDK practices. Finding ways to focus on the key components will reinforce the FDK 'constructivist' teaching approaches as described in the diagram below. Play-based Learning, Inquiry-based Learning, Experiential Learning, Child-centered Learning, and Environmental Education define the twenty-first century learning model for Kindergarten children embedded in the center as a focus of teaching and learning approaches and the ways to reach the outer developmental domains as well as how the child is nurtured by educators who guide the learning process from the outside.

Integrated Approaches: Shifting Kindergarten Teaching Approaches with FDK

Scholars and theorists (Froebel, 1887; Gardner, 1999; Malaguzzi, 1993; Montessori, 1964; Palmer 1993, 1998; Piaget, 1962; Steiner, 1994) acknowledged the importance of early years education. Identity, child-interests, and self-awareness are also important (Dewey, 1938; Miller, 2011; Miller, 2010; Wane, 2012). As children learn through play, experience and engage in inquiry, children are learning on a deeper level. Findings from the data show that teachers are starting to use holistic teaching and learning approaches, such as inquiry-based learning, to build on children's spontaneous desire for exploration. In inquiry-based learning, educators facilitate and guide students to become more focused and systematic in their observations and investigations. The practices in the classroom can vary from whole class, small group, and collaborative inquiry style learning approaches based on interests. Interaction and dialogue improve and allow for sharing thinking. Through the case studies presented in this research, it is evident that there are examples of FDK approaches in teachers' classroom teaching practice as described in the Ontario curriculum. Implications of this research, including curriculum expectations, will be discussed next.

Implications of the Research

According to previous brain research studies (Greenspan & Shanker, 2004; Pascal, 2009a; Shonkoff & Phillips, 2000; Mustard, 2006; Shonkoff, 2006), educational research (Cleveland et al., 2006; Cryan et al., 1992; ELECT, 2006; Pelletier, 2012; Sylva et al., 2004; Vanderlee, 2013), and different educational philosophies around the world, there are great benefits to early childhood education. The big investment in FDK with Bill 242 (Legislative Assembly of Ontario, 2010) has been based on various opinions of professional panels, educators, and researchers. Teachers in this research study all agreed that there are benefits with the FDK program as student achievement and learning are beginning to improve. Therefore, the continuation of the investment into FDK programs is of value.

A summary of key research implications providing quality FDK teaching and learning practices is important and can be based on the following features: (a) learning through play-based, inquiry-based and experiential-based exploration; (b) making the educational experiences child-centered and authentic; (c) building on children's past experiences, nurturing self-expression and identity; (d) strengthening relationships and connections; and (e) creating stimulating environments, both indoor and outdoor, for children's learning and development. This research study highlighted key areas for quality FDK.

This research did confirm that teachers also found improvements in child development, social skills, school readiness, and self-regulation. There was support from educators for FDK. However, many of them feel that FDK needs to be managed better and there needs to be a long-term plan that will allocate funds and ensure that the investment is focusing on helping the children. Older classrooms are being equipped with supplies and new ones are being constructed as an addition to existing school buildings. Current research (Ontario Ministry of Education, 2013; Vanderlee, M. L, Youmans, S., Peters, R., & Eastabrook, J., 2012) on FDK in Ontario is showing that school readiness skills and self-regulation are improving with FDK and children are benefiting from the investment in FDK programs in Ontario.

A major implication of this research is the need to improve the quality of FDK by reducing class size. The children are being placed into classrooms at an early age, but to improve the quality of care, there was a consensus on the need to reduce class size, provide more support for special needs children, and provide more ongoing training for teachers. School boards can also be more aware of the needs of teachers and advocate for smaller class sizes and improved learning partnerships. They also need to be conscious of how money is being spent and allocated. In the end, the children need best practices, quality educational programs, and supportive educators to ensure that they receive the true benefits of early years education. Thus, while the roll-out of FDK is almost near completion, there is still work to be done on effectively managing class size and the long term plans for sustaining this billion dollar investment.

Since the introduction of FDK in Ontario schools, teachers are more aware of twenty-first century teaching and learning practices such as play-based learning, inquiry-based learning, and experiential learning. As we build awareness of constructivist approaches in education (Wane, 2010; Miller, R., 1992; J. P. Miller, 2007, 2010), we also build support and confirmation of the positive effects of these approaches to teaching and learning. As the research has also shown, play-based learning is appropriate in Kindergarten. Children learn effectively in play-based learning (Perlmutter et al., 1995; Sylva et al., 2004) experiences. All the teacher participants also confirmed the value of play-based learning as a comprehensive and integrated approach in the Kindergarten years. There has also been some discussion on continuing play- learning approaches in Grade One. Further research and investigation is needed on the possible benefits in later grades. **For example, access to musical materials in a free open space for sound exploration in Kindergarten and other grades fosters creative engagement and reflects that music is one of the one hundred ways children can express themselves. It embraces the value of musical provocations and invitations. It encourages individual and personal expression. This is an area for future research and practice moving forward.

Administrators, school boards and policy-makers can also support and fund teacher training and provide more professional development opportunities. Pedagogical aspects can be evaluated and developed by providing clarity in the focus and direction of FDK implementation. Principals can learn more about the dynamics of FDK and become better informed about the importance of the Kindergarten years in education. Kindergarten information and orientations evenings and open houses provide ways to connect and communicate about FDK teaching and learning approaches. Outreach programs for parental and community involvement can be a priority in the school to build stronger partnerships.

Resources are available for teachers on an ongoing basis and encouraging stakeholders to develop interest, pursue, challenge, and discuss learning about FDK teaching and learning practices on an ongoing basis supports quality initiatives in FDK. The Ministry of Education published a list of resources, at http://www.edu.gov. on.ca/kindergarten/EL2013ResourceList.pdf, available for parents, educators, policy-makers and administrators, and they continue to stay abreast of information and updates on their Ministry of Education website as seen in Appendix C. One key insight in the process of examining FDK research is that the continuous interest in FDK sparks deeper connections and excitement, an evolution of learning about about how transformational practices can have an impact on both the teacher and the student, and how it prepares students for a life-long love for learning.

Examination of the physical environment of student learning is also critical as we understand the importance of physical space, materials and quality and variety in resources. The attention to both the indoor and outdoor environment at a school could mean more investment in outdoor spaces in education and to encourage more environmental education projects. The systemic monitoring, evaluation and reflection of activities within the classroom can also improve quality and bring attention to best practices. Documenting standards and quality assurance measures can provide consistency and sustainability of quality early years programs.

Future Research Recommendations

Looking into the future, we know that individual teacher experiences and qualitative research will help us realize and understand that the Kindergarten teaching practices are shifting. Taking a more in-depth look at equitable and inclusive practices may be one way to move toward more whole child education. Teacher participants did reveal some teaching approaches that engage children and get them involved in more 'free play' throughout the day. However, teachers can strengthen the way they teach to reflect greater intercultural understanding as well as culturally relevant and responsive pedagogy that builds identity and inner self development even as young as the Kindergarten years. As Montessori (1964, 1967, 1995) identified, the 'embryo of the child' as a core component of the child's spiritual aspect, and teachers need to be aware of this aspect to better understand the whole child. As the data findings revealed, JK students could start with the HDK program and SK students could be in the FDK. For example, one teacher stated, "JKs have a harder time with FDK" and another teacher participant said, "JKs do not have as much progress with the full day program."

Empowering teachers to support the change that is needed is possible by having more comprehensive professional development for teachers. Part of developing the FDK program will also mean attracting and retaining motivated staff and a diverse teaching force, to develop and deliver the program. Quality programs are developed by well-informed teachers. On the one hand, there is increased awareness of the needs for quality FDK programs, but on the other hand, the increasing complexity in establishing best practices leaves much to ponder. Teachers are key in disseminating information on implementation strategies that work best in the classroom and providing information that can address gaps and issues as we move ahead year by year in grounding best practices in the FDK classroom in Ontario.

This research implies that there are many areas for future research initiatives. While policies, procedures, and laws are being put into place, we need to continue examining the classroom practices and stay connected with teachers in order to make our work deeply connected. Supporting teachers to also become researchers is another way to bridge knowledge as we move forward. It is when you begin to see your classroom as an ongoing laboratory. Teachers articulated how insightful it was for them to share their experiences and to have opportunities for their voices to be considered. This was a good beginning and I think there is much more work to be done.

Research on the effectiveness and benefits of FDK can be further studied. Looking directly at how children are improving with academic performance and achievements, and comparing the direct effects of FDK on children's school life are areas for research. Parents' perspectives would uncover how home life is changing and the benefits and concerns parents have about FDK. Policy-makers can also gather more data across the province by investing in future research projects about FDK in Ontario. Union perspectives, successes and concerns that are grieved about would highlight more information and areas for improvements. Teachers can look closer at the impact of deeper connections with cultural awareness and self-identity and how this interconnectivity with learning affects overall student performance. Therefore, teachers' perspectives, along with other stakeholder perspectives can be grounds for future research direction and the deeper understanding of optimal learning and development.

Play involves a joyful engagement by allowing children to follow their natural instincts and letting them move freely. By not imposing the unnatural demand to sit for long periods of time confined to their desks and by recognizing their need to stretch, to walk, and to be free, play permitted the children to make a similar connection between the mind and the body. Play helped to create that sense of freedom and exploration and self-discovery. Play also built on the values of group exploration, cooperating with others, voicing ideas, and thinking. Play also may look different in the future as future generations of play are so heavily influenced by technological advances. Thus, continuing to look at how children are playing and engaging may mean adapting teaching and learning approaches to best fit the Kindergarten learners at that particular time.

Not all the connections associated with curriculum have been discussed with reference to the play themes. However, before concluding this chapter, I would like to make the following observations concerning play. Play should be spontaneous and in the control of the child. Any attempt to coerce the child to connect the play with school subjects would subvert the play, since it would now be the teacher, not the child, who would be determining the direction the play would go. Therefore, while teacher participants are actively integrating specific curriculum expectations set out by the Ministry of Education in Ontario, they need to understand the educational philosophies and the realm of early years practices and how it is important to learn and improve teaching and learning practices as they reflect on their own practice throughout the school year. Furthermore, giving children endless opportunities to try out ideas and to take risks will encourage them to pursue what interests them naturally at a young age.

FDK teaching approaches are characterized by an integrated and balanced approach that considers individual differences and the dynamics of relationships. As R. Miller (1991; 1992) argues, holism recognizes complexity and the many dimensions and layers in education. Looking at early years education by moving toward a model that can adapt activities and practices from the different educational approaches really works in the best interest of the children. This research shared the teachers' perspectives of child-centeredness, integrated teaching approaches, and FDK focus in Ontario which is moving from planned activities to the study of learning. .

Concluding Comments

Play is the core of Kindergarten learning. Play facilitates creativity, imagination, the expression of fantasies, and it enables children to deal with frustration and disappointment in a positive manner. When we keep our core strong and allow it to be the basis of our practice, we are building a strong foundation. At this core are teaching approaches in FDK based on key elements such as play-based learning, inquiry-based learning, and experiential learning. Child-centered core values that guide teaching and learning practices enrich the quality of educational programs. Our emotional state also reveals whether what we are doing is blending and fitting to our needs. Play is the landscape, but the child and the teacher support what happens during play and the direction it takes. Piaget (1962) maintains that imaginative, pretend play is one of the purest forms of symbolic thought available to a young child. Vygotsky (1978) extols the value of fantasy play arguing that this is when children are free to experiment, attempt, and try out possibilities. Play is a central teaching practice in all the teacher participant classrooms, and this research study showed some ways that play is developing in the FDK classrooms in Ontario.

By using a framework to contextualize the data, this research has shown that through play, we are able to meet the needs of the whole child in a more satisfactory way and that there is a spiritual domain that is important to recognize. The spiritual domain defines the uniqueness of each individual; it deepens understanding of the inner being, thoughts, morals, and values. The primary value of education and play lies in their contribution to self-awareness. Play can also help children discover their true selves, albeit in a more implicit manner. First, it provides children with the confidence needed to acquire self-esteem. Second, play facilitates a child's self-awareness. Through observing play, teachers can learn to care for children, to be mindful of them, and to enhance their own self-awareness.

In conclusion, I maintain that there are three goals of education that must be addressed if we are to provide children with all that they need. First, we have to attend to children's academic achievement by providing them with an education that will ensure that they acquire the knowledge and skills necessary for success. Second, we must focus on the emotional and social as well as the cognitive domains if we are to serve the needs of the whole child. Third, we have to provide children with the means for self-learning so that they are able to connect with their inner selves. To realize these goals, we must provide a balance of the philosophies and develop integrated and comprehensive practices in the classroom. In the Kindergarten years, we can nurture the joy and love for learning, thinking, creating, and using the imagination. Children are also capable of and can aim at reaching higher potentials.

The Kindergarten classroom will nurture a space for building a sense of wonder, awe, and curiosity. Children are naturally born with many curiosities and educators can build on this. Educators need to recognize that, in our enthusiasm for high achievement and the development of intelligence, the need for self-realization is crucial and perhaps paramount since so much of a child's performance is governed by his or her self-concept. Moreover, we can facilitate self-learning by slowing down the pace we have set for today's students. If we can allow them to enjoy a childhood in which they are free to control their world for at least part of the time, in which they are not solely concerned with the product of their effort, in which they are actively involved in their imaginative pursuits and enjoying the process, we can see the deeper connections being made and the valuable learning taking place.

Education practices include the need to understand the goals of whole-child education. With more emphasis on play-based and creative learning, educators are being more mindful of the whole child as well as the inner soul of a child. Child-centered approaches respect the natural tendencies and exuberance of young learners and give opportunities for children to grow and develop their natural curiosities as they fully engage in the learning. The Ministry of Education recognized the need for a balance between teacher-initiated and child-initiated activities:

> Each child grows and develops in various interrelated areas—physical, social, emotional, cognitive, and linguistic. In order to address the full range of each child's developmental needs, the Kindergarten program should provide opportunities for learning, self-expression, self-discovery in a variety of areas—for example, in music, drama, games, language activities, and cooperative activities with peers. Children need opportunities to learn in an appropriate manner and at an appropriate time in their development, and need to be given learning experiences that are within the range of things they can do with or without guidance [in their "zone of proximal development"].

(Ministry of Education, 2006, p.2)

The need to reach a balanced approach is critical because best practices are also part of quality practices. We are faced with a dominant technological culture in the twenty-first century. Children are using devices, electronics, cellular phones, and computers at younger ages and more often. There is a greater risk of disconnect and imbalance. Therefore, teachers can replenish the school life environment with both indoor and outdoor classroom practice, restore the love for nature and balance, and strengthen body, mind, and soul. More than ever before, we need to focus on laying a strong foundation and establishing fundamental connections that are so important for young minds and still facing the reality of technological stimuli in the environment that children are growing up in these days. There is a need to understand the real art of teaching happens in deeper connections and relationships, a pedagogy of relationships, between three protagonists – the child, the parent, and the educators.

Even if all the teacher participants were not clear about what 'holistic education' truly meant, their overall teaching practices reflected holistic educational approaches. As academics continue to advocate, and connect with policy-makers and educators, they can also move forward in the post-modern society with more awareness of truly understanding and defining holistic education. In the end, it really comes down to how well a teacher understands and believes in her work, and the way in which the teacher runs the Kindergarten program. These case studies revealed rich stories and teacher perspectives and how early learning experiences can make children thrive.

Constructivism, as we have come to understand I, is a powerful and essential role in play in both cognitive and moral development and it supplements our long standing awareness of play in socio-emotional development of children and we can articulate and advocate for its importance in childhood. The dynamic role of teachers in children's play is becoming better understood. The new wave of interest in facilitating children's play has reshaped the role of educators as partners, collaborators, facilitators, challengers, researchers, observers, scribers and communicators. Together we can build amiable communities for learning and teaching. There is great intellectual vitality through collaboration and finding teachers' voice.

Individual teacher's knowledge, skills, interests, and understanding vary, as do each of their teaching styles. There may be different ways that a teacher develops her Kindergarten program, and there may be emphasis in different areas. Although the task seems simple, teaching young children is actually quite complex. This research reveals more about the complexities. A lot of thought needs to be put into the setup, the materials, the types of activities, and the resources that can support the learning, understanding the individual interests and needs. Much thought also needs to be put into really tailoring an inclusive program to meet the cultural and linguistic needs of learners. Finally, creativity seems to emerge from multiple experiences coupled with a sense of freedom and space venture beyond the known and educators are emerging to provide this space and opportunity.

Since the policy push, there is clearly evidence of shifts in practice, embarkation on leading edge research, review of proven theories and experimentation and discovery of innovative approaches. There is action, interaction and reaction from pedagogists. Teachers like children feel the need to grow in their competencies, to try things out and interpret them. Teachers as researchers, facilitators and active change agents can redesign and build an educational climate that aims to enhance children's development, to nourish and sustain, grow and satisfy desires for creativity, social interaction, language development, and exploration. Working collaboratively, researchers and teachers can continue to study children, research Kindergarten best teaching practices, and advocate for continued improvements, funding and support for quality educational programs. During this heightened time in early years pedagogical evolution there is a stronger collaboration and professional educator community cultivation than ever before. We must continue to push our thinking with reflective practice. It is the conscious child that knows how to live in the moment, connect with the present, and flourish from within. It is the power of educators to know why this learning, for this child, in this way is important at this time.

In conclusion, there is no other time in human development when so much can be learned in so brief a period. The period from

3 to 6 years old constitutes truly fanatically formative years, marked by intellectual growth, rapid development of motor skills, increased social maturity, and emotional self-regulation. Kindergarten children are excited about the world, alert, high-spirited, and full of ideas and questions. With a renewed and heightened constructivist approach in learning we are mindful of the child and trust and follow their lead – to do nothing without joy. A nurturing environment, with indoor and outdoor spaces, where children can explore, play, and learn in the early years will give them the best possible start in their lives. It is the time for educators to be awakened to the need to connect, thrive and accelerate innovative teaching practices. It is a time to embody, absorb the transforming paradigm and empower with innovation, creation and imagination. As Albert Einstein consciously said, "It is the supreme art of the teacher to awaken joy in creative expression and knowledge."

REFERENCES

Aasen, G., & Waters, J. (2009). The outdoor environment as a site for children's participation, meaning-making and democratic learning: Examples from Norwegian Kindergarten. *Education,* *37*(1), 3-13.

American Academy of Pediatrics (2007). The Importance of Play in Promoting Healthy Child Development. *Pediatrics. 119 (1), 182-191.*

Bailey, A., Hutter, I., & Hennink, M. (2008). *Qualitative research methods.* London, England: Sage.

Banchi, H., & Bell, R. (2008). *The Many Levels of Inquiry.* Retrieved October 2012 from http://learningcenter.nsta.org/

Banfield, G. (2004). 'What's Really Wrong with Ethnography?' *International Educational Journal, 4*(2), 53-63.

Barbarin, O. A., Downer, J., Odom, E., & D. Head. (2010). Home-school difference in beliefs, support, and control during public pre-Kindergarten and their link to children's Kindergarten readiness. *Early Childhood Research Quality, 25*, 358-372.

Barr, R. (2002). *Mother and Child.* Millennium Dialogue on Early Child Development, November 12-14, 2001. Toronto, ON:

Atkinson Center, Ontario Institute for Studies in Education/ University of Toronto (OISE/UT).

Bascia, N. (2009). *Reducing class size: What do we know?* Toronto: Canadian Education Association.

Bergen, D. (2007). Play and the brain. In C. J. Ferguson &E. Dettore Jr. (Eds.), *To play or not to play: Is it really a question?* (pp. 11-22). Onley, MD: Association for Childhood Education International.

Bernhard, J., Lefebvre, M. L., Chud, G., & Lange, R. (1997). The preparation of early childhood educators in three Canadian areas of immigrant influx: Diversity issues. *Canadian Children, 22*(1), 26-34.

Best Start Expert Panel on Early Learning (2007). *Early learning for every child today: A framework for Ontario early childhood settings.* Toronto, Ontario: Ontario Ministry of Children and Youth Services.

Binder, M. (2008). Experiencing multiple literacies through picture books. In D. Booth (Ed.), *It's critical! Strategies for deepening and extending comprehension* (pp. 120-122). Portland, ME: Stenhouse.

Binder, M. (2011a). Contextual worlds of child art: Experiencing multiple literacies through images. *Contemporary Issues in Early Childhood,12*(4), 367-384.

Binder, M. (2011b). Remembering why: The role of story in educational research. *In Education, 17*(2), 42-56.

Binder, M. (2012). Teaching as lived research. *Childhood Education, 88*(2), 118-120.

Binder, M., &Kotsopoulos, S. (2011). Multimodal literacy narratives: Weaving the threads of young children's identity through the arts. *Journal of Research in Childhood Education, 25*(4), 339-363.

Bodrova, E., & Leong, D. J. (2007). *Tools of the mind: The Vygotskian approach to early childhood education* (2nd edition). Columbus, OH: Merrill/Prentice Hall.

Bogdan, R., & Biklen, S. K. (2006). *Qualitative research for education: An introduction to theories and methods.* Needam, MA: Allyn and Bacon.

Bredekamp, S. (Ed.). (1987). *Developmentally appropriate practice in early childhood programs serving children from birth through age 8.* Washington, DC: National Association for the Education of Young Children.

Bruner, J. (1961). The act of discovery. *Harvard Educational Review, 31*(1), 21-32.

Bruner, J. (1967). *On Knowing: Essays for the left hand.* Boston: Harvard University Press.

Bruner, J., Sylva, K., & Genova, P. (Eds.).(1976). *The role of play in the problem solving of children 3–5 years old.* New York: Basic Books.

Cadwell, L. (2003). *Bringing learning to life: The Reggio approach to early childhood education.* New York: Teachers College Press.

Canadian Council on Learning. (1996, 2007). *Report on the state of early childhood learning*. Ottawa, Ontario: Canadian Council on Learning.

Canadian Council on Learning—Early Childhood Learning Knowledge Center. (2006). Let the children play: Nature's answer to early learning. In *Lessons in learning*. Ottawa, Ontario: Canadian Council on Learning.

Cappon, P. (2006). Connecting the dots on lifelong learning: Canada's new Composite Learning Index. *Policy Options*. November Edition. Ottawa, ON: CCL. 79-82.

Chaillé, C., & Silvern, S.B. (1996). Understanding through play. *Childhood Education, 72*, 274-277.

Clandinin, D. J.,& Connelly, F. M. (1998). Asking questions and telling stories. In C. Kridel (Ed.), *Writing educational biography: Exploration in qualitative research* (pp. 202-209). New York, NY: Garland Publishing.

Cleveland, G., Corter, C., Pelletier, J., Colley, S., Bertrand, J.,& Jamieson, J. (2006). *Early childhood learning and development in child care, Kindergarten and family support Programs*. Toronto, ON: Atkinson Center at OISE/UT.

Cohen, L &Manion, L. (2000). *Research methods in education* (5ᵗʰ edition). New York, NY: Routledge. p. 254.

Cohen, L.,Manion, L., &Morrison, K. (2007). *Research methods in education* (6ᵗʰ Edition). New York, NY: Routledge.

Crain, W. (2000). *Theories of development: Concepts and Application*. (4ᵗʰ edition). New York: Prentice Hall.

Crain, W. (2004). *Reclaiming childhood: Letting children be children in our achievement-oriented society*. New York, NY: Holt Paperbacks.

Creswell, J. W. & Miller, D. L. (2000). Determining validity in qualitative inquiry. *Theory into Practice, 39*(3), 124-131.

Creswell, J.W. (2007). *Qualitative inquiry and research design: Choosing among five approaches*. Thousand Oaks, CA: Sage Publications.

Creswell, J. W. (2003, 2008). *Research design: Qualitative, quantitative, and mixed methods approaches*. London, UK: SAGE Publications Inc.

Creswell, J. W. (2013). *Choosing Among Five Approaches*. 3rd edition. Thousand Oaks, CA: Sage Publication Inc.

Cryan, J. R., Sheehan, R., Wiechel, J., & Bandy-Hedden, I. G. *(1992)*.Success outcomes of Full-Day Kindergarten: More positive behavior and increased achievement in the year after. *Early Childhood Research Quarterly, 7*(2), 187-203.

Curtis, D., & Carter, M. (2003). *Designs for living and learning: Transforming early childhood environments*. St. Paul, MN: Red Leaf Press.

Denzin, N. (2006). *Sociological methods: A sourcebook*. Chicago: Aldine Transaction.

Dewey, J. (1916). *Democracy and education: An introduction to the philosophy of education*. New York: MacMillian.

Dewey, J. (1929). Democracy in education. *Journal of the National Education Association, 18*(9), 291-295.

Dewey, J. (1938\1997). *Experience and education* (Original work published 1929 by New York, NY: Kappa Delta Pi). New York, NY: First Touchstone.

Dewey, J. (1933). *How we think.* Boston: D.C. Heath.

Diamond, A., Barnett, W.S., Thomas, J. & Munro, S. (2007). Preschool program improves cognitive control. *Science,* 318 (5855), 1387-1388.

Elicker, J., and Mathur, S. (1997). What do they do all day? Comprehensive evaluation of a full-day Kindergarten. *Early Childhood Research Quarterly,* 12(4), 459-480.

Edwards, C., Gandini, L., & Forman, G. (1993). *The hundred languages of children: The Reggio Emilia approach to early childhood education.* Norwood, NJ: Ablex.

Emerson, R. W. (1990). *Selected essays, lectures, and poems.* New York, NY: Bantam.

Emerson, R. W. (2003). *Selected writings of Ralph Waldo Emerson.* New York, NY: Signet.

Elementary Teachers Federation of Ontario (2010). *Playing is learning—Thinking it through: Teaching and learning in the Kindergarten classroom.* Toronto, Ontario: ETFO.

Elementary Teachers Federation of Ontario (2001).*Kindergarten matters: The importance of Kindergarten in the development of young minds.* Toronto, Ontario: ETFO.

Elementary Teachers Federation of Ontario (1999).*Kindergarten years: Learning Through play.* Toronto, Ontario: ETFO.

Forbes, Scott H. (2003) *Holistic education: An analysis of its ideas and nature.* Brandon, VT: Foundation for Educational Renewal.

Freebody, P. (2004). *The four resources model. Text Next: New resources for literacy learning.* Newtown, NSW: Primary English Teaching Association (PETA).

Froebel, F. (1887). *The education of man.* New York, NY: Appleton-Entury Crofts.

Froebel, F. (1889). *Autobiography of Friedrich Froebel.* Syracuse, NY: Bardeen.

Gandhi, M. (1927, 1929). *An autobiography: The story of my experiments with truth* (Published in two volumes). Gujarat, IN: Navajivan Publishing House.

Gandhi, M. (1938). *All men are brothers: Autobiographical reflections.* K. Kripalani (Ed.). New York, NY: Continuum.

Gandini, L. (1998). Educational and caring spaces. In Edwards, C., Gandini, L. & Forman, G. (Eds.) The 100 Languages of Children: The Reggio Emilia approach – Advanced Reflections (p. 161-178). Westport, CT: Ablex.

Gardner, H. (1975). *The shattered mind.* New York, NY: Knopf Publishing.

Gardner, H. (1983). *Multiple Intelligences: The theory in practice.* New York, NY: Basic Books

Gardner, H. (1987). Beyond IQ: Education and human development. *Harvard Educational Review, 57*(2), 187-193.

Gardner, H. (1999). *Intelligence reframed: Multiple intelligences for the twenty-first Century.* New York, NY: Basic Books.

Gardner, H. (2011). *Frames of mind: The theory of multiple intelligences.* New York, NY: Basic Books.

Glazer, S. (1999). *The heart of learning: Spirituality in education.* New York, NY: Jeremy P. Tarcher / Penguin Putnam.

Greenspan, S. & Shanker, S. (2004). *The first idea: How symbols, language and intelligence evolved from our primate ancestors to modern humans.* Cambridge, MA: Da Capo Press.

Gullo, D. F. (2000). The long term educational effects of half-day vs. full day kindergarten. Early Child Development and Care, 160, 17-24.

Haiget, W., & Miller, P. (1993) *Pretending at home: Early development in a sociocultural context.* NY: State University of New York.

Heard, Q., & McDonough, J. (2009). *A place for wonder: Reading and writing nonfiction in the primary grades.* Portland, ME: Stenhouse Publisher.

Hendrick, J., & Weissman, P. (2006). *The whole child: Developmental education for the early years.* New Jersey: Pearson Education Inc.

Herron, R., & Sutton-Smith, B. (1974). *Child's play.* New York: Wiley.

Herry, M. (1989). Inner voice experience: An exploratory study of thirty cases. *Journal of Transpersonal Psychology, 21*(1), 73-82.

Hough, D., & Bryde, C. (1996). *The effects of the Full-Day Kindergarten on student achievement and effect.* Paper presented at the annual conference of the American Educational Research Association, New York.

Johnsen, E.P., & Christie, J.F. (1986). *Pretend play and logical operations*. In K. Banchard (Ed.), *The many faces of play* (pp. 50-58). Champaign, IL: Human Kinetics.

Janus, M., Duku, E., &Schell A. (2012, October). McMaster, Offord Center for Child Studies. *The full-day kindergarten early learning program: Final report*. Hamilton:

McMaster University. Retrieved from:http://www.edu.gov.on.ca/kindergarten/ELP_FDKFall2012.pdf

Jones, E., & Nimmo, J. (1994). *Emergent curriculum*. Washington, DC: NAEYC.

Kabira, W. N., & Kimani, E. N. (2012). The historical journey of women's leadership in Kenya. *Journal of Educational Research and Policy Studies, 3*(6), 843-849. Nairobi, Kenya: Scholarlink Research Institute Journals.

Katz, L., & Chard, S. (1996). *The contribution of documentation to the quality of early childhood education* (ERIC Digest). Urbana, IL: ERIC Clearinghouse on Elementary and Early Childhood Education.

Kessler, Rachel. (2000) *The Soul of Education: Helping Students Find Connection, Compassion and Character at School*. Alexandria, VA: ASCD Publications

Kimani, E. N., & Wanjiku, C. (2004). Taking a gender perspective in the development process: A justification. In *Introduction to development studies in Africa* (pp. 45-53). Nairobi, Kenya : Acacia Publishers.

Kimani, E. N., & Mwikamba, K. (2010). Gender dynamics in science and technology. *Journal of Agriculture, Science and Technology.* 12(2).

Kostelnik, M. J., & Grady, M.L. (2009). *Getting it right from the start: The principal's guide to early childhood education.* Thousand Oaks, CA: National Association of Elementary School Principals and Corwin.

Lantieri, L. (2001). *Schools with spirit: Nurturing the inner lives of children and teachers.* Boston, MA: Beacon.

Legislative Assembly of Ontario. (2010). *Bill 242, Full-Day early learning statute law amendment act, 2010.* Retrieved from*www. ontla.on.ca*

Lee, V., Burkam, D., Ready, D., Honigman, S., & Meissels, S. *Full-Day vs. half-day Kindergarten: In which program do children learn more?* Anaheim, CA: American Sociological Association.

Lewin-Benham, A. (2006). *Possible schools: The Reggio Approach to urban education.* New York, NY: Teacher's College.

Malaguzzi, L. (1993). For an education based on relationships. *Young Children, 49*(1), 9-12.

Maslow, A. (1943). A theory of human motivation. *Psychological Review, 50*(4), 370-96. Retrieved from http://psychclassics. yorku.ca/Maslow/motivation.htm

Maslow, A. (1954). *Motivation and personality.* New York, NY: Harper and Row.

Maslow, A. (1970). *Motivation and personality* (2nd Ed.). New York, NY: Harper and Row.

Maslow, A. (1971). *Farther Reaches of Human Nature.* New York, NY: McGraw-Hill.

McCain, M. N., & Mustard, J. F. (1999). *Reversing the real brain drain: Early years study.* Toronto, Ontario: Publications Ontario.

McCain, M. N., Mustard, J. F., & Shanker, S. (2007). *Early years study 2: Putting science into action.* Toronto, Ontario: Council for Early Child Development.

McCain, M. N., Mustard, J. F., & McCuaig, K. (2011). *Early years study 3: Making decisions: Taking action.* Toronto, Ontario: Margaret & Wallace McCain Family Foundation

McQuail, S., Mooney, A., Cameron, C., Candappa, M., Moss, P., & Petrie, P. (2003). *Early years and childcare international evidence project, October 2003.* Nottingham, Great Britain: Department for Education and Skills, Sure Start.

Miller, E., & Almon, J. (2009). *Crisis in the Kindergarten: Why children need to play In school.* College Park, MD: Alliance for Childhood. Retrieved from http://files.eric.ed.gov/fulltext/ED504839.pdf

Miller, J. P. (1993). *The holistic teacher.* Toronto, Ontario: OISE Press.

Miller, J. P. (1996, 2007). *The holistic curriculum.* Toronto, Ontario: OISE Press.

Miller, J. P. (2000). *Education and the soul: Toward a spiritual curriculum.* Albany, NY: State University of New York Press.

Miller, J. P. (2006). *Education for wisdom and compassion: Creating conditions for timeless learning.* Thousand Oaks, CA: Corwin.

Miller, J. P. (2010). *Whole child education.* Toronto, Ontario: University of Toronto Press.

Miller, J. P. (2011). *Transcendental learning: The educational legacy of Alcott, Emerson, Fuller, Peabody and Thoreau.* Charlotte, NC: IAP Inc.

Miller, J. P.,& Seller, W. (1990). *Curriculum, perspectives and practices.* Toronto, ON: Copp Clark Division, Longman.

Miller, R. (1991). Introduction. In. R. Miller (Ed.), *New Direction Education* (pp. 1-3). Brandon, VT: Holistic Education Press.

Miller, R. (1992). *What are schools for? Holistic education in American culture.* Brandon, VT: Holistic Education Press.

Miller, R. (1995). *Educational freedom for a democratic society: A critique of national goals, standards, and curriculum.* Banton, VT: Holistic Educational Press.

Miller, R. (2000). *Caring for new life: Essays on holistic education.* VT: Foundation of Educational Renewal.

Miller, R. (2002). *Free Schools, free people: Education and democracy after the 1960s.* Albany, NY: State University of New York Press.

Miller, R. (2006). Reflecting on spirituality in education. *Encounter: Education for Meaning and Social Justice, 19*(2), 6-9.

Ministry of Children and Youth Services. (2006). *Ontario's best start action plan: A progress report.* Toronto, Ontario: Government of Ontario.

Montessori, M. (1936/1972b). *The secret of childhood*. New York, NY: Ballantine.

Montessori, M. (1946). *Education for a new world*. Oxford, UK: Clio Press.

Montessori, M. (1949/1972a). *Education and peace*. Chicago: Henry Regnery.

Montessori, M. (1967, 1973). *To educate the human potential*. Madras, India: Kalakshetra.

Montessori, M. (1995). *The absorbent mind*. New York, NY: Henry Holt and Company.

Mustard, J.F. (2006). *Early child development and experience-based brain development: The scientific underpinnings of the importance of early child development in a globalized world*. Washington, DC: Brookings Institute.

National Scientific Council on the Developing Child. (2007). *Young children develop in An environment of relationships*. Cambridge, MA: Harvard University Press.

Nimmo, J., & Hallett, B. (2008). Childhood in the garden: A place to encounter natural and social diversity. *Young Children, 63* (1), 32-38.

Ontario Ministry of Education (2003a). *Early reading strategy: The report of the expert panel on early reading in Ontario*. Retrieved from http://www.edu.gov.on.ca/eng/document/reports/reading/reading.pdf

Ontario Ministry of Education (2003b). *Early math strategy: The report of the expert panel on early math in Ontario*. Retrieved from http://www.edu.gov.on.ca/eng/document/reports/math/ math.pdf

Ontario Early Years (2004). *Achieving cultural competence.* Toronto, Ontario: Ministry of Children and Youth Services.

Ontario Ministry of Education. (2006a). *Early learning for every child today: A framework for Ontario early childhood settings.* Toronto, Ontario: Queen's Printer for Ontario.

Ontario Ministry of Education. (2006b). *The Kindergarten program.* Toronto, Ontario: Queens's Printer for Ontario.

Ontario Ministry of Education. (2009). *Realizing the promise of diversity: Ontario's equity and inclusive education strategy.* Toronto, Ontario: Queen's Printer for Ontario.

Ontario Ministry of Education. (2010). *The full-day early learning Kindergarten program* (Draft Version). Toronto, Ontario: Queen's Printer for Ontario.

Ontario Ministry of Education. (2012). *Full-day Kindergarten: Memo summary.* Toronto, Ontario: Government of Ontario. Retrieved from www. edu.gov.on.ca

Ontario Ministry of Education (2013a). *Full-day Kindergarten study evaluation.* Toronto, Ontario. Retrieved from http://www.edu. gov.on.ca/kindergarten/theresearchisin.html

Ontario Ministry of Education (2013b). *A meta-perspective on the evaluation of full-day Kindergarten during the first two years of implementation.* Toronto, Ontario: Queen's Printer for Ontario.

Ontario Ministry of Education (2013c). *Think, Feel, Act: Lessons from Research about Young Children*. Toronto, Ontario: Queen's Printer for Ontario.

Ontario Ministry of Education (2014) *How does learning happen? Ontario's Pedagogy for the Early Years*. Toronto, Ontario: Queens's Printer for Ontario.

Orr, D. (2011). *Beautiful and pointless: A guide to modern poetry*. New York, NY: Harper

Palmer, J. A. (1998). *Environmental education in the twenty-first century: Theory, practice, progress, and promise*. London, UK and New York, NY: Routledge.

Palmer, P. J. (1993). *To know as we are known: Education as a spiritual journey*. San Francisco, CA: HarperCollins.

Palmer, P.J. (2004). *A hidden wholeness: The journey forward on individual life*. San Francisco, CA: Josey-Bass.

Palmer, P. J. (2007). *The courage to teach guide for reflection & renewal*. San Francisco, CA: Wiley.

Pascal, C. (2009a). *Every child, every opportunity: Curriculum and pedagogy for the early learning program*. Toronto, Ontario: Government of Ontario.

Pascal, C. (2009b). *With our best future in mind: Implementing early learning in Ontario*. Toronto, Ontario: Government of Ontario.

Pellegrini, A. (1976). *The future of play theory: A multidisciplinary inquiry into the contributions of Brian Sutton-Smith*. New York, NY: State University of New York.

Pelletier, J. (2012a). *Key findings from year 1 of Full-Day Early Learning Kindergarten in Peel.* Toronto, Ontario: Dr. Eric Jackman Institute of Child Study, Ontario Institute for Studies in Education.

Pelletier, J. (2012b). *Key findings from year 2 of Full-Day Early Learning Kindergarten in Peel.* Toronto, Ontario: Dr. Eric Jackman Institute of Child Study, Ontario Institute for Studies in Education.

Pelletier, J. (2014). *Key findings from year 3 of Full-Day Early Learning Kindergarten in Peel.* Toronto, Ontario: Ontario Institute for Studies in Education.

Perlmutter, J. C., &Burrell (1995). Learning through play as well as through work. *Young Children Young Children, 50* (5), 14-21.

Piaget, J. (1927). *The first year of life of the child. British Journal of Psychology, 18,* 92-120.

Piaget, J. (1950). *The psychology of intelligence.* London: Routledge and Kegan Paul.

Piaget, J. (1952). *The child's conception of number.* London: Routledge and Kegan Paul.

Piaget, J. (1962). *Play, dreams, and imitation in childhood.* New York, NY: Norton.

Piaget, J. (1969). *The mechanisms of perception.* London: Rutledge and Kegan Paul.

Piaget, J. (1972). *Science of education and the psychology of the child.* New York, NY: Viking.

Ramsey, P. G. (1979). Beyond ten little Indians and turkeys: Alternative approaches to Thanksgiving. *Young Children, 41*(60), 60-67.

Ramsey, P. G. (1982) Multicultural education in early childhood. *Young Children, 37*(2), 13-24.

Rousseau, J. J. (1979). *Emile or on Education.* Geneva, Switzerland: Library of Congress Cataloging in Publication Data

Rushton, S., & Larkin, E. (2001). Shaping the learning environment: Connecting Developmentally appropriate practices to brain research. *Early Childhood Educational Journal, 29*(1), 25-33.

Rutledge, D. (2000). Neurons and nurture in the early years. *Education Canada, 39*(4), 16-19.

Samuels, M., & Samuels, N. (1975). *Seeing with the mind's eye: The history, techniques and uses of visualization.* New York, NY: Random House.

Saracho, O., & Spodek, B. (Eds.). (1983). *Understanding the multicultural experience in early childhood education.* Washington, DC: NAEYC.

Schirrmacher, R. (1998). *Art and creative development for young children* (3rded.). Albany, NY: Delmar.

Shonkoff, J. P., & Phillips, D.A. (2000). *Neurons to neighbourhoods: The science of early childhood development.* Washington DC: National Academy Press.

Slade, A. (1994). Making meaning and making believe: Their role in the clinical process. In A. Slade &D. P. Wolfe (Eds.), *Children at play: Clinical and developmental approaches to meaning and representation* (pp. 81-107). New York, NY: Oxford University Press.

Smith F. (1982) *Understanding reading*. New York, NY: Holt, Rinehart & Winston.

Sobel, D. (1996). *Beyond Ecopobia: Reclaiming the heart of nature education*. Great Barrington, MA: The Orion Society.

Sprung, B. (1978). *Perspectives on non-sexist early childhood education*. New York, NY: Teachers College Press, Columbia University.

Stake, R.E. (2005). Quantitative case studies. In Denzin, N.K. and Y.S. Lincoln (Eds.),*The handbook of qualitative research* (3rd ed.). Thousand Oaks, CA: Sage Publications.

Stake, R.E. (1995). *The art of case study research*. Thousand Oaks, CA: Sage Publications.

Steiner, R. (1965). *Education of the Child*. London: Rudolf Steiner Press.

Steiner, R. (1994). *Theosophy: An introduction to the spiritual processes in human life and in the cosmos*. New York, NY: Anthroposophic Press.

Sutton-Smith, B. (1966). Piaget on play: A critique. *Psychological Review, 73*,104-110.

Sutton-Smith, B. (1976). *The future of play theory: A multidisciplinary inquiry into the contributions of Brian Sutton-Smith*. New York, NY: State University of New York.

Sutton-Smith, B. (1997). *The ambiguity of play*. Cambridge, MA: First Harvard University Press.

Sylva K., Melhusih, E. Sammons, P., Siraj-Blatchford, I., & Taggart, B. (2004). *The effective provision of pre-school education (EPPE) Project*. London: OFES/Institute of Education. University of London.

The Laboratory School at the Dr. Eric Jackman Institute for Child Study. (2011). *Natural curiosity: Building children's understanding of the world through environmental inquiry*. Kingston, ON: Miracle Press Ltd.

Thompson, R. A. (2006a). Conversation and developing understanding: Introduction to the special issue. *Merrill-Palmer Quarterly, 52*, 1-16.

Thompson, R. A. (2006b). The development of the person: Social understanding, relationships, self, conscience. In W. Damon & R. M. Lerner (Eds.), *Handbook of child psychology* (6th Ed., pp. 24-98), Vol. 3. Social, emotional, and personality development (N. Eisenberg, Vol. Ed.). New York, NY: Wiley.

Thompson, R. A. (2006c). Nurturing developing brains, minds, and hearts. In R. Lally& P. Mangione (Eds.), *Concepts of care: 20 essays on infant/toddler development and learning* (pp. 47-52). Sausalito, CA: WestEd.

Thompson, R. A., Goodvin, R., & Meyer, S. (2006). Social development: Psychological understanding, self-understanding, and relationships. In J. Luby (Ed.), *Handbook of preschool mental health: Development, disorders and treatment* (pp. 3-22). New York, NY: Guilford.

Thompson, R. A., & Lagatutta, K. (2006). Feeling and understanding: Early emotional development. In K. McCartney

& D. Phillips (Eds.), *The Blackwell handbook of early childhood development* (pp. 317-337). Oxford, UK: Blackwell.

Thoreau, H.D. (1999). *Uncommon learnings: Henry David Thoreau on education*. Boston, MA: Houghton Mifflin.

United Nations Educational, Scientific and Cultural Organization (UNESCO). (2004). *Education for all: The quality imperative. EFA global monitoring report 2005*. Paris, France: *UNESCO*.

United Nations Educational, Scientific and Cultural Organization (UNESCO).(2008). *Inclusive education: The way of the future*. UNESCO International Conference on Education. November 25-28. Geneva: UNESCO.

UNICEF. (2010). *Fact Sheet: A summary of the rights under the convention on the rights of the child*. Article 31. Retrieved from http://www.unicef.org/crc.files/Rights_overview.pdf, accessed March 4, 2013.

United Nations—General Assembly. (1989). Session 44 Resolution 25. Convention on the Rights of the Child. 20 November 1989.

Van den Berg, A.R. (1986). Play theory. In Q. Fein& M. Rivkin (Eds.), *The young child at play*. Washington, DC: NAEYC.

Vanderlee, M.L, Youmans, S., Peters, R., & Eastabrook, J. (2012). Queen's Study. *Final report: Evaluation of the implementation of the Ontario full-day early learning-kindergarten program*. Kingston: Queen's University. Retrieved from http://www.edu.gov.on.ca/kindergarten/FDELK_ReportFall2012.pdf

Vygotsky, L.S. (1934, 1986). *Thought and language*. A. Kozulin (Ed.). Cambridge, MA: MIT Press.

Vygotsky, L.S. (1978).*Mind in society: The development of higher psychological processes.* M.Cole, V. John-Steiner, S. Scribner, & E. Souberman (Eds.). Cambridge, MA: Harvard University Press.

Vygotsky, L. S. (1987). Thinking and speech. In R. W. Reiber & A. S. Carton (Eds.), (Trans., N. Minick), *The collected works of L. S. Vygotsky.* Vol. 1: Problems of general psychology. New York, NY: Plenum Press.

Vygotsky, L.S. (1998). *The collected works of L.S. Vygotsky.* R.W. Reiber (Ed.). Vol. 5: Child psychology. New York, NY: Plenum Press.

Walston, J. & West, J. (2004). *Full day and half day in the U.S.: Findings from the early childhood longitudinal study-Kindergarten class of 1998-99.* US Department of Education. National Center for Educational Statistics, Institute of Educational Science. Washington, DC: US Government Printing Office.

Wane, N. (2010). *Spirituality and schooling: Sociological and pedagogical implications in education.* Toronto, Ontario: Canadian Scholars' Press.

Wane, N., Maryimo, E.,& Ritskes, E. (Eds.). (2011). *Education, spirituality and society: An integrated approach.* Boston, MA: Sense.

Wane, N., Kempf, A., & Simmons, M. (Eds.). (2011). *The politics of cultural knowledge.* The Netherlands: Sense Publishers.

Wane, N. N. (2007). *Theorizing empowerment: Canadian perspectives on black feminist thought.* Toronto, Ontario: Inanna Publications and Education.

Wane, N. N. (2008). Mapping the field of indigenous knowledges in Anti-colonial discourse: A transformative journey in education. *Race Ethnicity and Education, 11*(2), 183-197.

Wane, N. N., & Chandler, D. J. (2002). African women, cultural knowledge and environmental education with a focus on Kenya's indigenous women. *Canadian Journal of Environmental Education, 7*(1), 86-98.

Wane, N. N., & Waterfall, B. (2005). Hoops of spirituality in science and technology. In P. Tripp & L. Muzzin (Eds.). *Teaching as activism: Equity meets environmentalism* (pp. 47-64). Montreal, Quebec, Canada: McGill-Queen's Press.

Wardle, F. (2001). Supporting multiracial and multiethnic children and their families. *Young Children, 56*(6), 38-39.

Washington, V. (2002). Why early childhood matters now more than ever. *Early Childhood Today, 17*(3), 5.

Wien, C. (2005). Six short reasons why pedagogy matters in schools. *Canadian Children,30*(1), 21-26.

Wien, C. (1995). *Developmentally appropriate practice in "real life": Stories of teacher practical knowledge.* New York, NY: Teachers College Press.

Wien, C. (Ed.). (2008).*Emergent curriculum in the primary classroom: Interpreting the Reggio Emilia approach in schools.* New York, NY: Teachers College Press.

Weininger, O. (1979). *Play and education: The basic tool for early childhood learning.* Springfield, IL: Charles C. Thomas Publisher.

Willows, D. M. (2002). The balanced literacy diet. *The School Administrator,* 59(1), 30-33.

Willows, D. M. (2008). Reducing literacy failure through teacher development: Implementing a balanced a flexible literacy diet. *Education Canada,* 20-24.

Zull, J.E. (2002). *The art of changing the brain: Enriching the practice of teaching by exploring the biology of learning.* Stylus Publishing: Sterling, VA.

Appendix A

GLOSSARY OF TERMS

Audit Trail: a collection of work from the beginning of the student year until the end. It includes things like a series of photos of children at play, writing samples, a journal, a portfolio of student work, binder of assessments and logging of one-to-one assessments and conversations with the child.

Co-construction: a way of developing activities and centers where a teacher brainstorms with students to decide centers to create, materials needed, things to do, and what to do. With much child input the teacher facilitates the creation and implementation of a center in class.

Critical Thinking: thinking about ideas or situations in order to understand them fully, identify their implications, and make a judgement that can guide decision-making. Critical thinking skills include questioning, predicting, hypothesizing, analyzing, synthesizing, examining opinions, identifying values and issues, detecting bias, and distinguishing alternatives.

Differentiated Instruction: a method of instruction in which the teacher considers the needs of each child at his or her current stage of development, and then uses a learning approach with that child that responds to his or her individual needs. As a result, each child's growth is maximized.

Diversity: differences and uniqueness that each child brings including values, beliefs, culture, ethnicity, language, ability, education, life experiences, socio-economic status, spirituality, gender, and age.

Document Panel: a collection of photographs, student quotes, sample work in order to understand student thinking. It is created by compiling and capturing the process of learning rather than just showing the end product.

Environmental Education: teaching about the natural environment, sustainability of the environment, and how humans can conserve, protect, and manage behaviors to maintain ecosystems, plant, and animal life.

Experiential Learning: making meaning in learning through direct experience and self-exploration. It is more connected to hands-on learning, action and doing.

Fine-Motor Control: control over muscles that regulate small movements of fingers, hands, and wrists. It can be enhanced by activities such as working with blocks, threading beads, drawing with markers or crayons, fastening buttons, snaps, and zippers, cutting with scissors, and doing puzzles.

Focused Exploration: A method of instruction in which children use the materials and equipment available in the classroom in ways of their choosing. The teacher observes and listens while children are exploring, and provides guidance as needed. For example, posing a question, prompt for deeper thinking, or introduce new vocabulary.

Gross-Motor Control: control over the larger muscles in the arms, legs, and torso. Activities to develop gross-motor skills include walking, running, throwing, lifting, and kicking.

Inquiry-based Learning: learning through noticing, wondering, playing, exploring, questioning, planning, reflecting, sharing, and discussing.

Intentional Teaching: involves educators being deliberate, purposeful, and thoughtful in their decisions and actions. Intentional teaching is the opposite of teaching by rote or using traditional methods simply because things have always been done that way.

Manipulatives: objects that children handle and use in constructing their own understanding of skills and in demonstrating that understanding. Manipulatives may also be called concrete materials.

Modeling: a demonstration by the teacher of a routine task, or strategy to children. Children become aware of the processes needed to do a task. The teacher may "think aloud" to make the process clearer.

Observation: the process of watching, listening, and being attuned to children's behaviour, emotional states, interests and abilities, and patterns of development in order to meet their needs and evaluate their development and learning.

Play-based Learning: a vehicle for learning and lies at the core of innovation and creativity. It is during play that children are most receptive, and play is linked to problem-solving, language acquisition, literacy and numeracy development, and the development of social, physical, and emotional skills. Children manipulate objects, act out roles, experiment with materials, and explore with song, dance, games, toys, and arts.

Problem-Solving: students engage in a task or activity that is not familiar and students must draw on previous knowledge and try out different strategies to make connections and reach a conclusion.

Real-Life Contexts: originate from the child and comprise all their preschool experiences with family, community, and culture, as well as school-based experiences and media influences.

Scaffolding: a process involving the provision of opportunities for play and interaction that relate to children's experiences and support from educators to help children move beyond their current levels of understanding. The idea that scaffolding is a temporary structure that can be gradually removed to develop students.

Transformational Learning: Teaching practices and learning that include changing the way one interprets an idea, experience or interaction with the world.

Sources: (1) Ontario Ministry of Education. (2012). *Full-Day Kindergarten Key Facts.* Toronto: Queen's Printer; (2) Ontario Ministry of Education. (2006a). *Early learning for every child today: A framework for Ontario early childhood settings.* Toronto, Ontario: Queen's Printer for Ontario; (3) Ontario Ministry of Education. (2006b). *The Kindergarten program.* Toronto, Ontario: Queens's Printer for Ontario.

List of Acronyms

Canadian Council on Learning	CCL
Canadian Education Association	CEA
Developmentally Appropriate Practice	DAP
Early Childhood Educator	ECE
Early Development Index	EDI
Early Learning for Every Child Today	ELECT
Early Learning and Kindergarten Team	EL-K
Elementary Teachers Federation of Ontario	ETFO
English as a Second Language	ESL
English Language Learners	ELL
Full-Day Kindergarten	FDK
Full-Day Early Learning Kindergarten Program	FDELKP
Half-Day Kindergarten	HDK
Knowledge Building	KB
Ministry of Education	MOE
National Association for Education of Young Children	NAEYC
Ontario College of Teachers	OCT
Organization for Economic Cooperation and Development	OECD
Ontario Institute for Studies in Education	OISE
United Nations Educational Scientific and Cultural Organization	UNESCO

Appendix B

FDK IN ONTARIO: INFORMATION, REPORTS AND FACTS

On September 7, 2010, Ontario made history as Boards launched Full-Day Early Learning Kindergarten in 600 schools across the province. Approximately, 35,000 four and five-year-old children benefitted from the first phase of full-day learning as part of the Province's plan to build a stronger school system and a well-educated workforce. The Province has made a commitment to fully implement the Full-Day Kindergarten Program in all schools by 2015-2016.

For the first time ever elementary teachers and early childhood education teachers were working in partnership to deliver a play-based full-day program guided by *The Full-Day Early Learning Kindergarten Program (Draft version, 2010-11)* which incorporates principles from the Ontario Early Years Framework. Ontario government investment in early years initiative reached over $1 billion dollars - an increase over 90% since 2003.

There was curriculum restructuring that also led to revised curriculum documents put out by the Ministry of Education. Not only was there was greater accessibility and availability of child-care and education for the early years, there was also more clarity on the content of the program and plans for improved quality of education.

Some useful Ontario early years reports that supported Kindergarten program development included: 1980-To Herald a Child; 1984-Early Primary Education Project; 1994-Royal Commission on Learning; 1998-The Kindergarten Program; 1999-Early Years Study; 2005-Best Start Initiatives; 2006-The Kindergarten Program (revised);

Percentage of Children in FDK Program with phased in roll-out of FDK

- *September 2010*: 35,000 four and five year olds entered the first year of Full-Day Kindergarten—about 15 per cent of the total Kindergarten population
- *September 2011*: 50,000 four and five year olds enrolled in nearly 800 schools—about 20 per cent of Kindergarten children
- *September 2012*: 1,700 schools offer the program to 49 per cent of Kindergarten students—about 122,000 children
- *September 2013*: 2,600 schools will offer FDK program to approximately 75 per cent of Kindergarten students
- *September 2014*: 3,800 schools will offer FDK program to approximately 95 per cent of Kindergarten students

Funding Facts:

- $200 million in support from the Ministry of Education for the program in year 1, $300 million in year 2 and $675 million in year 3
- To date, the government has allocated almost $1.4 billion in capital funding to support the implementation of full-day kindergarten
- Research says every $1 spent on early learning repays a seven-to-one return on investment

Source: Ontario Ministry of Education. (2012). *Full-Day Kindergarten Key Facts.* Toronto: Queen's Printer

Appendix C

MINISTRY'S COMMITMENT TO THE FULL-DAY KINDERGARTEN LEARNING

Early Learning Program –Full-Day Early Learning-Kindergarten Program Memorandum 2010: EL5 from Grant Clarke and Jim Grieve April 13, 2010

The Ministry is committed to providing a Full-Day of learning to four- and five-year-olds as part of the province's plan to build a stronger school system and a well-educated workforce.

Implementation of the *Full-Day Early Learning-Kindergarten Program (Draft version)* in selected school sites will begin in September 2010. The program will be expanded in phases and the goal is to implement it in every school by 2015-16. The finalized document for the *Full-Day Early Learning-Kindergarten Program* will be released in June 2011.

The development of the draft *Full-Day Early Learning-Kindergarten Program* document involved building on *The Kindergarten Program (Revised) 2006* and considering an analysis of the *Early Learning for Every Child Today* (ELECT) program and other frameworks as well as the advice in Dr. Pascal's report, *Every Child Every Opportunity*. The draft program document was completed using the Ministry's standard approach to curriculum development and the consultation process was expanded to include the Early Childhood Education (ECE) community. An integrated extended day program that is complementary to the instructional day program is also in development. The extensive consultation process included teachers, early childhood educators, principals, program staff, faculties of education, colleges, teacher affiliates, the College of Early Childhood Educators, Association of Early Childhood Educators, and other ministries such as the Ministry of Children and Youth Services.

Ministry of Education	Ministère de l'Éducation	
Office of the ADM	Bureau du sous-ministre adjoint	
Business & Finance Division	Division des opérations et des finances	
20ᵗʰ Floor, Mowat Block	20ᵉ étage, édifice Mowat	
Queen's Park	Queen's Park	
Toronto, ON M7A 1L2	Toronto ON M7A 1L2	

2009: B12

MEMORANDUM TO: Directors of Education

FROM: Nancy Naylor
           Assistant Deputy Minister

DATE: October 27, 2009

SUBJECT: **Early Learning Program –
               Planning for 2010-11 and 2011-12**

As announced by the Premier today, the first phase of Ontario's plan for a province-wide Early Learning Program (ELP) is the implementation of full-day early learning for four- and five-year-olds.

The program will be offered in a number of schools throughout the province starting in September 2010. The goal is to make the program available over time to all four- and five-year-old students. This multi-year, phased-in approach will help ensure a smooth transition to a mature ELP, while recognizing current economic and fiscal realities.

As noted in today's memorandum from the Deputy Minister of Education, entitled *Implementation of Early Learning for four- and five-year-olds: Year One*, the purpose of this B-memorandum is to provide school boards with information about the initial planning steps that boards must take to prepare for Years One and Two of ELP implementation (2010-11 and 2011-12). Appendix 1 lists the initial board-by-board planning allocations of ELP pupil places for these two years.

The government has committed $200M in 2010-11 to support the first year of full-day early learning for up to 35,000 four- and five-year-olds – 15 percent of the Junior and Senior Kindergarten (JK/SK) population. This investment will grow to $300M in 2011-12 to expand the full-day program to approximately 20 percent of the JK/SK population. The goal is to have early learning fully implemented in all schools by 2015-16.

As the ELP is a school-based initiative, school boards will have a lead role in achieving the province's vision for early learning. The Ministry of Education will work with and support school boards in this leadership role. Successful implementation of the ELP will require boards to consult with their school communities and other key partners, including coterminous boards, Best Start networks, and Consolidated Municipal Service Managers and District Social Services Administration Boards.

To support this collaborative approach and address the needs of the childcare sector, the Ministry will also work closely with the Ministry of Children and Youth Services.

Early Learning Program – Planning for 2010-11 and 2011-12   Page 1 of 8

A. PROGRAM MODEL

Overview – two basic components

The ELP will be offered during the school year. The program model has two basic components:

1. A *core* component that will be offered each school day during the hours of the instructional program (for example, 9:00 a.m. to 3:30 p.m.). In each classroom, an educator team of one certified teacher and one early childhood educator (ECE) registered with the College of Early Childhood Educators will work side by side to deliver the program.

2. An *extended day* component that will be available before and after school (for example, 7:00 to 9:00 a.m. and 3:30 to 6:00 p.m.). A student's participation in this component of the program is at the option of parents and guardians, but boards must offer the program where there is sufficient enrolment to make a program viable. This component of the ELP will be led by ECEs. It will be funded through parent fees set on a cost-recovery basis, with subsidies available for families who need help with the cost. Further information about fees will be provided in the near future.

Class size and child-adult ratio

The class size standard for the ELP will be an average of 26 students on a board-wide basis, which provides for an average child-adult ratio of 13:1.

While this standard gives boards flexibility, boards are expected to conform closely to the standard and organize ELP classes so that almost all these classes have 26 students.

As with current JK/SK class sizes, boards will report ELP class sizes, which will be published on the Class-Size Tracker. However, ELP classes will be excluded from each board's calculation and reporting of primary class sizes and board-wide elementary class size average. JK/SK classes outside the ELP will continue to be subject to the primary class size standards and will be included in the calculation and reporting of class sizes at the primary and elementary levels.

B. EARLY YEARS LEADER

The implementation of the Early Learning Program is a priority throughout the next year. Each board must ensure that it is assigning sufficient resources to planning, management and reporting activities.

To provide leadership at the board level, the Ministry asks that each board appoint a senior official as its Early Years Leader. The primary responsibilities of the Early Years Leader will be to co-ordinate the board's implementation of ELP, facilitate board consultations, and act as a link to the Ministry. Boards are encouraged to begin the selection of an Early Years Leader as soon as possible.

Sections of the Memo from Jim Grieves, Assistant Deputy Minister dated May 5, 2010

Bill Introduction

I am writing to inform you that Bill 242, "The Full-Day Early Learning Statute Law Amendment Act, 2010," was passed in the Legislature on April 27, 2010. Once in force, this legislation will establish the legal framework governing the long-term implementation of the government's full-day learning initiative. Specifically, it:

- Requires boards to deliver Full-Day JK/K programs,
- Requires that there be a teacher and early childhood educator (ECE) team in JK/K classrooms,
- Requires boards to deliver extended day programs for four- and five-year old son instructional days, and
- Provides the government with authority to enter into agreements with municipalities, or other persons or entities, to administer subsidies related to the extended day program.

Role Information

Roles and responsibilities of teachers and ECEs

The legislation creates section 264.1 in the *Education Act* to establish a duty for teachers and ECEs to co-operate and co-ordinate in the following areas:

- Planning and delivery of the JK/K program,
- Assessment and observation of children,
- Communicating with families, and
- Maintaining a healthy social, emotional and learning environment.

Ministry of Education responsibility for child care

The government has announced that is it implementing some of the other recommendations in Charles Pascal's report, *With Our Best Future in Mind*. A key part of this announcement that impacts most directly on the Ministry of Education is that responsibility for child care has been transferred from the Ministry of Children and Youth Services to the Ministry of Education within the Early Learning Division. The transfer will occur through a phased approach. Effective immediately, responsibility for childcare policy and program will transfer to the Ministry of Education. Contract management will be transferred in fall 2010, and child care licensing will remain with the Ministry of Children and Youth Services, at this time.

The transfer of child care to the Ministry of Education is a significant step in the government's plan to enhance seamlessness between the two systems and integrate programs and services for young children and their families. Putting the care and education of our children under one ministry will make them more coherent, consistent and responsive to Ontario's families' needs.

Appendix D

TIPS FOR TEACHERS

Tips for teachers include:

- Find ways to develop calm, alert and happy children in your classroom
- Develop creativity and imaginative play daily into classroom learning, centers and activities; allow time for children share their work, their ideas and thinking.
- Encourage children to persevere in a world of challenge and change; provide resources, time and space to get deepen and broaden learning experiences
- Develop a questioning style that respects student thinking, extends learning, and is open-ended to provide challenging and differentiated learning opportunities
- Transform everyday circumstances into opportunities to activate self-expression, student voice, problem-solving, critical and creative energies
- Creative ways are not always about art, find ways to encourage personal voice, ideas and make problem-solving a part of creative and critical thinking focus throughout the day
- Follow the child's lead and interests in play and inquiry; provide opportunities for hands-on exploration,

cross-curricular experiences, play embedded with literacy and numeracy extensions in an authentic and purposeful way that is mindful of the child's experience

- Nurture personal interests, individual identity and the uniqueness of each child
- Recognize cultural diversities in the classroom, welcome parents as guest speakers and include the family as a partner in the learning of the child
- Educational partnerships are not only the ECE and the teacher, but connect and create positive relationships with lunch room supervisors, planning time teachers, teaching assistants and administrators, extended care professionals, community support services and most importantly the families of the children.
- Encourage self-regulation with hunger but also remind children not to eat all of their lunch at snack time but leave a little food for later
- Talk things through with children when it comes to self-regulation, be patient and let them see why it makes sense to do things a certain way
- Find varied ways and strategies to regulate behavior, emotions, attention, and physiological states of the children in the classroom as required
- Establish clear classroom expectations - what does good tidy-up look like; establish clean-up routines, give ongoing feedback and gentle reminders and hints as they do so; manage and model hygiene expectations with the food routines; washing hands properly
- Model good social skill development by teaching them about when to share ideas, when to listen and then when its best to talk; engage in the process of resolving problems – don't just solve conflicts for them; foster caring and thoughtfulness by modeling it

- Write/use child created pictures / actual student photographs and discuss and co-create rules and even posting them at centers (e.g. wear a smock at paint center – have a picture of smock and two / three word reminders – 'wear smock' – written by a student ideally)
- Give more time as needed and slow things down to deepen the learning and engagement
- Avoid sitting quietly for too long and add in movement with songs and dance throughout the day for daily physical activity and as a strategy for classroom management; use a child as a 'barometer' and if they are not engaged, respond, adjust and move as needed
- Minimize transitions and interruptions to work towards a seamless day
- Deepen empathy, ethical and inclusive relationships and practices throughout the year
- Making transitions easier by giving warnings and giving clear expectations;
- Use signals (both verbal and non-verbal) and establish routines that work best with the child's interests and behaviors in mind.
- Provide opportunities for role play activities for social skills and oral language development and model and discuss how it is best to interact with others as need arises.
- Using a buddy for ESL learners that speaks the child's home language; support ESL learners by providing dual language learning experiences where possible, connect with them and their families and encourage them to express themselves and feelings in class
- Using a timer or visual and communicate with educational partners for smooth transitions
- Provide varied learning experiences based on different levels and interests of the children at that this time in your classroom; adapt and accommodate to meet learners needs

- Use pedagogical documentation to generate questions not always find answers; make the learning process visible and welcome perspectives, student thinking and new ways
- Children love songs for routines (e.g. clean-up song, lullaby for coming to the carpet, line-up); use teacher and student voice creatively in the classroom to engage and excite
- Pictures with labels in the classroom encourage things to be put back where they belong
- Setting up centers so that children are playing in small groups all around the room
- Proximity as a way to manage behaviors and starting to introduce a time out as needed
- Getting support where needed and identifying children who need close supervision early can build support from colleagues and administration right from the beginning.
- Frequently introduce new materials, books, activities and ideas to engage the learner
- Build outdoor learning into your program and encourage inquiry into nature
- Bring the outdoors in and let the learning continue and curiosities build and develop
- Build a positive rapport between the ECE and Teacher - it is an ongoing relationship that you need to adjust to - be flexible and professional with interactions, and welcome ideas
- Connect with parents, using social media, in-person conversations, informal meetings and get to know their families and the children who you are teaching
- Be at the child's level for face-to-face interactions; use a calm and gentle voice; simple words and make eye contact in a warm and responsive way; child as engaged learner
- Let the learning environment be the third teacher, create it as child-owned not adult focused; invite investigation, spark curiosity; provided open-ended materials; fluid, free-flow

spaces that are continually re-evaluated to adapt to the best way, at the time for that child; see children as curious, complex and competent learners and reflect in classroom

- Co-construct and collaborate in responsive teaching and practices; not restrictive practices but reflective practices
- Develop professional learning communities and opportunities to share, dialogue and connect with other educators and look at the Kindergarten program as a study of learning; rethink the way you work and learn together with other adults – a growth mindset-

Appendix E

SOME TEACHERS PERSPECTIVES WHEN APPLYING EDUCATIONAL THEORY

✓ **Bruner's unstructured play**

- Unstructured play would be just the ability to use your imagination, to show leadership, maybe cooperation.
- There is a greater variety in the student output during open-ended activities. The free-flow of imaginative play unfolds as they engage.

✓ **Vygotsky's social talk**

- They talk while building Lego structures; they share ideas. Talking is important in learning.
- As the teacher once children are at centers this is my time to walk around listen in and ask guiding questions to facilitate conversation and dialogue around their experimenting and learning.

✓ **Dewey's Experiential Learning**

- Anything tactile works well. For example, like play dough, this week they do play dough shapes, numbers and letters.
- We notice the kids are not using the math manipulatives in the math area then we put them in the block area. We see what they are doing.

✓ **Reggio Emilia – The Environment as a Third Teacher**

- We go out for outdoor play, walk, sit under a tree…I will bring out different bins of things at different times.
- As a teacher my role is as a researcher, observing, documenting, analyzing, scaffolding and making meaning of what I see and finding ways to hone the learning for the individual students.
- We use natural tones, wicker baskets, wooden containers, plants in the classroom and remove bright colors and plastic materials.

Appendix F

CREATIVITY – WAYS TO BUILD IT IN THE CLASSROOM

- **Teaching Approaches**

1. Integrating learning with activities - All eight participants adapted center-based learning. Interactive, experiential and hands-on approach - "Play as significant" (*Play-based* and *Experiential Learning Opportunities*)

- **Physical Space**

2. Room layout, set-up, access, materials, variety of play – carpet area, floor space, the table top and counter designed and used for activities to engage the children, with 'quiet space' and 'loud space' in mind. (*Child-centered*)

- **Integrated Curriculum**   3. Inquiry-based learning, problem-solving and critical thinking opportunities by asking guided questions in learning process. Use of senses to guide the types of activities and 'extended the learning' and 'deepen thinking' (*Inquiry-Focus*)

- **Holistic Practices**   4. Whole-child focus, Focus on natural sciences. 'Looking at their perspective' and bringing a 'child's ideas' into the classroom and 'more nature in learning' (*Environmental Education*).

Appendix G

QUESTIONS FOR EDUCATORS TO THINK ABOUT:

1. How can I bring more creativity into a child's life? Throughout the day?
2. How can I enhance imaginative play experiences?
3. What are the different materials and loose parts to introduce to children?
4. How can the environment encourage choice and excite children to learn?
5. Am I facilitating opportunities to think, ponder and engage deeply?
6. Is the child building on natural curiosities and leading the inquiry?
7. Does the learning experience go beyond intelligence and rekindle enthusiasm?
8. Does the learning nurture student's personal confidence and self-esteem?
9. Are there learning experiences to share ideas and encourage dialogue?

10. Can the learning experience be extended in a different ways at different levels?
11. How can educators strengthen learning partnerships with all stakeholders?
12. What are some ways to professionally manage conflicts and difference of opinions?
13. How can the relationship with families be more meaningful and supportive?
14. Does our questioning respect student thinking and enhance the learning?
15. How can we change the environment to reduce the children's stress levels?
16. Are there different ways to keep children calm, alert and engaged in learning?
17. How can learning partners co-construct and collaborate in better ways?
18. Can we make mundane tasks more interesting, and provide smoother transitions?
19. Have we been organic in the flow of the day, being mindful that each day is different?
20. Is this learning, for this child, in this way, most engaging at this time?

ACKNOWLEDGEMENTS

As a teacher and researcher, I was inspired by many for the impetus for change and search for innovation in teaching practice; making this a true endeavor of awe, wonder and inquiry. I would like to thank the Ontario Institute for Studies in Education which provided an academic arena for research. I am also indebted to the Kindergarten teachers and principals at participating schools in my study. The eight teacher participants played a major role in this research project and were open to sharing experiences and I am grateful for their insight into FDK classroom practices.

I remember how important the first day of Kindergarten was to me and my children. I found the most joy in seeing them explore, discover and adapt to the change in their environment. I cherished the artwork that came home and just imagined how those little hands were creating so many marvelous things. I am thankful to all the memories with all the students for being such an inspiration and for showing me how much nature means to them. The children's excitement at the sight of bugs, butterflies, grasshoppers, snails, and fish made me dig further into inquiry-based learning practices. The joy of seeing children at play and their deep sense of engagement and excitement in their learning stayed dear to my heart.

This book really led me to see the natural curiosities and inner spirit of a child. It brought me deeper into inner exploration about the important things in life, awakening my senses, the value of relationships, and getting me back in touch with meditation, nature, and giving generously with time and knowledge to students and following my passion for the love of learning.

My two dear children inspired me tremendously for this endeavor when they entered my life. This journey took on more meaning over the years as I honored the roles of being a mother, teacher and researcher. It was evident to me the importance of nurturing the authentic spark within each one of my own children and each and every student in my classroom. The love, laughter, and hugs from my own children connected me deeply to the life of children, understanding them, and just being with them each day. I learned how to tap the true potential that lies within children. Each learning experience was about finding opportunities for self-expression, voice and creativity that began to build a child's self-esteem. Both my son and daughter, along with my niece and nephews, continue to teach me to be a better person. Just being in their presence reminds me to live each day with happiness and gratitude. As they change and grow, so do I.

In addition, to my dear husband, generous, loving, warm and supportive, always behind me all the way as I explored and developed my interests in elementary education, academic research and worked towards publishing my book. My mom and dad instilled strong values of my culture which resonate with me. My parents grounded me and in-laws supported me. I can also recollect amazing childhood memories with my brother and sister that shaped who I am today. To all my family members who continue to always be there for me with their unwavering and never-ending support and love. I am most blessed by the presence of all of you in my life.

ABOUT THE AUTHOR

Dr. Ella Karia, is a certified elementary school teacher with the Ontario College of Teachers, and received her Doctorate in Education from the University of Toronto in 2014. She has taught Kindergarten for over eight years in public schools in Ontario and her research interests are educational policy change, philosophy of education and social justice education. She is an expert in the field of Kindergarten education and has worked with two major university research projects at the Ontario Institute for Studies in Education (OISE). In 2011, she worked as the Early Years Coordinator at the Department of Applied Psychology and Human Development, focusing on literacy development practices and the value of professional development through the use of technology. In 2012, she worked on the project Women and Leadership in Higher Education at the Department of Humanities, Social Sciences and Social Justice Education. In 2015 she was selected to join a curriculum writing team at the board level whose goal was to publish an Educator's Guide to Transformative Early Year Programming. She is committed to finding ways of seeing pedagogy reflect the needs of young children and being mindful of the spirit of a child. *Fostering Creativity* is based on her own steadfast pursuit of early years educational research. In this book she designed and presented the EYE (Early Years Education) Model which represents some of the key elements for understanding how learning happens within Ontario's Full-Day Kindergarten Early Years Program. She began her career as a teacher and has since embraced the role of a researcher. Email her at fosteringcreativitywithkids@gmail.com.

Printed in the United States
By Bookmasters